The Ernest Hemingway Companion

Edited by

Somdatta Mandal

SARAT BOOK DISTRIBUTORS

Kolkata-700 073

The Ernest Hemingway Companion
Edited by : Somdatta Mandal

ISBN-81-87169-17-6

First Published : March, 2002

Published by : SAS Enterprise
FD-462/4, Salt Lake, Kolkata-700 106
E-mail : smandal@vsnl.com

Distributed by : Sarat Book Distributors
18 B, Shyamacharan De Street
Kolkata - 700 073, Phone : 241-8389

Printed at : The Saraswati Printing Works
2 Guruprosad Chowdhury Lane, Kolkata-700 006

Price in India : Rs.200/-
Outside India US $10

To all Hemingway *aficionados*

About the Editor

Somdatta Mandal teaches English and American Literature at Vivekananda College, Madhyamgram and at the postgraduate department of the University of Calcutta. Graduating from the University of Calcutta, she obtained her M.Phil and Ph.D. degrees from Jadavpur University. A Fulbright scholar, she has participated in several national and international seminars and workshops, including the prestigious Salzburg Seminar and the British Council Cambridge Seminar. Her research articles have appeared in several national and internationally reputed journals. Her publications include *Reflections, Refractions and Rejections: Three American Writers and the Celluloid World* (2002). Among her editorial ventures are *F. Scott Fitzgerald: A Centennial Tribute (2 vols)* 1997; *William Faulkner: A Centennial Tribute (1999); The Diasporic Imagination: Asian American Writing (3 vols) 2000.*

Note

The following articles were originally published elsewhere. They are reprinted here with the necessary copyright permissions.

"Papa and All His Children" in *US News and World Report*, June 1, 1998.

"The Mode of Hemingway's Rhetoric" by E. Nageswara Rao in *Ernest Hemingway: A Study of His Rhetoric* .New Delhi: Arnold Heinmann, 1983.pp.61-81.

"A Reader's Guide to Pilar's Bullfighters: Untold Histories in *For Whom the Bell Tolls.*" by Miriam Mandel in *The Hemingway Review* Vol.15 no.1 1995. All rights reserved.

"Humor in *The Sun Also Rises*" by Scott Donaldson in *New Essays on The Sun Also Rises*. Ed. Linda Wagner-Martin. Cambridge University Press. pp.19-41.

"Picasso, Hemingway and the Bull" by Indrani Haldar in *Indian Journal of American Studies* 16.1 (Win'86) pp.27-32.

"Exchange Between Rivals: Faulkner's Influence on *The Old Man and the Sea*" by Peter L. Hays in *Ernest Hemingway: The Writer in Context*. Ed. James Nagel. The University of Wisconsin Press. pp.147-164.

"*Waste Land* Parallels Unifying *In Our Time*: Hemingway's Confirmation as a Modernist" by Bickford Sylvester in *Up in Michigan: Proceedings of the First International Conference of the Hemingway Society*. Eds. Joseph Waldmeir & Ken Marek. Traverse City, MI: The Hemingway Society, 1983. 11-19.

CONTENTS

INTRODUCTION

'There is Never an end to Papa'

Somdatta Mandal

Ernest Hemingway's literary reputation reached a boom with his birth centenary celebrations on July 21st 1999,enhancing and clarifying the image of the grizzled "Papa" in the public eye. Perhaps no other American writer of the twentieth century achieved the combination of international celebrity and literary stature that Ernest Hemingway did during his lifetime. Hemingway had very early trapped himself into the stereotype of the romantic and virile literary "man of action," very American in essence. His effect on reviewers and readers alike had been set right from October 18, 1925 when the anonymous critic of *The New York Times* reviewed "In Our Time" with words and phrases like, "lean and pleasing, with tough resilience," "fibrous," "athletic," "fresh," "hard," "clean" – justifying the fact that a prose style dramatically different demanded equally new ways of describing it. Between 1925 and 1961, Hemingway changed the face of American fiction and became a widely recognized public figure. His obituary in *The Times*, July 2, 1961, echoed the promise of its book review a lifetime earlier, describing his "lean and sinewy prose," and his "laconic, understated dialogue." Now he has become an American icon. whose picture needs no identifying caption, for his face and his name, both ubiquitous, are the very definition of "the writer" to many people. It is no secret that during Hemingway's later years the more he became a popular symbol of "art" in the United States, the more his serious reputation declined – perhaps, as Maxwell Geismar suggests, because he himself no longer appeared to be serious as an artist. Perhaps this was due to the unfortunate *persona*, or public mask, which Hemingway chose for him during his later career, the benign "Papa" of American fiction, who, however benign, brooked little interference and less criticism. Though the boundaries of Ernest Hemingway's literary reputation had contracted since the first glowing period of his advent, it reemerged itself with greater zeal once again in the last two decades of the twentieth century and more so with the celebration of his birth centenary in 1999.

Among the scores of tributes that filled the pages of journals and newspapers reporting this event, this author chose to quote an extract from "Hemingway in Our Times", a Web-Only Essay on the Hemingway Centenary by Michael Reynolds, which offers a brilliant retrospective on the life and work of Ernest Hemingway, the quintessentially American writer that he was.

> Ernest Hemingway became and remains an American icon and one embodiment of America's promise: the young boy from Oak Park who set out to become the best writer of his time, and did just that. His ambition, intensity, creative drive, sense of duty, belief in hard work, and faith in the strenuous life carried him to the pinnacle of his profession and provided him with worldwide recognition and considerable wealth before destroying him when he could no longer meet the demands of his public life. It is an old story, older than written words, a story the ancient Greeks would have recognized.
> Hemingway told us that pursuit was happiness, and that any story followed far enough would end badly. He lived constantly on the edge of American experience and constantly in the public eye. He wrote books that influenced two or more generations, and was awarded not only with prizes, including the Pulitzer and the Nobel, but also with fame such as few writers have known or have had to endure. He remodeled American short fiction, changed the way characters speak, confronted the moral strictures confirming the writer, and left behind a shelf of books

telling us how we were in the century's first half and leaving a record for those who come after. At the end of the next century, the basic human struggle with universal demons that Hemingway put down with such clarity will still be read, and men may still take heart, knowing that they are neither the first nor the last to face their fate.

So much has already been written about Ernest Hemingway before this that it has been understandably difficult for critics to say or write anything original about him. Attempts to sum him up (or put him down) begin to sound as familiar as Hemingway's own famous – and often parodied – prose style. Nevertheless, this anthology is aimed at bringing within reach of the Indian students of American literature some of the best articles written on Hemingway during the last two decades. I hope it will prove useful to teachers, students and researchers in Indian universities, who cannot have easy access to recent critical material on Hemingway. I am also painfully aware that some eminent Hemingway scholars, who have done monumental work on the writer, delving deep into the manuscripts and coming up with significant discoveries, do not figure in this anthology.

The very first article, "Papa and All His Children" is a special report on how Hemingway's style left a deep imprint on the landscape of prose. This short but impressive survey traces the biographical and literary history of the making of this great American writer, stressing on the fact that the literary style he forged was strikingly original – "Mark Twain had begun the naturalistic rebellion against Romanticism four decades earlier but it was Hemingway who finally cleared the adjective-clotted arteries of mainstream writing." The article ends with the belief that though the realistic novel within the tradition of the Great American Novel died a natural death with Ernest Hemingway and from the sixties' onwards "journalism chose this juncture to invade literature's turf," even the later post electronic generation failed to inspire the reader of the realistic novel. Hence, Hemingway is here to stay.

E. Nageswara Rao, in his "The Mode of Hemingway's Rhetoric," discusses Hemingway's stylistic practices such as verbal irony, figurative language, repetition of motifs and structural patterns of plot and action, use of epigraphs, and selection of titles. He demonstrates how Hemingway communicates his vision and influences our thinking about it through several forms of verbal irony like parody, sarcasm, understatement (sometimes in the guise of meiosis), and ingénue irony with suitable illustrations.

After this general survey of Hemingway's narrative style, we come to articles where most of the time single fictional pieces are focused upon. Bickford Sylvester argues, in his "*Wasteland* Parallels Unifying *In Our Time*: Hemingway's Confirmation as a Modernist," that Hemingway was a modernist who, wearing a low-brow mask, craftily demonstrated that he could adopt the allusive narrative approach and much of the vision and perspective that brought Joyce and Eliot the enviable respect of the intelligentsia. He maintains that Hemingway made his debut as the manipulator of a continuous juxtaposition between the twentieth century emotional and spiritual alienation and the four hundred years of Christendom with *In Our Time* rather than with *The Sun Also Rises*. Sylvester quotes the full Evening Prayer and demonstrates how the stories and interchapters of *In Our Time* are experienced as a rueful expansion of the prayer with an ironic difference. The composite protagonist (variously named but mostly Nick), like the many-voiced speaker of *The Waste Land* becomes a universal 20th century questor/victim.

After establishing Hemingway as a modernist deserving a place on the same shelf as Joyce and Eliot, the next two articles take us into a comparative study of the writer across the continent again and find similarities between his art and that of the Russian master, Ivan Turgenev. In the short article, "Hemingway and Turgenev: An Introduction," Kelley Dupuis draws our attention to the fact that Hemingway's youthful reading largely centered around the great Russian masters – Tolstoy, Dostoeivski, Turgenev, Gogol and Chekhov. Hemingway first read Turgenev's *A Sportsman's Sketches* by borrowing it from

Sylvia Beach's bookshop and he never made his admiration for the writer a secret. According to Dupuis, Turgenev's stories "are snapshots of places, characters, situations and Hemingway's *in our time*, a product of 'modernism' written not long after he had been reading Turgenev in Paris, works in much the same way." He even finds a lot of similarity between the endings of Turgenev's "The Raspberry Water" and Hemingway's "The Battler."

Hemingway's *The Torrents of Spring* has always been associated to be a parody of Sherwood Anderson's *Dark Laughter*. Critics have not attempted to explain Hemingway's use of the Turgenev novella in this context. In her article, "Half a Century and Half a World: Turgenev's and Hemingway's *The Torrents of Spring*," Judy Henn focuses our attention to the fact that the history of the comparison of the two works is new and relatively unexplored. Though there is no indication in Hemingway's writings as to the reason for his appropriation of Turgenev's novel published way back in 1872, Judy tries to examine the nature of, and the extent of Hemingway's utilization of Turgenev, using the theoretical vehicles of parody/satire, intertextuality and Bakhtinian theories of dialogism. Apart from the similarity in nature of the Byronic hero, and the importance of art to life, Hemingway's praises for the Russian predecessor is unanimous –"Turgenieff (sic) to me is the greatest writer there ever was.....Turgenieff was an artist."

In an interesting essay written on April 29, 1951, "25 Years of a Hemingway Classic", Carlos Baker states, "Twenty five years ago Ernest Hemingway awoke one autumn morning in Paris to find that the sun had also risen. It could hardly have been anything but a welcome sight." *The Sun Also Rises* was admired and in some quarters adversely criticized but it has remained a genuine classic of modern American fiction. There is also one legitimate sociological reason. Though he was not the first to present the "lost generation," Hemingway gave it a local habitation, a brilliant dramatization, and an extension in social space that over-reached its ostensible national boundaries of France and Spain. He made his Paris and his Pamplona, with its bullfighting into microcosms, which relentlessly

embodied a considerable part of the social history of the
Nineteen Twenties along with F. Scott Fitzgerald's *This Side
of Paradise*. Though quite in different ways, both books
anatomized the desperate gaiety with which the Jazz Age
masked its incipient melancholia. Watching the
complications at work under the quick narrative flow of
The Sun Also Rises, one understands that the book has kept
its vitality as much by virtue of its richness in symbolic
suggestiveness as by its sturdy moral backbone. The
following two articles discuss different facets of this
important novel.

Hemingway is not generally known as a humorous
writer, and a novel like *The Sun Also Rises*, which is a grim,
sad story of the 'lost generation', is normally not associated
with humor. But Scott Donaldson, in his "Humor in *The
Sun Also Rises*," points out that Hemingway started out
trying to be funny in this novel, with the dual epigraphs
suggesting an intricate mixture of humorous and serious
elements, and argues that the primary technique of humor
in the novel is that of incongruous juxtaposition, the
juxtaposition of "high-brow speech against the vulgate." He
says that Jake, who has few illusions about anyone
including himself, adopts a posture of irony, sarcasm, and
cynicism, and is capable of seeing the humor in the way
others react to his wound. His tone is not only ironical but
also humorous even as the novel opens with a description
of Robert Cohn. Donaldson calls Bill Gorton the most
consistently funny character (modeled on the humorist
Donald Ogden Stewart, who was one of the group at
Pamplona), who seems to have discovered how to live in
this world. Jake wonders, "All I wanted to know was how to
live in it," and Bill provides the answer.

Treating the same novel from a different point of view,
Chidananda Bhattacharya discusses "The Alternate Titles
of *The Sun Also Rises*." Published in October 1926, *The Sun
Also Rises* (or *Fiesta* as it was called in England), was
Hemingway's first major novel and it established him as a
literary force and proved that he could maintain the
intensity and control of his stories in the longer form of
the novel. By keeping the biographical details in mind,

Bhattacharya traces the making of the novel and shows us how Hemingway experimented with various titles to finally come to the one with Biblical overtones. After discussing several related issues, the writer comes to the conclusion that the common belief of the novel being a faithful mirror of the directionless 'lost generation' is not entirely true. Instead, according to him, Hemingway seemed to rise to some length "from the morass of personal trauma and disillusion and artistically exploited them to some constructive end." War, moral perversion, and anarchy, were all temporary phases and the ultimate message that Hemingway tries to convey through this novel is that "the earth abideth forever and the sun also riseth."

The themes of love and war are the basic tenets upon which most criticism of *A Farewell to Arms* is usually based. This is truer especially after the papers of Agnes Von Kurowsky were published a few years back. In a completely different vein, Amitabha Sinha discusses the "Opening of *A Farewell to Arms*". According to Sinha, who focuses his attention only upon the opening paragraph of the novel, Hemingway paid special attention to the use of language, metaphors or tropes – most of'which are overlooked by the average reader engrossed in a story of love and war. He also tries to explore how the novelist uses subtle repetitions, even sense of rhymes and syllabic-cum-numerological methods in his narrative technique and for this the entire novel's 'arrangement' or 'organization' is very important.

A scholar who has earnestly dedicated her research to Ernest Hemingway's writings, Miriam Mandel has over the years, painstakingly tried to locate the facts behind all the characters, incidents, places, described in Hemingway fiction. In her article, "A Reader's Guide to Pilar's Bullfighters: Untold Histories in *For Whom the Bell Tolls*," she continues it. According to her, just as access to the novel's political background enriches our reading of it, so can knowledge of the cultural figures that dominated pre-Civil War Spain help us understand the characters shaped by those figures. Spanish culture enters the novel through Pilar's stories, in which she mentions famous singers, dancers, musicians, and most importantly, bullfighters.

Focusing upon two of Pilars's narratives that are particularly rich in cultural references, (and through which Hemingway is able to perform the necessary task of introducing the cultural landscape of peacetime Spain in the novel), Miriam elucidates the life histories of eight bullfighters, with special emphasis upon Jose Gomez Ortega, who for many years and by many critics was considered the best matador of the twentieth century. In conclusion she feels that when we recontextualize the bullfighters Pilar mentions, we can recover some of the Spain described so poetically in Hemingway's other "Spanish" book, his neglected masterpiece *Death In the Afternoon* (1932).

Published in 1952 after a ten-year literary drought, *The Old Man and the Sea* was Hemingway's last major work of fiction. Written in his characteristically sparse prose, it received the Pulitzer Prize for fiction in 1953 and the Nobel Prize in 1954. In this short novel, or novella, Hemingway celebrated the familiar theme of the solitary individual drifting on a blind and hostile sea of life: a watery Darwinian universe of shark-eat-shark, and winner take nothing. As serious Hemingway scholars have already noted, the apparent simplicity of the tale is misleading. That Santiago is spent but triumphant at the end of the story speaks a lot about Hemingway's philosophy of life. Apart from being the most popular Hemingway text being read and taught in India, this last work possibly is open to the maximum number of interpretations and comparative studies. The following five essays in this anthology bear ample testimony to the multifaceted nature of literary criticism today:

In the first article entitled "Intertextualities: *The Old Man and the Sea* and *Islands in the Stream.*" Sobha Chattopadhyay feels that one approach that has been so far overlooked is to relate *The Old Man and the Sea* to the longer novel, *Islands in the Stream*, of which it was originally a part. "The Sea Book," which later became *Islands in the Stream*, originally had four sections, namely, (a) "The Sea When Young," (b) "The Sea When Absent," (c) "The Sea in Being," and (d) "The Sea Chase." The third section, "The Sea in Being" was then severed from the rest of the tale and published separately as the novella under discussion.

A close study of the two novels, therefore, reveals striking resemblances and links in themes, motifs, symbols and images. They share some characteristic themes like love, the need for reciprocal human relationships, creativity and the artists' concern for craft, the theme of life as a struggle for existence, and a preoccupation with death. Also, the symbols of the sea, fish, and shark, and the use of literary sources like Dante make them a close kin to each other. Though they stand as separate, independent novels today, *The Old Man and the Sea* and *Islands in the Stream* do share a unity, and the study of one illuminates the other.

The love-hate relationship between F. Scott Fitzgerald and Ernest Hemingway is well known. In the next article, "Exchange Between Rivals: Faulkner's Influence on *The Old Man and the Sea*", Peter L. Hays focuses our attention towards the antagonism that Hemingway proclaimed towards William Faulkner. He draws our attention to the fact that Hemingway had told both James T. Farrell in 1936 and Jean Paul Sartre in 1944 that Faulkner was a better writer than himself. In *Death in the Afternoon*, he praised Faulkner while mocking *Sanctuary*. The two authors' works curiously intertwined and their loves too reveal curious likenesses. Among the two, Faulkner was, according to Hays, "consistently milder in his comments and more respectful of both Hemingway and his work." A larger section of this essay also concentrates upon the similarities between The *Old Man and the Sea* and Faulkner's "The Bear" where both authors pay tribute to seascape and landscape respectively, and more significantly, "both authors make gods or demi-gods of the animals their protagonists hunt." Again, Hays also finds another link between the two writers at that point in their career – both emphasize 'endurance.'

Dipendu Chakrabarti's article presents an inter-textual encounter between Hemingway's novella and J.M. Synge's one-act play, *Riders to the Sea*. After a detailed discussion of the various issues, he comes to the conclusion that the two texts challenge each other at so many levels, yet at the end they look like two supplementary angles for mapping the site of humankind's age-old struggle with nature. The next article is Priyadarshi Patnaik's "*The Old Man and the Sea* in the Light of the *Rasa* Theory: An Indian Reading of Hemingway." *Rasa* theory (which can be roughly translated as aesthetic emotion or rapture) is the most popular and significant reading tradition in ancient Indian aesthetics. The writer begins by describing the theoretical background of the school of aesthetics, which was expounded for the first time in *Natya-Sastra* of Bharata (1st to 4th Century), who stated, "Without *rasa* there can be no drama." What is implicit in the statement is the fact that a literary work does not achieve completion or merit unless it contains the elements of *rasa* and results in the *rasa* experience. Patnaik then attempts a reader's response to *The Old Man and the Sea* from within this theory, especially showing how Santiago features under the theory of *vira rasa*. The features listed under *vira rasa* are very interesting (at least from a Western point of view) since they indicate qualities such as valor, humility, courage, patience, endurance etc. all together.

The last article of this section is also another analysis of Santiago's character and predicament. As the very title of Pralhad A. Kulkarni's short article "Santiago: A Sinless *El Campeon*" suggests, the protagonist of the novel is treated as a champion who fights for the right of a life worthy of humanity.

One of the fortunate Hemingway scholars from India who visited the J.F.K. Presidential Library in Boston, Massachusetts, and had the opportunity to go through the Hemingway manuscripts housed there, P.G. Rama Rao in the next article focuses upon the manuscripts of the posthumously published work, *The Garden of Eden* (1986). Composed forty years earlier in 1946, this novel deals at great length with the idea of role-reversal and androgyny. Knowing how meticulous an artist Hemingway was, the finished product would have been definitely different from the form in which we find the novel today. In fact, according to Carlos Baker, Hemingway had confessed to Buck Lanaham that he wrote the novel at enormous speed. In this article, Rama Rao focuses upon the manuscript version of the text and feels that the 1189 pages contain certain interesting passages that are vital to the structure of the novel and should not have been omitted.

From its use of Christian motifs in the development of character, and the forging of consonances with scriptural situation and mood, to its appropriation of images, directly or indirectly related to both the Testaments and its frequent adoption of the rhythms of the King James' Bible, the Hemingway short story demonstrates a closeness with the Authorized Version that virtually begs investigation. The Biblical echoes in Hemingway's short fiction, though not overwhelmingly overt in their consistency, may yet be recognized as mythic multivalences of character and style, which yield resonance far in excess of their materials, even as they generate ironies and resolve ambiguities in the manner of most provocative fictions. Ajanta Paul's essay, "Biblical Resonance In Hemingway's Short Fiction: Moving Testaments to His Art," analyzes this predicament in details.

My own article "*True at First Light*: Our Centennial Gift" attempts to place the recently published 'fictional memoir' within a historical context. Beginning with Hemingway's love of East Africa, his penchant for big-game hunting and the subsequent expression of those experiences through various pieces of fiction and non-fiction, I come to the great volume of debate and criticism that has evolved regarding the posthumous publication of this work. These include critics who feel that Hemingway, the perfectionist that he was, would never have approved the present form as opposed to the justifications from Patrick Hemingway, who admitted that he did not change a single word written by his father while editing the 850-page manuscript. What is interesting in this work is that apart from the mainstream narrative on Africa and a lion hunt, Hemingway also muses on the act of writing itself and the author's role in determining the truth. I conclude with the remark that however unrevised, unpolished it might be, in this book Hemingway also offers a compendium of his familiar old symbols, themes, moods, feelings and details.

In her book of reminiscences, *Portrait of Hemingway*, Lillian Ross quotes Hemingway as having said, "I learned to write by looking at paintings in the Luxembourg Museum in Paris." Indeed, in interviews, letters, as well as in his writing, he repeatedly referred to painters and paintings, stressing at the same time his indebtedness to them even as he attempted literary equivalents of the innovative techniques the artists resorted to. The indebtedness was of various sorts. His stylistic indebtedness was to the Impressionists, Cézanne in particular, but thematically or subject-wise, he was indebted to the Spanish artists Goya and Picasso, whose bullfight paintings he was distinctly drawn to as an *aficionado* of the bullring himself. His hesitant response to the final step in modernistic innovation – total commitment to the geometricized abstraction of Picasso or Gus (both of whom he admired and studied) – becomes most evident. In her article "Picasso, Hemingway, and the Bull," Indrani Haldar shows us how for both Picasso and Hemingway, the bullfight is of complex and ambiguous significance equally as visual experience and metaphor. Both depict the actual drama in all its crude reality but infuse it with patterns of symbolic meaning. After detailed discussion of these issues, she come to the conclusion that for both the artists the bull, bullfighter, and bullring seemed to crystallize the human experience of living in a world of chaotic, destructive, and indifferent by turns, and yet, simultaneously suggest the means of redemptive transcendence.

Ernest Hemingway's love-hate relationship with Hollywood and the motion-picture industry is too well known. Though he ranked first among the American writers to have the maximum number of films adapted from his fiction, his personal relationship with the sunny Californian town was rather skeptical. One of the reasons for this dissatisfaction was the feeling that the author had to surrender his hegemonic control of the text to the filmmaker. In her article "The Real, The Imaginary and the Hyperreal Text: Hemingway's Fiction and Hollywood's Visual Fiction" Sanjukta Dasgupta examines the various problems related to adaptations and filmic representations.

Beginning her argument by quoting from Jean Baudrillard, who categorically accuses the cinema for destroying the real and the imaginary, history and fiction, through its projections of cinematic myth as real and thereby producing the hyperreal, she then tries to relate why Hemingway could never reconcile himself to the transcreation of the narrative image into a visual image that appeared to be recognizably different. Discussing various individual adaptations, she comes to the conclusion that it would not be inappropriate to distinguish between Hemingway's fiction and visual fiction in Barthesian categories as the difference between the fictional text of *jouissance* (bliss) and the filmic text of *plaisir* (pleasure) respectively.

The last article in this anthology is an attempt to compile a bibliographical overview of Ernest Hemingway in the Indian context. Being the most popular American writer to be read and taught at various institutions throughout India, the flurry of articles and books (all of which, I fear to say, are not of great standard) bear testimony to the impact he left upon the psyche of Indian researchers and scholars. This list, I must admit, is not complete in all respects as I am sure there are scores of articles published in the regional languages and local journals that could not be accessed. Nevertheless, it can serve as a ready reference for all Hemingway *aficionados*, so to say. After all, as the title of this introduction reinforces the idea, there is really never an end to 'Papa'. It must also be mentioned that no anthology is ever complete and justice could not be done to several important fictional works and research areas. I think this holds true of any anthology.

To conclude it has to be admitted that the impact of Hemingway upon a generation of writers cannot be overemphasized. I cite just one instance here. In an article written on July 26, 1981, Gabriel Garcia Marquez reminisces about one rainy spring day in 1957 in Paris when he met Ernest Hemingway by chance at Boulevard St. Michel. "He looked so alive amid the secondhand bookstalls and the youthful torrent from the Sorbonne that it was impossible to imagine that he had but four years left to live." Unable to decide whether to ask him for an interview or cross the avenue to express his "unqualified admiration for him," Garcia withdrew because at that time he was a 28-year old newspaperman with a published novel and a literary prize in Columbia, but "was adrift and without direction in Paris." He admits that the two leading influences in his life had been that of William Faulkner and Ernest Hemingway –"the ephemeral man who had just said goodbye to me across the street, leaving me with the impression that something had happened in my life, and had happened for all time." Marquez went on to say that "Faulkner is a writer who had much to do with my soul, but Hemingway is the one who had the most to do with my craft – not simply for his books, but for his astounding knowledge of the aspect of craftsmanship in the science of writing." What greater tribute can one writer give to another? Garcia Marquez concludes his article with an even more interesting anecdote:

> Some years ago, I got into the car of Fidel Castro – who is a tenacious reader of literature – and on the seat I saw a small book bound in red leather. "It's my master Hemingway," Fidel Castro told me. Really, Hemingway continues to be where one least expects to find him – 20 years after his death – as enduring yet ephemeral as on that morning, perhaps in May, when he said "Goodbye, *amigo*" from across the Boulevard St. Michel.

Papa and All His Children

"Hemingway's style left a deep imprint on the landscape prose."

In the years after the First World War, the Young Man Who Lived and Loved Hard and Wrote Well revolutionized American literature. His prose was a symphony of short, strong, sonorous sentences. His heroes were men broken by the world but left "strong at the broken places." His women were both strong and weak, and they were always very beautiful in their summer dresses. The Young Man Who Lived and Loved Hard and Wrote Well lied out of his mouth and told the truth out of his typewriter. He defied courage better than any writer ever had before. But he died a coward's death by his own hand, his brains and blood staining the foyer of house on the slopes of the Rockies one fine Sunday morning in July. This is the legend of Ernest Hemingway in 130 words, as he might have written it himself if he had been a minor character in one of his own novels.

The doctor's son from Oak Park, Illinois, was so perfectly suited to the aborning literary age that perhaps only an education in a college English department could have kept him from becoming the most influential figure in the 20th century writing. Instead, Hemingway matriculated at age 18 at the Kansas City *Star*, where the style sheet instructed : "Use short sentences. Use short first paragraphs. Use vigorous English." They were rules he never forgot. He picked up other pointers from the King James Bible, from dead writers like Mark Twain and Stephen Crane, and from living luminaries such as Ezra Pound and Gertrude Stein, at whose feet he sat after becoming the *Toronto Star*'s mustachioed 22-year-old correspondent in Paris.

For all that, the literary style he forged was startingly original. The Victorian tradition, which still held sway in many quarters, dressed up prose in ornate finery to blunt the starkness of life. Hemingway stripped prose to its union suit to lay bare life's futility. He found power in simplicity and poetry in the rhythm of ordinary speech. Mark Twain had begun the naturalistic rebellion against Romanticism four decades earlier, but it was Hemingway who finally cleared the adjective-clotted arteries of mainstream writing. The *New York Times* Pronounced his short stories "fibrous and athletic, colloquial and fresh, hard and clean." After publication of his first novel, *The Sun Also Rises*, in 1926, a reviewer wrote in the *Atlantic* that Hemingway "writes as if he had never read anybody's writing, as if he had fashioned the art of writing himself,"

Hemingway invented more than a style; he invented "the Hemingway hero." Here too, he owed a debt to Twain. Nick Adams in numerous short stories, Frederick Henry in *A Farewell to Arms* (1929), Robert Jordan in *For Whom the Bell Tolls* (1939), and other Hemingway heroes were Huckleberry Finn grown to manhood. They were American innocents negotiating the river of life wherever it took them: to Italy, to Spain to Africa, to the Carribbean, wounded men laughing through the pain, sometimes risking their skins but never sacrificing their honor. It was a river into which countless writers would thrust their paddles, Hemingway's *oeuvre* was not large, yet he became the great American water buffalo of stylists, his spoor spread by imitators across the landscape of prose from journalism to pulp fiction to literary novels. The Hemingway hero grew into a stock figure on the movie screen as well.

But the most vivid and complex character Hemingway created was himself. The greatest terror of the world held for him was a blank sheet of paper in his typewriter—or so he wished the world to believe. All his life he was gripped by a compulsion to demonstrate the magnitude of his *cojones*. He hunted lions in Africa, fished for marlin in the Caribbean, scouted for Nazi submarines with his yacht, aided the French Resistance in World War II, drank enough to fell a field army, and in Key West, his only longtime U.S.

haunt, he was wont to invite patrons of Sloppy Joe's to box with "Papa" (as he liked to be called).

Hemingway did something else to prove his prowess: He lied. Shamelessly. He claimed, for example,to have slept with the World War I spy Mata Hari (forgetting she had been shot before he reached Europe). In a fragment of prose found among his papers after his death, he wrote : "It is not unnatural that the best writers are liars. A major part of their trade is to lie or invent...Lying to themselves is harmful, but this is cleansing away by the writing of a true book." Hemingway had four wives, cheating on each with the next in the line of succession. Despite his he-man airs, for nearly his entire adult life he had a spouse on hand to comfort him (of which he had much need, being so accident prone that most photos show a bandage on some parts of his body). He backbit friends and feuded with former mentors. Yet men and women alike craved his company, and not only because of his fame. Charisma poured off him. Like the heroes in his books, Hemingway seemed to bear some secret psychic wound. His heroic posturing lessened the pain, but the only true anesthetic was writing well. A writer is like a gold mine, he wrote in an unpublished musing. He must "exhaust the mine each time or he will sicken and die." In 1954, two years after his lyrical masterpiece, *The Old Man and the Sea*, Hemingway won the Nobel Prize. But his failing health soon sapped his writing skills. By 1961, his typewriter lay inert beneath his fingers. Hereached for a new pain killer, a double-barreled shotgun.

Realism vs. reality

Hemingway went to his grave at time when growing numbers of intellectuals were convinced that the realistic novel as an art form might follow him. No longer did the literati talk of the Great American Novel—as they had since the Civil War—the single work that would synthesize the American experience. At the start of the 1960s, Philip Roth defined fiction's challenge : Reality suddenly seemed more gripping than the conjuring of any writer's imagination. Many younger writers of "serious fiction" held back from painting the social panorama. They wrote stories of small scope or abandoned realism altogether for absurdism, fables, or other postmodern ventures.

Journalism chose this juncture to invade literature's turf. Hatching almost overnight like a brood of cicadas, the New Journalists commenced to feed on the carnival of 1960s America with a deafening buzz. Whether examining the sexual revolution, the Mafia, auto racing, racial strife, or the life of a celebrity, Tom Wolfe, Gay Talese, Jimmy Breslin, and many others tried to marry the literal truth of journalism and the psychological truth of fiction. They filled their novelistic narratives with true-life scenes, sharply observed sociological detail, and long snatches of dialogue. They tried to get inside their subjects' heads in a way few journalists had had the cheek to do before.

Wolfe, in particular, became for a time the most imitated writer since Hemingway. His prose crackled with irony and attitude and smarty-pants élan. He spewed out dots, dashes, and exclamation marks—!!!!—as a blowtorch spews out sparks. Wolfe and Talese liberalized sartorial standards in a trade in which resembling an unmade bed was a traditional mark of authenticity. Wolfe wore a white suit and swung a cane ; Talese dressed like a Fifth Avenue dandy even when his only date was with his typewriter. No longer would journalists be content to be, in Wolfe's word, the "lumpenproles" of the writing game while novelists sported aristocratic airs.

Norman Mailer and Truman Capote became another type of literary cross-dresser. Already novelists, they merely took their sticks with them into journalism. Capote coined the term "nonfiction novel" for his *In Cold Blood*, a true-crime saga serialized in the *New Yorker* in 1965. Published in hard cover in 1966, it spawned a true-crime genre that henceforth would compete with fictional potboilers. By 1973, Wolfe was hooting that journalism—as practiced in *New York, Esquire, Harper's*, other magazines, and in books—had "wipe[d] out the novel as literature's main event." On the campuses, meanwhile, deconstructionists, multiculturalists, and neo-Marxists were pulverizing the traditional mystique of the novel. Works of literature, long

given succor and worshiped in academe as windows on
beauty and moral truth, were now to be studied primarily
as mere cultural artifacts produced by the prejudices,
illusions, ethnic hubris, and economic or gender realities
reigning at the time of their creation.

Not literature alone, but the entire print culture felt
undr siege in the last quarter of the century as electronic
media proliferated. On the surface, the situation was not
dire. Some magazines died, others were born. Some
newspapers died, others were born. By the 1990s, 50,000
new books were being published each year in the United
States—five times as many as when Scribner's issued
Hemingway's first novel.

Yer cries of panic arose. Alvin Kernan's *Death of
Literature* (1990), David Marc's *Bonfire of the Humanities*
(1995), and Sven Birkerts's *The Gutenberg Elegies* (1995)
resounded with apocalyptic gloom about the future of
literacy. Partly, it was nostalgia and future shock. But what
disturbed the dwindling partisans of the print culture most
was the new lost generation—lost to literature. Kids'
language skills had sunk for three decades. Fewer and fewer
read except when forced to. Opinion was divided on what
the brave new world would bring. The pessimists saw an
"electronic hive,"and addictive collective consciousness
geared to shortened attention spans and ruinous to the
reflectiveness, mental coherence, and sense of self that
books had fostered in the cream of pre-electronic
generations. The optimists saw a glorious new age of
instant information and discourse, a coming surge of
computer interactions that would bolster literacy and
thinking skills and uncover new levels of human potential.

The Mode of Hemingway's Rhetoric

E. Nageswara Rao

Hemingway's early syntax is his most deliberate choice of a rhetorical strategy, a choice dictated by the circumstances of his experience and training. His syntax is his major procedure for attaining his goal of accurately reporting what he observed in life. The importance of this syntactic method to Hemingway is attested by the fact that in his early fiction that syntax seems to become virtually his rhetoric. While Hemingway demonstrates the rhetorical potential of parataxis as it is to be compared to more complex syntactic forms, a careful analysis of his early work shows that he has also adopted several conventional practices such as verbal irony, the use of the ingénue, the manipulation of characters, the employment of symbols and figurative language, the repetition of motifs and structural patterns of plot and action, the repetition of significant terms, the prefixing of epigraphs, and the selection of titles not merely as means to disclose his vision to us, but agents for persuading us to that vision. Such an analysis also reveals to us how Hemingway shaped these conventional devices for his own needs. Parody, for instance, is used basically to demolish views and attitudes he does not share; sarcasm is used for discrediting clichés and slogans. Meiosis and ingénue irony are the shock devices to sharpen what appeared to him to be the blunt sensitivities of the reader. Characters are manipulated to serve as disclosing and persuading agents. Their dialogues, commentaries, monologues, and postures are expository devices which function rhetorically also in Hemingway's early fiction. Symbols, epigraphs, and titles are used as

reinforcing devices while the skillfully managed technique
of repetition keeps Hemingway's vision before our eyes
constantly. Since most of these are customary ways in
fiction for persuading the reader to a particular view, as
Wayne Booth has brilliantly demonstrated in *The Rhetoric
of Fiction*, we may say that these devices together constitute
Hemingway's rhetorical mode.[1] It seems appropriate to
consider not only the devices Hemingway adopted, but also
the ways in which he adapted them for his own ends.

The most overt way by which Hemingway seeks to
communicate his vision and influence our thinking about
it seems to be through several forms of verbal irony such
as parody, sarcasm, and understatement. Bill Gorton's
parody of contemporary moral clichés and the narrator's
parody of the hackneyed descriptions of the bullfight critic
in "The Undefeated" illustrate what Hemingway thought
was false and hence worthy of his disapproval and
discrediting. When Bill Gorton talks of "Road to hell paved
with unbought stuffed dogs," (*The Sun Also Rises*, 73) he is
indirectly pointing out that the moral language of the past
has become inappropriate to the lost generation. He
accomplishes this through ridicule and by putting the old
slogans in an incongruous, but modern, context. The
criticism implied in these parodies indicates to us what
Hemingway attempted to exclude from his vision because
he was apparently convinced that these (the objects of his
parody) are untrue in his experience. How this process of
ridicule in Hemingway's parody works may be illustrated
by an analysis of *The Torrents of Spring* where he works to
undercut Sherwood Anderson's naïve and sentimental
attitudes towards love and sex. Scripps O'Neil, a Harvard
aesthete, the story's "hero," complains (like Anderson's
heroes) to all who would listen that his first wife has
deserted him. His subsequent love affair with the waitress
named Mandy is portrayed in high sentimental fashion.
As Scripps and Mandy express their mutual love, they break
into tears, and she declares, "You are my man and more
than my man. You are all of America to me" (*The Torrents
of Spring*, 70). Hemingway's judgment was that Anderson's
characters appear to live in an unreal world of their own

making because of their affectations, naivety, and romanticized mysticism. By exaggerating Anderson's manner in repeating his beliefs, Hemingway would expose their essential vapidity. In this derogation is the implicit suggestion that reality is different from Anderson's presentation of it in such novels as *Dark Laughter*. Thus, parody becomes an instrument of dissuasion. At this point in Hemingway's development as a literary artist, he was interested in demolishing views and attitudes, which his experience had demonstrated to be untrue, and for this purpose, parody is well suited.

Sarcasm, which involves an "inversion of meaning"[2] in that it implies the opposite of what is actually said, is used occasionally by Hemingway to expose to us what he thought was a distorted view. Fredric Henry's accurate reporting of the battle police's words to the retreating lieutenant colonel on his patriotic duty is an obvious instance where the narrator betrays his sarcastic intention: "It is because of treachery such as yours that we have lost the fruits of victory" (*A Farewell To Arms*, 223). In choosing to record precisely these words, Henry is, of course, expressing his own bitterness; he is also warning us, as he himself is in the process of learning, that the attitude of the battle police deriving from a conventional sense of patriotism and justice is invalid when put to the test of reality. He works to convince us not only that that attitude was wrong, but also that its very basis is questionable by evoking our contempt for trite sayings through sarcasm and by indirectly drawing our attention to his own authoritative knowledge of the events of the battlefield.

Understatement in the guise of meiosis is a third form of verbal irony, which Hemingway uses for transmitting his vision and for persuading us to it. In meiosis something is deliberately represented as much less than it really is. By intentionally dwarfing the big events, meiosis works as a shock device and this can be useful in "situations that call for a strong emotional response"[3] because it can shock those who have grown insensitive to disaster by its frequency, brutality, and magnitude. The shock can sharpen the blunted sensitivities and thereby release more appropriate reactions. In this way, meiosis helps the author to manipulate our reactions to events.[4] Jake Barnes and ·Frederic Henry underplay disasters, both personal and general. Frederic Henry whose own sensitivity is obviously blunted by the horrors of war speaks coolly and casually of a great disaster: "At the start of the winter came the permanent rain and with the rain came the cholera. But it was checked and in the end only seven thousand died of it in the army" (*A Farewell To Arms,* 4). Although the death of a large number of soldiers is not a matter for alarm or concern to the narrator, he unwittingly shocks us by his manner, and the shock underscores the magnitude of the disaster. Similarly, Jake understates his personal anguish in *The Sun Also Rises.* Although the entire action of this novel centers on his unique injury, Jake never, expresses his misery or sexual jealousy publicly even when he is provoked. He is "hardboiled" and, in Bill Gorton's phrase, he never gets daunted in public. To the prostitute Georgette's persistent questioning about his lack of response to her gestures of love, he simply replies he "got hurt in the war" (*The Sun Also Rises,* 17). He tells Brett that what happened to him was supposed to be "funny" (26); to Bill Gorton, he says, "I just had an accident" (115). This laconic style, the statement of just the bare facts, and the studied avoidance of ornamental language are an inevitable consequence of war and similar harsh experiences.[5]

Even when Jake is under great emotional stress, as he undoubtedly is after he contrives a meeting between Romero and Brett at her insistence, he understates his own emotions by giving a brief, objective, matter-of-fact description of the scene after Brett and Romero have gone: "The coffee-glasses and our three empty cognac-glasses were on the table. A waiter came with a cloth and picked up the glasses and mopped off the table"(187). Instead of directly telling us what his emotions are on this occasion, he resorts to the indirect means of the "objective correlative" to communicate those emotions. The external facts, which in Jake's description are the "empty" glasses and the waiter's mopping the table, suggest through a process of association that Jake too was "empty" because he was let down by Brett. By her departure with Romero, Brett has figuratively mopped him off as the waiter and done the table. Jake's feelings of loneliness, desperation, and sexual jealousy on this occasion are communicated through the frugal and indirect means of the "objective correlative" and we are persuaded to sympathize with his plight through the minor, but still felt, shocks administered by his pertinent understatement.

The method of indirection, which is at the core of understatement, works superbly in many of Hemingway's stories. In "Hills Like White Elephants," for example, an American and his girlfriend discuss the tabooed subject of abortion without mentioning the taboo word. They manage to do this because, like Lady Brett, they are also masters of the art of "talking around" a subject rather that "talking about" it. Hemingway, like his characters, also uses the same indirect means in some of the other stories. Nick's shocks when he is exposed to violence are never stated openly; the impotence of Mr. Elliot is not mentioned at all in "Mr. And Mrs. Elliot," the American wife's yearning for femininity is not expressed directly in "Cat in the Rain," and Butler's crookedness is not even named in "My Old Man." And yet we understand Hemingway's meaning on all these occasions. Although Hemingway does not choose to talk directly about the central issue in his stories, he draws our attention to them by indirectly referring to them. And his indirect methods are forceful enough to merit our attention.

Less overt, but employing the same shock device, is the use òf ingénue irony[6] in which a naïve young man is exposed to the chaotic world so that the contrast[7] between his own innocence and the violence and hypocrisy which encounter it (the innocence) reveals the conflicts and jolts us into accepting the gross reality. As Muecke observes, "The effectiveness of this ironical mode comes from its economy of means, mere common sense or even simple innocence or ignorance may suffice to see through the complexities of hypocrisy or expose the irrationality of prejudice."[8] The Hemingway hero's experience of "the way it was" is a passage from naivete to knowledge, from blissful ignorance to an awareness of the actual state of the world. After obtaining such knowledge, the young man characteristically becomes disillusioned. For example, Nick Adams' growing up is so inseparable from his encounters with violence and evil. After witnessing two unhappy events in the Indian camp in quick succession, Nick asks his father a number of innocent questions about death and killing:

> 'Is dying hard, Daddy?'
> 'No, I think it's pretty easy, Nick. It all depends.'
> (*Short Stories*, 95)

Nick's initial shock is reinforced by further shocks which he received later in life such as his unpleasant meeting with Ad Francis and his disturbing encounter with the killers in Summit. After these successive psychological "blows" to his innocent assumptions about the world comes spinal injury on the battlefield, which deepens his disillusionment. Cumulatively, the harshness, force, and frequency of these "blows" are implicit lessons to Nick on the nature of life. He is shocked into sense by his traumatic experiences.

The use of the ingenue as a rhetorical device enables Hemingway to present "the real thing" through the eyes of an innocent young man since such a view is presumably uncorrupted by the falsifications and overstatements of romantic fiction. This is by implication a determination to uncover the incongruity between appearance and reality, and to know this incongruity is essential for passage from a state of innocence to a state of experience.[9] To be experienced is to be disillusioned in Hemingway's world. Harold Krebs in "Soldier's Home" suffers this disillusionment after participating in the war. His midwestern, middle-class home in Oklahoma is conformist and conventional and understandably Krebs received his early training in pious platitudes and illusions. His early

Heming-3

conformity is indicated not only by his picture with his fraternity brothers, all of whom wore exactly the same collar, but even by his enlistment in the Marines. After he has seen the war and returned home, "nothing was changed in the town except that the young girls had grown up" (*Short Stories*, 147). His mother's platitudes "embarrassed" him. She is so steeped in her smug conventions that Krebs "couldn't make her see"(152) that after his homecoming, he does not love anybody. Like Krebs, Joe, the boy-narrator in "My Old Man," is also disillusioned. He is fond of his jockey-father, Butler. Travelling with him to horseraces, he comes to know of the corruption of the jockeys who are bribed to keep excellent horses from winning a race. Added to this is the shock of Joe's discovery that his father was also dishonest and that some of his father's colleagues thought Butler's death on the tracks a fitting retribution for "the stuff he's pulled"(205). Whether it is war or sport, the exposure of the older generation's hypocrisy and corruption had disillusioned young men like Krebs and Joe because they were brought up to believe in conventional morality and order. When the reality is genuinely known, the appearance can no longer be believed. Jake Barnes's disillusionment comes partly at least from his awareness of the gap between potential fulfillment and actual accomplishment in his affair with Lady Brett. He loves her and she returns his love, but they can do nothing more about it. Frederic Henry's bitterness comes with his unreasonable injury, the misery of the gigantic Caporetto retreat, and the terror of the Italian battle police, and it increases with his helplessness in the face of Catherine's death in childbirth. He had hoped that in Switzerland he would have the happiness and peace of mind in the company of his beloved Catherine, but it was a vain hope. This discrepancy between his hope and the shocking, undeserved misery of his life at the end made him totally disillusioned. Robert Jordan feels that the Spanish Civil War was a sort of education for him: "Sure, Gaylord's [the Madrid hotel which the Russians took over] was the place you need to complete your education. It was there you learned how it was all really done instead of how it was supposed to be done. He had only started his education, he thought" (*For Whom the Bell Tolls*, 230). His association with the guerillas for four days was also instructive. As he says at the end, "I wish there was some way to pass on what I learned, though. Christ, I was learning fast there at the end"(467). This "education" is a process of shedding one's illusions about war and human motivations. Jordan's participation in guerilla activities brings him into touch with reality as nothing else has done before. In these characters, Hemingway is simply reflecting his own fascination with that which lay beneath the surface of appearance. His own education, his own disillusionment, was based on his intense perception of the jarring, discordant elements in experience. The ingenue's education, awareness, or even awakening, makes us pause and ponder over his world because he is skillfully manipulated to that end by the author.

The actual process of manipulation of the ingenue may be illustrated by an analysis of "The Battler," a story ostensibly narrated in the third person. Here Nick and Bugs are used as devices to disclose the strange world of Ad Francis, which largely reflects the world of irrational violence often encountered by Hemingway. It is Nick who through various means lets us know all that we need to know about the battler. As a reporter of what he sees, as one who asks relevant questions, as one who elicits the necessary information, and as a target for the crazy man's intended attack, Nick became the chief instrument of disclosure in this story.[10] The situation is reported in the third person, but it is told essentially as Nick sees it. We see the battler through Nick's eyes in the beginning. Nick watches him from a distance and reports to us that the battler was sitting by the fire, that he seemed to be alone, and that he was looking into the fire. On a closer view, Nick reveals to us what he saw: his "misshapen" face, "sunken" nose, "slit" eyes, "queer" lips. To Nick's shocking embarrassment, he learns that the battler has only one ear, the other a stump. We also know through the battler's answers to Nick's questions that he is Ad Francis, the ex-prizefighter, and that he is "crazy." We even get some proof.

of his "craziness" when Nick unwittingly becomes the butt of Ad's threatened attack, and Nick is saved by the violent and timely intervention of Ad's Negro companion, Bugs, who provides more facts on the battler while answering Nick's questions. Bugs explains that Ad Francis had become crazy because "he took to many beatings," because of the "unpleasantness" of his marriage to his manager, and because of "disagreements" with his wife. As a climax to these shocking revelations, Bugs adds that he and Ad Francis became friends in a jail and that they are now tramping the country supporting themselves with the money send by Ad's wife. This sordid story of Ad Francis is disclosed to us largely through Nick's inquisitive questions and Bugs' answers. Whatever may be the emotional impact of the unexpected and sickening encounter with Ad Francis on Nick, he is Hemingway's device to communicate to us the eccentric world of the demented prizefighter. Nick also reveals to us the irrational violence which characterizes Hemingway's world: he is the victim of the brakeman's practical joke when he is busted; he is shocked by the deformed appearance of Ad Francis; he is threatened by Ad for no apparent reason, Ad himself is hit by the Negro while Nick looks on stunned. Bugs reveals his companion's past life and his own dubious relationship with him. Thus, the story of the battler is actually disclosed through the two minor characters, in the naïve questions of the one and the alarming answers of the other. The narrative functions of disclosure and commentary, which apparently belong to an omniscient third person narrator in "The Battler", are actually assigned to and fulfilled by the two minor characters. Each revelation about Ad Francis is a fresh shock to Nick as well as to us. The ingenue is here manipulated as an unwitting agent of disclosure, and his disclosures as well as his own stunned reactions must influence our view of the world.

Hemingway manipulates his characters in an attempt to mould our beliefs through the fictional narrator's commentaries. Such commentaries also serve as important means for disclosing his vision. The first person narrators in *The Sun Also Rises* and *A Farewell to Arms* are

rather convenient technical devices not only to make us
see, but also to make us appreciate, certain things. For
instance, Jake tries to convince Brett that the bullfight is
"more something that was going on with a definite end,
and less of a spectacle with unexplained horrors"(*The Sun
Also Rises*, 167). He guides her by focusing her attention
constantly on what he considers to be most essential so
that she might appreciate it as an art form. Here Jake
successfully merges his dual roles, character in the novel
and narrator, and under the pretext of instructing Brett on
the bullfight, Hemingway is in fact addressing and guiding
the reader. He chooses his facts and incidents carefully
and allows us to see only what he wants us to see. Jake
has already established his authoritative, knowledge of not
only the bullfight, but of the streets, bars, and restaurants
of Paris, and of the relative cost of things in France and
Spain; he has demonstrated his skills in finding bait-worms
for trout-fishing, in packing trout with ferns and in the
native method of drinking wine from leather bottles at the
fiesta. Such evidence of his knowledge and skills works on
our habit of accepting views, which come from those whom
we consider authorities, and on our tendency of approving
expertise. He has also made a favorable impression on us
by his meticulousness, his tolerance, and his
understanding in the early chapters of the novel. Without
his explicit commentary and expert knowledge, it would
not be easy for us to appreciate how Romero is to be favorably
distinguished from other bullfighters. Jake tells us that
Romero gave "real emotion" because he "had the old thing,
the holding of his purity of line through the maximum of
exposure" (168). He praises Romero's style of working close
to the bull under the gravest danger to his own life. The
long account of Belmonte's method of bullfighting is an
analogy meant to show Romero in the best light: "Romero
did always, smoothly, calmly, and beautifully, what he,
Belmonte, could only bring himself to do now
sometimes"(215). Such commentary, because of its
favorable nature and approving tone, helps to establish
Romero as one of the moral norms in the novel. His fight
with Cohn, far from diminishing his stature or tarnishing

his character, enhances them because his physical courage and grace in the bullring are matched, as the narrator works to reveal to us, by his moral courage when he refuses to admit defeat in his fight with Cohn. He is not daunted in public and he gives a brilliant performance the next day. The point, which Hemingway wishes to make through Jake's authoritative commentary, is that Romero's code is one decent way to live in a harsh and hostile world.

Jake's habit of thinking aloud on lonely nights is also a sort of commentary which, besides providing us glimpses into Hemingway's vision, influences us by rousing our sympathy for Jake. Two of his nocturnal ruminations are caused by Brett's promiscuous conduct. On the first occasion, she has left him in order to flirt with Count Mippipopolous and on the second, she is in bed with Mike Campbell, while Jake is in the adjacent room. His despair on both these occasions prompts him to muse over his life and we see here the workings of his mind. He tells us, "I try and play it along and just not make trouble for people" (31). He wants to get along with his friends as best he can. He is "hardboiled about everything in the daytime,"(34) but at night when he is alone and when his mind works, the world appears differently to him. The "fine philosophy" which is based on a simple exchange of values is useful for a while as a practical way of living, but such "fine philosophies" have hardly any permanent validity in a mutable world. As a practical man he is concerned about "how to live" rather than the largely speculative question of "what it was all about." He is not sure about abstractions like "morality" and "immorality," yet he feels them to be "large statements," and finally "a lot of bilge." To avoid such nonsense, he prefers the speech of his British friends who "talked with inflected phrases. One phrase to mean everything"(149). This is a "central statement on morality"[11] especially when considered in relation to his later sarcastic references to the simplicity of living in France because of its "clear financial basis"(233). No clear answers to abstract questions appear possible to him. Jake's thinking aloud is a method of unfolding Hemingway's vision to us and a subtle way of winning our sympathy for his position. It is a subtle appeal because while he appears to be only musing, he is, in fact, making a powerful appeal to our emotions. When he expresses his distrust of abstractions and "large sentiments" when he describes the bullfight in artistic terms, when he denotes his preference for fishing in the Irati river to living in the midst of the din of Paris, when he complains of insomnia, and when he speaks in an ironical manner, one suspects that the sympathy we feel for Jake is being transferred to the views and attitudes he (Hemingway) expresses.

Like Jake's, Frederic Henry's commentaries also accomplish the same purpose through similar appeals. His outspoken denunciation of abstract words is not simply his personal reaction to Gino's conventionally patriotic sentiments, but a deliberate attempt to use an opportunity to influence our minds on the specific question of abstractions. He cites what he has "heard" during the war and what he has "seen" on the battlefield as reliable evidence to condemn the use of abstract words. His sarcastic insistence upon the misplaced idealism and blind loyalty of the Italian battle police who were shooting down officers in the name of abstraction, ("the sacred soil of the fatherland"), is an indication of his contempt for such unwarranted abstraction. Observe his telling remarks:

> I was obviously a German in Italian uniform. I saw how their minds worked, if they had minds and if they worked. They were all young men and they were saving their country.....The questioners had that beautiful detachment and devotion to stern justice of men dealing in death without being in any danger of it. (*A Farewell to Arms*, 224-5)

In the context of his injury, and the death of Passini at Fossalta, of Aymo during the retreat, and of countless men at Udine, wounding and killing have come to seem sudden, unreasonable, and gratuitous. So many examples of violent death both provide and emphasize the likelihood that his considered view of the world can be taken as true. The parallels between Henry's injury and Hemingway's injury,

between Henry's love affair with Catherine Barkley and
Hemingway's love affair with Agnes Von Kurowsky during
World War I,[12] and their shared distrust of abstract words
lead us to believe that Hemingway is dramatizing his own
situation in Frederic Henry and is using Henry to voice
his own views. Thus, the first person narrators, Jake and
Henry, are used to dramatize the author's own situation,
to give us some idea of his vision, and to convince us largely
through the authority of their knowledge, personal
experience, and by their comments on the moral and
intellectual qualities of the other characters.

Some minor characters like Bill Gorton and Count
Greffi, and the so-called "code" heroes like Pedro Romero
and Robert Wilson, are also skillfully handled to become
instruments for disclosing the affirmative aspects of
Hemingway's vision to us, since these men are endowed
with a certain force of character, they work as instruments
of his rhetoric too. For instance, Bill Gorton is a moral
neutral in so far as he is the only one among Jake's friends
who is not Jake's rival for Brett. His success as a novelist,
his travels in Europe, his interest in fishing and in
bullfighting testify to his wide knowledge and range of
interests. He speaks in the imperative form to Jake and
reminds him of what he should or should not do. Morton L.
Ross has argued that Bill is "the voice of Hemingway's code,"
and that he "is in fact the novel's preacher functioning
very much as does the speaker in Ecclesiastes."[13] At least
three of Bill's imperatives have the ring of commandments
and these suggest practical ways of getting along in a not
too friendly hopeful, or adequate world. When he asks Jake
to "Show irony and pity," he refers to the burlesque act of
the Fratellinis which reference suggests that in an
irrational world one needs a sense of detachment to survive.
A comedy act such as the Fratellinis to which the friendly
banter of Bill and Jake is analogous is one way of forgetting
at least temporarily, the hostile outside world.[14] Bill's
second command, "Utilize a little," which directly echoes
Ecclesiastes[15] stresses the importance of sensuous life,
which he and Jake are celebrating at the time of this mock-
sermon. We know that the gratification of the senses is an

important way for Hemingway to combat *nada*. Bill's third command, "Let us not pry into holy mysteries of the hencoop with simian fingers," forbids metaphysical speculation as dangerous. Bill is once again echoing Ecclesiastes: "For in much wisdom is much grief: and he that increaseth knowledge increaseth sorrow."[16] Bill's moral authority and his intimate relationship with Jake – he is both confessor and physician to Jake – invest his imperatives with a certain respectability and force which cannot be easily ignored. Like Bill Gorton, Count Greffi in *A Farewell to Arms* influences through the force of his character and moral stature. He is a man of "discipline" who is full of the zest for life even at the advance age of ninety-four. His gracious conduct towards Henry with whom he plays a "lovely game of billiards" (260) serves essentially the same therapeutic purpose as Jake's fishing trip with Bill Gorton. It is the Count's love of life that impresses us most as his unaging spirit revives the self-assurance of Henry who has complained to Catherine a short while before that he felt like a "criminal" after deserting the army (251). In the Count's healthy attitude to life, one may sense a solution to the problem of living in a troubled world just as Bill's commands show Jake how to live.

Hemingway uses the "code" heroes as exemplars of the values he wishes to defend and these values are an intrinsic part of his vision. Pedro Romero and Robert Wilson are the most prominent of these men. They are men of action rather than of words. Being professional experts in their own fields, they concentrate on perfection in their work. Belemonte and Joselito, the two great bullfighters of the decadent period who are praised by Hemingway for their *pundonor* (*Death in the Afternoon*, 68-9), emphasized the style of fighting rather than the actual killing of the bull. They provide through their dignified conduct public norms of behavior. In his own profession of bullfighting, Romero made no contortions and hence he could give pure emotion. Romero's self-respect and dignity is also evident in his behavior towards Robert Cohn after Cohn knocked him down. As Morton L. Ross notes, he is the only character in *The Sun Also Rises* who never gets daunted, "neither by the

bulls, nor by Cohn, nor by Lady Brett."[17] The integrity and
self-discipline of the other characters in this novel can be
assessed by the extent to which they approach Romero's
norm. Thus Jake never gets daunted in public; rather he
would cry in the privacy of his room, however intense his
agony might be. Mike is too talkative, Bill too ironical, and
Cohn too romantic to measure up to Romero. The other
'code" hero, Robert Wilson, is a hunter who has high
professional standards which include discipline and grace.
He teaches fearless shooting, (or the code), to Francis
Macomber and thereby makes a man of him. He considers
talking about his hunting accomplishments unprofessional
and therefore warns Macomber not to talk "too much" about
his elation on killing a buffalo. The repeated delineation of
"code" heroes in successive works underscores their
central role in Hemingway's scheme of things.

Even the wounded hero becomes a device for
communicating Hemingway's vision through frequent
repetition of this character type in ways designed to arouse
our sympathy. For instance, Jake is placed in situations
where his wound makes him a helpless onlooker while
Brett flirts with several of his friends, situations which
naturally move us to pity. Nick and Jake are also victims
of insomnia and unhappy night thoughts. By showing
repeatedly that their sleeplessness, helplessness,
hopelessness, and bitterness are the consequence of their
physical or psychological injuries Hemingway evokes our
compassion for them. He also seems to be raising questions:
why should it happen to a non-combatant like Frederic
Henry and why should Jake be wounded the way he was?
This irrationality is typical of the atmosphere of unreason
which led to the war, and war which recurred so often for a
single generation has itself become a symptom of the times.
The violence of modern times is not merely irrational, but
impersonal in that people are killed by machines which
make no discrimination between good and evil, between
the innocent and the guilty. It is this state of the world
which Hemingway seeks to convey to us through the
repeated portrayal of the wounded man. The wounded heroes
from Yogi Johnson in *The Torrents of Spring* to Thomas

Hudson in *Islands in the Stream* appear to be specimens of
the general scheme of things in Hemingway's world. Most
of these men, notably Nick, Jake, and Henry, are injured
on the battlefield under circumstances which make such
injury seem gratuitous. The wound, besides dramatizing
the author's own injury, is a constant reminder of a world
at war with itself. The shell-shocked soldier, the gored
bullfighter, the injured pirate, the hurt fisherman who
inherited the earth represent Hemingway's world
eloquently because they bear the visible marks of violence.
Even as they are crippled by the loss of a limb or some
other vital organ, the world too is crippled by the mass
slaughter of the war. Jake's sexual wound represents the
state of much of western Europe after World War I when it
became in Eliot's well-known phrase, "the waste land". The
desperate predicament in which the lovers, Jake and Brett,
find themselves is a commentary on the peculiar problems
of the modern world. So the figure of the injured man
reflects an essential segment of Hemingway's vision and
the condition of that man evokes our sympathy.

The state of Hemingway's world is depicted through
carefully chosen symbols, which are also assigned
persuasive functions. The symbols, dust and dry leaves, in
the first chapter of *A Farewell to Arms,* for instance, not
only foreshadow events in that novel, but also serve to
establish the mood of impending doom. The strong
emotional connotation of "dust," as Carlos Baker[18]
indicates, indirectly alludes to the Old Testament and the
funeral service. Falling leaves suggest approaching winter,
which has its own burden of death and disaster. Winter
brings the permanent rain, which, in turn, brings cholera.
And cholera, in the narrator's quiet understatement, killed
only seven thousand soldiers. These symbols are reinforced
by other recurring symbols like rain in this novel. Rain
usually portends disaster for the Italian army and for
Frederic Henry and Catherine Barkley. The sense of doom,
disaster, and death, which informs the novel, is indicated
to us by the connotations implicit in symbols such as dust,
falling leaves, winter, and rain. The religious and
emotional connotations of some of these symbols are meant

to affect our emotional responses to the character and events.

Recurring images, metaphors, motifs, structures, and patterns of action help to clarify Hemingway's vision to us and by the very force of repetition attempt to convince us of it. Repetition has three concurrent functions in Hemingway's work. It reflects the repetitive pattern in his vision; it shows how deeply Hemingway believed in his vision. More importantly, by using the technique of repetition in a variety of situations and in a number of ways Hemingway transforms it into a rhetorical instrument. When we see Hemingway's men and women trapped under different circumstances in successive novels, when the metaphor of game is repeated in various forms, when the motifs of luck and catharsis recur in almost all his major works, when the circular structure forms the basis of many of his novels, and when the cyclical pattern of action is recreated in several works, we are given the means to obtain a better understanding of Hemingway's world-view. Hemingway has worked with various types of characters in various situations and with different temperaments, but most of them come to the same conclusions about the world. Skilful repetition[19] may be seen in the game metaphor,[20] which recurs in the bullfight, big-game hunting, and fishing. In all these games, the animal is trapped or cornered, hooked or baited, then killed not through superior strength or courage, but through skill and expertise. In the baseball game also the player is metaphorically trapped and punished before he has time to learn the rules and as Frederic Henry observes; "They threw you in and told you the rules and the first time they caught you off base they killed you" (A Farewell to Arms, 327). It is this inevitably and gratuitousness of death that Hemingway constantly emphasizes through the game metaphor. These metaphors body forth the analogy between life and game. The use of analogy, explicit or implicit, whether in the game metaphor or the image of the trap, attempts to influence our mind in a certain way. It is a well-known fact how the important motif of luck and the circular structure recur in much of Hemingway's work.

The cyclical pattern of action is perhaps best illustrated in *For Whom the Bell Tolls* at the end of which, Robert Jordan, the hero, is literally back where he started, the pine-needled forest in exactly the same "flat" posture. The entire action in this novel revolves round the bridge. Starting with the debate in the guerilla camp on the wisdom of, and the necessity for, destroying the bridge, the action proceeds to enlisting the support of El Sordo's band, to preparation for demolition, and to the actual demolition itself. As Allen Guttman notes, the bridge is "the centre of a series of concentric circles."[21] Jordan believes that the bridge is "the point on which the future of the human race can turn" (*For Whom the Bell Tolls*, 43). The principal characters in the novel are differentiated by their attitude to the bridge. Pablo opposes its demolition for sound tactical reasons; Pilar ardently supports destruction by identifying with the Republic: "I am for the Republic.....And the Republic is the bridge"(53). Robert Jordan considers himself the "instrument" for its demolition; he is a "bridge-blower now. Not a thinker"(17). The other guerillas are too weak to resist the emotional appeal of Pilar. The circular action is also stressed by Jordan's essential re-enactment of Kashkin's role. He is somehow identified with Kashkin in the minds of the guerillas, because both are "dynamiters" sent to the guerillas for sabotage operations. When Jordan describes to El Sordo and Pilar how he had shot the incapacitated Kashkin, El Sordo looks at Jordan strangely. Pilar who has seen "nothing" in Jordan's palm earlier claims that she could smell death in Kashkin and that she saw his death in his face "as though it were burned there with a branding iron"(251). Jordan also imaginatively identifies himself with his predecessor by his close association with Kashkin, by metaphorically wearing his mantle as a "dynamiter," and by carrying Kashkin's German gun with him. The circular analogy is complete even in the manner of Jordan's death. He is also unable to escape to Gredos with the other guerillas after the destruction of the bridge because of the bad wounds. The same "gray gelding" ridden by a Fascist cavalryman whom he had killed only the previous day crushes him. Thus the wheel of action comes full circle once again. The repeated cyclical pattern of action along with the other recurring features in Hemingway's work helps focus his vision so that we may understand, and perhaps be convinced of, the importance of that vision as an expression of Hemingway's world-view.

The technique of repetition is supplemented by the analogous technique of redefinition of certain terms, which are crucial to an exposition of Hemingway's views. We know that he disputed the contemporary meanings and usages of certain words because these did not, in his view, correspond to contemporary realities.[22] His redefinitions of terms like "morality" and "defeat" are demonstrated first by dramatized situations and then by exposition. Brett fashions a morality of her own when she was initially infatuated by Romero. She tells Jake on this occasion: "I don't say it's right. It is right though for me" (*The Sun Also Rises*, 184). When she finally leaves Romero, after deciding not to be a bitch that ruins children, her morality becomes for her a substitute for God. The same morality is at work when Cayetano Ruiz, the gambler refuses to divulge the name of his assailant to the police, or when Ole Andreson keeps cool after learning of his impending assassination. This dramatized morality is summarized in his expository work, *Death in the Afternoon*: "What is moral is what you feel good after and what is immoral is what you feel bad after"(4).

The seemingly minor items like the titles of stories and novels, and epigraphs are tactical items in Hemingway's calculated verbal strategy to persuade us by putting us in a proper frame of mind before we actually read the fiction. Titles like *In Our Time* which allude to the Book of Common Prayer expose us to the workings of the author's mind through the ironic contrast between peace implied in the allusion and the violence of the modern times. Similarly, the title and one of the epigraphs of *The Sun Also Rises* with their biblical origins provide us with inklings of what Hemingway thought of the world he lived in. Both in the title and the epigraph from *Ecclesiastes*, Hemingway is clearly indicating his considered view of the world. No generation is "lost," but the passing of generations is part of a continuous cyclical pattern that may be observed in many natural phenomena like the rising and setting of the sun, the blowing of the wind, and the flowing of the rivers. The circular motion suggested by the title and the epigraph actually foreshadows the circular journeys of Jake and Brett. The essential story of this novel, as James Rouch[23] observes, is circumscribed between the two cab rides and aimless wanderings symbolic of the purposeless, desperate life of Jake's generation. Together, the rides indicate the circularity in the lives of Jake and Brett. No matter where they go, Paris, Pamplona, or Madrid, they come back to the same point. Brett may run away with Robert Cohn to San Sebastian, or with Pedro Romero to Madrid, but she keeps coming back to Jake Barnes because she knows that he alone could comfort her. Jake moves from one café to another in Paris, and from Paris to Burguete for fishing, to Pamplona for bullfighting, to San Sebastian for swimming, but he ends the same way as he begins, riding a cab with Brett. Both of them have had another forced ride on the "vast wheel" and have returned to the starting point, and nothing seems to have been accomplished at the end of the novel. Jake remains impotent, verily "time's eunuch,"[24] a phrase used by Gerald Manley Hopkins to describe the condition of modern man. This return to the initial situation of the novel underscores not only the circularity, but also the meaninglessness of life for a desperate generation. It may be argued that the titles and epigraphs of the novels and stories are similarly strong pointers to the author's views, and therefore they are valuable instruments of disclosure and they are also significant attempts to condition our attitude to the story somewhat in advance.

Thus, Hemingway's rhetorical mode draws from the whole repertoire of customary rhetorical practices. Several forms of verbal irony, including parody, sarcasm, and understatement, and indirection are parts of his verbal strategy to shape our beliefs. The introduction of the ingénue influences our thinking while the other characters are used as instruments of disclosure and persuasion either through their questions, answers, commentaries, monologues, or postures. Symbols, images, metaphors, motifs, structures, and cyclical action, which recur, serve to focus on his vision and convince us of it. Redefinition of terms and thoughtful selection of epigraphs and titles are small, but important tools for giving glimpses of Hemingway's world-view and for putting us in a perceptive frame of mind. Hemingway's rhetorical mode, then, is a combination of a variety of customary technical resources, which he deems effective for the presentation of his vision.

NOTES AND REFERENCES

1. *The Oxford English Dictionary* defines "mode" as "a prevailing fashion or conventional custom, practice or style."
2. David Worcester, *The Art of Satire.* New York: Russell & Russell, 1960. 78.
3. D.C. Muecke, *The Compass of Irony.* London: Methuen, 1969. 80.
4. On the origin, nature, and function of understatement in Hemingway, it is instructive to know Ihab Hassan's views: "Hemingway's understatement stems from a private conviction that good things deserve to remainunexpressed; it ends by serving an artistic purpose. Understatement requires omission, and the art ofomission is one that he learns from the Great Impressionist painter, Cézanne particularly.....Omission compels participation. Thus the house of fiction, with its spaces, is finally inhabited." See his *The Dismemberment of Orpheus.* 89.
5. G.W. Turner's comments on this topic are perceptive: "What I have called 'deadpan theory' has permanent if limited usefulness. It is a necessary part of wartime slang. If a soldier calls a murderous battle 'a bit of a dust-up', it is because there is no danger among soldiers that the irony in the   understatement will be misunderstood. Warfare and other harsh experiences need and produce popularlaconic styles. Such styles are a feature of hard frontier life and appear in America and Australia as they appeared and became great literature in the Early European frontier region, Iceland." See his *Stylistics.* Harmondsworth: Penguin Books, 1973. 221.
6. D.C. Muecke argues that ingénue irony is different from

romantic irony and that some American critics have "widely
misunderstood and misrepresented " the latter. Some of
the American critics like Sedgwick and Worcester identified
the ingénue with romantic irony. I think Mueke's
distinction is validand useful. See *Irony*. Critical Idiom
Series. London: Methuen, 1970. 20.

7. Contrast as a recurring structural principle in Hemingway
 .   is studied by Keisuke Tanaka who observes hat it is "well
    employed as a rhetorical device and a structural technique
    and is very effective in creating balance and unity in his
    works." See his "The Bipolar Construction in the Works
    of Ernest Hemingway," *Kyushu American Literature* 12:
    Jan'70: 32-44.

8. *Irony*. 58.

9. Maurice Z. Shroder argues that the matter of the novel is
    traditionally "the passage from a state of innocence to a
    state of. experience," and that irony is peculiarly
    appropriate to the novel. See "The Novel as Genre,"
    Massachusetts Review, 4:1963. 291-308.

10. I am indebted to R.S. Crane for this approach. See his
    discussion of "The Killers" in *The Idea of the Humanities
    and Other Essays, Critical and Historical*, Vol.II. Chicago:
    University of Chicago Press, 1967. 303-314.

11. Claire Sprague, "*The Sun Also Rises*: Its Clear Financial
    Basis," *American Quarterly* 21(Sum'69): 260.

12. For a full account of Hemingway's affair with Agnes Von
    Kurowsky, see Carlos Baker, *Ernest Hemingway: A Life
    Story*. 68-80.

13. Morton L. Ross, "Bill Gorton, the Preacher in *The Sun
    Also Rises*," *Modern Fiction Studies* 18 (72-73): 519.

14. See Robert O. Stephens, *Hemingway's Non Fiction: The Public
    Voice*. Chapel Hill: The University of North Carolina Press,
    1968. 243.

15. *Ecclesiastes*, 3: 1-15 urges: "And also that every man should
    eat and drink and enjoy the good of all his labour, it is the
    gift of God." Bill Gorton seems to be indirectly referring to
    this passage of the preacher.

16. *The Bible for Students of Literature and Art*, selected with
    an introduction by G. B. Harrison. Garden City, N.Y.:
    Anchor Books, 1964. 294.

17.   Morton L. Ross, "Bill Gorton the Preacher in *The Sun
    Also Rises*," *Modern Fiction Studies* 18: (7273): 523.

18. *Hemingway: The Wrier as Artist*, 95.

19. Skillful repetition as an effective tool of persuasion amply demonstrated in the story in the *Panchatantra* in which a Brahmin was persuaded through repetitive and organized lying that the goat he was taking for a *yajna* (fire-sacrifice) was a dog, which a Brahmin cannot even touch. Persistent and judicious repetition is a common method of persuasion even today.

20. J.J. Benson considers game as an important metaphor for emotional control in Hemingway's work. See *Hemingway: The Writer's Art of Self-Defense*. Minneapolis: University of Minnesota Press, 1969. 70-98.

21. "Mechanized Doom: Ernest Hemingway and the Spanish Civil War," in Baker ed. *Ernest Hemingway: Critiques of Four Major Novels*. New York: Scribner's, 1962. 98.

22. Joseph Conrad, like Ezra Pound, has noted the rhetorical strength of the right word in these words: "He who wants to persuade should put his trust not in the right argument, but in the right word." Quoted by John Holloway, *The Victorian Sage: Studies in Argument*. London: Archon Books, 1962. 16.

23. "Jake Barnes as Narrator," *Modern Fiction Studies*, 11:Win'65-66. 369-70.

24. Gardner, W.H. & Mackenzie, N.H. Eds. *The Poems of Gerald Manley Hopkins*. London: OxfordUniversity Press, 1967. 4th edn. 107.

Waste Land Parallels Unifying In Our Time: Hemingway's Confirmation as a Modernist

Bickford Sylvester

Tracing in *The Sun Also Rises* Hemingway's carefully-wrought appropriations of *The Waste Land*'s themes and methods, Richard P. Adams lamented in 1959 ("Sunrise Out of *The Waste Land*," *Tulane Studies in English*) what amounts to a widespread bias against viewing Hemingway as a consciously *literate* writer. This is, in other words, a bias against seeing Hemingway as the modernist he was, the student of Pound and rival of Joyce and Eliot, who craftily demonstrated (too craftily, perhaps) that he could adapt to his unique style the allusive narrative approach and much of the vision and perspective that brought Joyce and Eliot the enviable respect of the intelligentsia. We have come a long way since 1959; but the bias has lingered, causing even a valuable corrective effort like Hugh Kenner's (1975) to portray Hemingway's world as more "homemade"—more autonomous and intuitive—than it is. Hemingway's persona has not helped, of course. Believing in the writer's right to lie for effect, he no doubt felt justified in his lifelong masquerade, even before close colleagues like MacLeish, as the uniformed artisan who must "think good with [his] bones" because he cannot think with his head (*Letters*, 545). And Hemingway's matching evasiveness about the philosophical intention of his works has not encouraged us to look for learning in them. Thus it is only now, when we are beginning to take fresh stock of everything about Hemingway – his relationships, his enormous, disciplined reading, his manuscripts, his art collections, his letters, *and* his books – that we are ready to accept all that is there in his texts. Michael Reynolds has called for a spirit of scholarly exploration whenever evidence points to obvious, uncharted regions in Hemingway's work ("The Next Ten Years," *College Literature* [Fall,1980]). And the favorable reception of Robert Gadjusek's recent observation of "close and deliberate" parallels between *In Our Time* and *Dubliners* (*Hemingway Review* [Fall, 1982]) is a welcome example.

Accordingly, I want to show that quite apart from the many *Dubliners* parallels Mr. Gadjusek has so thoroughly traced, there is in addition a great deal more of *The Waste Land* in Hemingway's first major work than the presence that has often been noticed in "Big Two-Hearted River." Indeed, in noticing certain parallels between the overall structure and central theme of Eliot's poem and those of the book, we can discover in Hemingway's collection a larger unifying context than we have been aware of. We can recognize a context more thoughtful, more informed than has been suspected, one within which the unifying patterns of detail already explicated by various admirable studies take on fresh significance.

It was with *In Our Time*, rather than with *The Sun Also Rises*, that Hemingway made his hitherto unacknowledged debut as the manipulator of "a continuous parallel between contemporaneity and antiquity" used as "a way of controlling, of ordering, of giving a shape and a significance to the immense panorama of futility and anarchy which is contemporary history." The quoted words are of course Eliot's in *The Dial* of November, 1923, describing Joyce's (and his own) monumental accomplishments a year earlier in *Ulysses* and *The Waste Land*. And when Eliot's formulation appeared, Hemingway had not only read Pound's copy of *The Waste Land*, but was shortly to begin selecting, adding to, and organizing the collection of stories and vignettes he would soon publish as the full *In Our Time*.

The most central "continuous parallel between contemporaneity and antiquity" in Hemingway's book is between the twentieth-century emotional and spiritual alienation in American and Europe (which his composite protagonist must progressively admit, contribute to, and start to withstand, as we shall see) and the four hundred

years of Christendom represented by the entire Evening
Prayer of which Hemingway's title is an allusive fragment
– like the hundreds of quoted "fragments" of cultural
tradition Eliot uses. The process is the same as Eliot's,
whose parallels often stress, not merely similarity, but
ironic contrast between earlier times of belief and the
degraded present, and whose multiple earlier worlds are
also outside the text itself, to be evoked, from the reader's
fund of associations, by relevant "fragments" "shored
against" the present ruin.

We have always limited ourselves to the obvious
ironies about peace and war suggested by this fragmentary
title alone. But we would do well to examine the total context
of Hemingway's titles, for they were chosen from a deeper
background of reading than we have assumed. We should
approach them as we do Eliot's allusions, and Joyce's and
Pound's, for example. The Versicles and Responses from
the Order for Morning and Evening Prayer, from the Book
of Common Prayer of the Church of England, were shared
daily wherever the British Empire stretched, marking the
coalescence of metaphysical certainties inherited by the
twentieth century and shattered by the great war:

Priest	O Lord, shew thy mercy upon us.
Answer.	And grant us thy salvation.
Priest.	O Lord, save the King.
Answer.	And mercifully hear us when we call upon thee.
Priest.	Endue thy Ministers with righteousness.
Answer.	And make thy chosen people joyful.
Priest.	O Lord, save thy people.
Answer.	And bless thine inheritance.
Priest.	Give peace in our time, O Lord.
Answer.	Because there is none other that fighteth for us, but only thou, O God.
Priest.	O God, make clean our hearts within us.
Answer.	And take not thy Holy Spirit from us.

The prayer shows the "people" of that earlier mortal
community acknowledging the human vulnerability
besetting those in our time, but sustained by their shared

conviction that the sources of authority and security in society will protect and guide them as long as these functionaries are in turn protected and given purpose by God. He is asked to make the institutions in the hierarchy function, to "save the King," to "Endue [His] ministers with righteousness" (with a sense of their responsibility as intermediary authorities), in each case for the ultimate comfort of the people, and then to grant peace and purity of heart to the people themselves. The order of concern is from the top of the hierarchy to the bottom.

Now the stories and interchapters in the body of the text, when read with the entire titular prayer in mind, are (among many other things, of course) experienced as a rueful expansion and elaboration of the prayer, with an ironic difference. In the book the supplication is everyman's inborn, unarticulated yearning for guidance, protection, and belief; it consists of the indirectly-expressed longing of all the alienated protagonists and/or speakers of the stories and vignettes. The prayer, on the other hand, is a believers' ritualized, shared address to a known source of order in an age of consubstantial myth; and in the book the central orderer is not there to "save" and "endue....with righteousness" the various members of the human hierarchy to whom the composite protagonist turns. Thus the composite protagonist (variously named Nick or Marjorie, etc., or typenamed – "the American wife"—much liked the many-voiced speaker of *The Waste Land*), becomes a universal twentieth-century figure as the stories and vignettes accrue; and he is portrayed as a questor/victim like Eliot's speaker. He begins as the littlest of the people and as he grows up is progressively failed by every source of guidance, security, and authority (both individual and institutional) that he has inherited a need to believe in – inherited as representative human being, as American and European romantic idealist, and as twentieth-century man set up and betrayed by the western tradition, the failed faith of his consequently failing, psychically-wounded and impotent leaders.

The order of concern in the prayer is reversed in the book to suit the expanding awareness of the protagonist in a *bildungsroman*. We move upward and outward from father, then both parents, through various functionaries (including cabinet "ministers") and emptied institutions encountered as the protagonist matures (love, marriage, parenthood, patriotism, justice, etc.), to dwell once again in "My Old Man" upon failed fatherhood, from the point of view now of a near-adult. Thence, after "Big Two-Hearted River," we end with a parodic portrait of a king – that chief human father-figure, not only in the prayer providing Hemingway's continuous parallel but, conveniently, in the myth providing Eliot's. The "king" of "L'envoi" accepts his political impotence with blithe irresponsibility because he is of our time, and thus un"saved," not endued with a sense of purpose beyond personal survival. The fairy-tale *hortus conclusus* to which he is confined is a far cry from the fallen reality imprisoning his abandoned "people" outside the garden. And a far cry from any rejuvenation bringing renewed life to his people will be his resurrection across distant waters, possibly as the proprietor of a Greek-American restaurant. So much for the foundation of our western "inheritance," the Apollonian tradition whose degradation Pound had lamented in "Hugh Selwyn Mauberley," *his* work ending with an "Envoi." (And so much, at a related level, for the Old World perspective sought by the questing protagonist as American Abroad. The journalist in "L'envoi" speaks as the last and most knowing of several such voices in the book, and seems to realize that the boon he has sought afar is sought in his backyard by elders as lost as he.)

Both poem and book portray the same psychological connection between failure of faith and failure of others. In *The Waste Land*, as it is approached by Cleanth Brooks in *The Well-Wrought Urn* (1936), and Kimon Friar in his superb notes of *Modern Poetry, American and British* (1951), the mythic and legendary association of spiritual, emotional, social, and physical disease is seen by Eliot to reflect a universal causal relationship. In times when there is no commonly shared myth, or explanation of the world, human beings become so preoccupied by personal anxiety (over the unmentionable "overwhelming question" of

"Prufrock") that in both their public and their private lives
they are inaccessible to those who would depend upon them;
and their victims in turn become inaccessible to others. It
is as the products of a complex legacy of self-absorption
thus passed on, that Eliot's emotionally-paralyzed lovers
introduce us to the modern wasteland. It is as the ultimate
recipient of just such a legacy (traced from the beginning
of the book) that the recently shattered Nick Adams of "Big
Two-Hearted River"sets forth, utterly alone at last, to learn
how to feel without having his feelings spin into madness.

The two opening stories dramatize the inadequacies
of the code that has turned his representative *fin de siecle*
parents in upon themselves to start the process. Their
Victorian assumption that the human will can deny the
emotional component of man's mixed nature leaves them
so ironically dominated by repressed feeling that they
shame their son by their hypocrisy as well as remain blind
to his feelings—as they are to each other's, and as the
doctor is to his patients' emotions. (These consequences
of the Victorian synthesis are re-experienced when the
composite protagonist, as Krebs, reaches early manhood.)
Nick in turn cannot later respond to Marjorie's adult needs
or release his own. Nor, in his other male identities, can
the composite protagonist surrender himself as husband
or father in the stories of the marriage group. Without
examples of sexual or ethical completeness he is afraid of
commitment; and deprived, by his parents' manifest self-
deception, of even their generation's illusory spiritual belief,
he is distracted by general anxiety. Thus each of the
protagonists in the stories and chapters, whatever his
particular identity, sex, or nationality, and whatever the
corresponding expectations he inherits, can only retreat
into himself in his way, as Nick does in his father's way.

In addition to those like the various wives who are
failed by their husbands, there are in many stories,
obviously, other characters whose past, present, or future
betrayals parallel the central character's. (There are the
mother and baby in "Indian Camp," Eddy Boulton, Bill,
perhaps, Bugs and Ad and possibly Ad's sister, Luz, Peduzzi
and his daughter, and the local mother-to-be in "Cross

Country Snow," for example, not to mention the two unborn children or any child unfortunately born to the Elliots. Simultaneously, in the interchapters military officers, political leaders, matadors, priests, and police show, by their indifference to those who might depend upon them in a world of dislocation and violence, the inadequacy of the conspectus of codes they profess.

As a result, when Joe Butler says, at the end of the penultimate story, "When they get started, they don't leave a guy nothing," we feel the "they" referring not only to destiny, but to all the failed sources of security in the book. Joe speaks, not just for himself, but for the composite twentieth century youth of the collection, admitting at last that life inevitably takes away every external permanence one is born to expect, and in the cruel process destroys the capacity for pleasure that accompanied one's illusions and that allowed one to respond to others. Re-enter Nick Adams, alone.

Nick fights to keep from "thinking" because that would mean "mixing memory and desire" (as the opening lines of *The Waste Land* puts it). And the feelings associated with Nick's traumatic loss are too powerful to be defended against by depressive apathy like that of Eliot's speaker; for "the thing left out" is more than that Nick Adams had experienced violence in combat and rejection in love, or even that as the individual called Nick he is the child of a destructive marriage. It is all of these, of course. And it is also that the war ended for his whole world the assumptions of order and permanence that permitted the spontaneous pleasures Nick remembers sharing with earlier comrades. For the reader Nick's losses are identified with the betrayals experienced by all the others in the book, as are Joe's. But the most shattering blow left out yet communicated by the story is Nick's discovery, since the protagonist spoke as Joe, that the human bio-psychic organism cannot normally bear as much reality as Joe perceives, that when one is betrayed by all the external sources of order, one's own emotions betray him, so that he cannot even trust himself. Consequently Nick has had to accept the harsh fact that survival in our time begins with a self-discipline more rigorous and difficult than any demand in times of belief.

This is not the attempted evasion of feeling of Nick's Victorian parents, stripped only of its self-deluding piety, that Young (*Ernest Hemingway*, 1952) and some others come close to defining, and that would merely begin another cycle of self-imprisonment and betrayal. Nor is it the beginning of renewed faith, as others wish. Rather, what we see in "Big Two-Hearted River" is a thoroughly worked out application of *Damyata*, "Control," the last and (I think) the most fundamental of the three Sanskrit disciplines making up Eliot's prescription at the end of *The Waste Land* for emotional revival without revival of belief. Indeed, I suspect that, critical bias notwithstanding, *In Our Time*'s partial explication of this celebrated poem's resolution might have been noticed after Cowley clarified "Big Two-Hearted River" (*The Portable Hemingway*) had there not always been considerably confusion about the meaning of Eliot's ending.

At any rate, according to Friar (and apparently as it was read by Hemingway), the poem suggests that we can find in the fragments of works from times of belief the kinds of emotion all people need, and that we can practice these feelings. In so doing we can keep ourselves emotionally alive, even though without belief. Thus we can sustain the extra burden of twentieth-century man, the need to create for ourselves feelings which came automatically to those who lived in the ages of belief from which the quoted fragments come. Eliot selects from past cultures three techniques he considers essential emotional abilities shared by men and women in all periods of belief. He finds them defined succinctly in the three Sanskrit words "*Datta, dayaddhvam, damyata*," meaning "give, sympathize, control" (both self-control and control of others). And he concludes his poem by explicating each of these techniques or precepts individually and then placing them together just before the final words, "*Shantih, shantih, shantih*," "*Peace, peace, peace*," meaning "the peace that passeth understanding."

Datta. Dayadhvam. Damyata.

Shantih   Shantih Shantih

The words are arranged to suggest that the three abilities lead to the peace that will relieve our present paralysis. (Of the words "left out" in Hemingway's title, "peace" is the one most associated by readers with his quoted fragment; and in the Christian incantation invoked by Hemingway the word, of course, shares its primary, spiritual meaning with its counterpart in the Sanskrit incantation invoked by Eliot.)

In explicating the final portion of the poem (11.392-434), Friar explains the process whereby we may develop in ourselves the all-important openness to others stressed by the first words of the formula – an openness "endued" as a matter of course in times of belief and that can be developed by vigilant practice to break the legacies of self-absorption and betrayal of others central to the poem and the book:

> Suddenly the cock crows, dispelling fear and illusions, the rain *does* begin to fall, and God speaks out of the thunder to give us the disciplines for living. Give, Sympathize, Control ("*Datta, Dayadhvam, Damyate).* The first injunction is to give of ourselves in self-surrender and self-sacrifice, but as Eliot says in "East Coker" we are filled with the "fear of possession, / Of belonging to one another, or to others, or to God." If, in an awful moment we do dare to give of ourselves, we spend the rest of our lives trying to retract this daring, erasing it from our obituaries, leaving no memento of it on our tombstones or record of it in our last will and testament. And how can we learn to "Sympathize," to forget ourselves by immersing ourselves in the problems of others, for always we are locked up in the prison of our own egos and personalities, unable to leave it except for those moments of ethereal illumination which may relieve even such an arch-individualist as Coriolanus. *If we can learn to give of ourselves and to live in sympathetic identification with others, perhaps we may also learn the art of self-control and thereby prepare ourselves to take on the most difficult of responsibilities; that of giving destinies and perhaps those of others, as an expert helmsman controls a ship.* This is the vision seen in

the midst of the Waste Land by the pure in heart, by
Parsifal; by which the Fisher King may be healed,
and by which his land and people may be brought to
prosperity. *But we are reminded that the Waste Land is
still about us, that the vision and its application are to
be striven for time and again in a land which is falling
apart in broken images, without tradition, a bundle of
fragments. Amid all this catastrophe, there is only the
trying ("East Coker"), the fishing in an arid land, the
attempt to put land and life in order.* (*Modern Poetry*,
492-93; italics mine)

Nick, who is at the first stage of his progress out of
distraction and possibly toward eventual contact with and
responsibility for others, has been betrayed by too many "a
moment's surrender" to his need for love, guidance, and
belief (the "other needs" mentioned in the story). He has
been imprisoned by his nerves' chaotic reaction to these
disappointments in a world where everyone needed is "in
his prison" of the self. But Nick's spontaneity can be
released; he can "respond" once again to life's limited
pleasures (like those of skiing, of Joe's racetrack world,
etc.), if he becomes "expert" at managing his emotions.
Perhaps eventually that accomplishment may give him the
confidence and the freedom to commit himself to others
and know their delight in a life-giving guidance he has
never received. (By using this language from the poem,
incidentally, I do not suggest that Hemingway's story is a
gloss of Eliot's lines 402-23, but merely that the situations
are parallel.) Yet the control of others through giving and
sympathizing is too much to ask of Nick now. (It will be
accomplished – as we shall see—by Jake Barnes in his
final scenes with Brett in the novel immediately following
this work.) "Big Two-Hearted River" is confined to an
extended psychologically-detailed dramatization of the
discipline of self-control alone, that is synoptically presented
by *The Waste Land*. We see Nick deliberately practicing
rudimentary attitudes leading to that ancient capacity for
self-control which in subsequent Hemingway heroes we
refer to as "grace under pressure." The genesis of that

quality in the Hemingway hero is here. It parallels *The Waste Land*'s theme that, deprived of the satisfactions of that large order we all desperately need, we can "at least set our lands in order" by emulating the immemorial disciplines of those who felt the inner peace of earlier times.

Nick's preliminary step is to set each day in order, of course. He does this by constructing for himself, out of nature's immediate offerings, an orderly, simplified structure of predictable, achievable satisfactions, satisfactions at best only partially compensating for the deeply-longed-for completions with others and with the universe that those of his generation had expected others to provide for them. Many details of the pattern of compensation in the story have been discussed, certainly, yet without taking into account this religious dimension involved. Accordingly, the fundamental parallel between *The Waste Land* and this story has been overlooked, even when some similarities of setting and plot have been noticed.

In Hemingway's realistic analysis and in the poem's abstract one, modern man's struggle must be to regain both feeling and composure in the face of inevitable disbelief (to develop the ability to see "nothing that is not there and nothing that is" without becoming Wallace Stevens' snow man). The method Nick uses is to confront the specific frustrations of innate need that have pushed his feelings beyond control, and by gradually increased exposure "desensitize" himself, as we would put it today. (Hemingway's favorite, Conrad, referred to it, of course, as immersing oneself "in the destructive element.") As we have seen, these needs (the "other needs" Nick quietly acknowledges [p. 179] are for the various kinds of human connection we have been tracing throughout the book, and especially for the greatest of all connections, that between the self and the unseen mysteries of the created universe, the connection lost in our time that would have freed others from the self-absorption they have passed on to Nick. It is in the episodes of direct contact with fish that "Big Two-Hearted River" portrays Nick openly confronting this vital need, and I think we can gain fresh understanding of the story's theme and resolution by focussing more than we have on the two most important fish Nick plays: the huge trout and the "good" trout.

The metaphor of connection I have just been using reflects the fundamental, visceral origin of that ancient association of fishing with not only sexual, but spiritual completion – the association that created the myth of the Fisher King. Even thinking of casting his line into an opaque, watery medium and feeling and answering tug of vitality creates for Nick, as for all true fishermen of all times, an "old feeling" of satisfaction (p.178), a feeling older and deeper than any merely personal memory. Conversely, the loss of that connection as a line goes slack is a sensation that goes beyond ego and eros; it is a feeling of emptiness, telling beyond logic or sense. To some extent the size of the quarry determines the intensity of each feeling. And Nick must bear the extremes of both sensations almost as soon as he starts fishing – with the second fish he hooks.

Without warning, as life presents such a thing, and without a chance to work up to it as he has deliberately prepared for everything else in the story, Nick must test himself in an ordeal of promised fulfilment and inevitable loss reflecting the very heart of his trauma (and that of the composite protagonist in the collection). He is therefore in considerable emotional danger: the rod comes "alive and dangerous"––reminding us of the price of feeling; the pull of the line is "dangerous" – (p.203) – it forces him to deal with the sensations of vulnerability and loss that have sickened him. Everything is nervewracking, "too fast," the strain "too great," "the hardness too tight"; and "Of course" this fish is gone (p.203). That has been inevitable, given his association in the story, as in the myth, with man's deepest need and most cruel loss.

Appropriately, as all life leaves the line it becomes "dry and hard," and when it goes slack it leaves Nick's mouth "dry" (p.203). This is language associated with spiritual desolation in Part V of *The Waste Land*, while the language used to describe the fish is that used in the poem to describe the longed-for-combination of water (fertility) and rock (Peter, the church) that represents vitalized, or presently

tenable, divinity. "here is no water but only rock/Rock and
no water....If there were only water amongst the rock
(11.231-38)

At least in the immediate natural world of the story
this connection occurs, if only ultimately to tantalize Nick.
Even his small first fish settles in the water "beside a stone"
and that phrase is repeated (p.201). As for the huge trout:
"By God, he was the biggest one I ever heard of"; he was
"solid as a rock. He felt like a rock, too"; and now he rests
again on the bottom – a rock in the water, vital and holy at
once (p. 204). But his connection to Nick could not
realistically have been hoped for: "There was a heaviness,
a power not to be held" (p.204). This is the twentieth
century.

Still Nick is not pushed beyond control by this sudden
and dangerous proffering and withdrawal of feelings
associated with the greatest completion man can envision
("He was the biggest one I ever heard of"). Refusing to "rush
his sensations" (no mean feat), he is able to return to that
disciplined focus on non-threatening details that he has
used all along; and he waits as the "disappointment" after
the "thrill' slowly does drain away (as we assume it would
not have earlier, before he had developed his obvious skill
at emotional management). He can see the humor in the
tiny trout and the match. He will complete a cigarette; it is
not the completion he would prefer, but he uses it wisely.
And then he ties up again; he will go on.

He has been deeply shaken, however: "His hand was
shaky...The thrill had been too much. He felt, vaguely, a
little sick, as though it would be better to sit down" (p.204).
It will be some time and take considerably more practice
before he can "fish the swamp," where there are more such
reminders of the difficult plight of modern men. And let me
stress that plight again: the tantalizing need for spiritual
completion remains (the very biggest fish get on and can
be felt); yet satisfying systems of belief are rendered
implausible by modern experience (the great fish are found
only "in places impossible to land them" [p.211]..

To understand this "tragic" fishing without feeling
aversion to the "deep wading" in the messy water, and

without being shaken by the inevitable exposure and betrayal, is to cope fully with both hearts, both sides, of the life man is offered. The most attractive, most needed, and most painful side cannot be evaded. And to avoid it is to be distracted (as were Nick's parents and all but a very few of the other characters in the book – and in Eliot's poem), diverted from exploiting the *other* side, those offerings of life that can provide limited pleasures — less-satisfying, but realizable, completions. It is this heart of nature and life that is represented by the "one good trout"(p.207) that rewards Nick's ability to go on, after his experience of unattainable felicity (to paraphrase Melville's Ishmael). It is not the great fish, but it is landed. Nick has it, it is "good" and it is "one" – it is a start. Nick follows it with another, and with this balance comes small order. There is also reassurance that he can have further rewards for understanding the lesson of *Eccleciastes* that informs Hemingway's next book (*The Sun Also Rises*): it is better to enjoy the good things one likes, than be distracted by yearning for the better things one would prefer. Strengthened by more "good" fish and the prolonged practice of humility and honesty they will require (attitudes that came automatically to men of faith), he will eventually be able to "fish the swamp," and thus live feelingly, if without faith, in this century. I would like to think that this is the "undefined aspect of the human condition" that Oldsey feels hovering "in the air, moving well beyond the physical stopping place of the story's ending."(*College Literature* , Fall, 1980).

Nick must struggle to construct this limited order, shoring against his ruins direct visceral experiences of the old truths that Eliot's speaker found reflected in inspiring literary fragments. And fighting against the loss of control that threatens, as must Eliot's fabricator ("Hieronymo's mad againe"), this composite, representative modern character turns for help to ancient discipline and thinks of peace – in our time.

Hemingway and Turgenev : A Brief Introduction

Alexander Kelly Dupuis

One has to be very careful taking Ernest Hemingway at his word. Fiction was his metier, and one of the dictionary definitions of fiction is "something invented or imagined." The impulse to embellish was powerful in him. Hemingway seldom let facts get in the way of a good story, either on paper or while entertaining a crowd at lunch. Add mental breakdown, alcoholism, repeated head injuries and depression to that tendency, and you have some of the reasons why *A Moveable Feast*, Hemingway's memoir of his life in Paris with his first wife during the early 1920s, is undeniably a wonderful "read," (I fell in love with this book, and with Hemingway's art, when I was 16) but it's also a book that has to be taken not just with any grain of salt, but with a grain of the kind of salt they use to de-ice freeways.

And not only did Hemingway love to embroider around facts, but like many self-educated men, he wore his erudition on his sleeve. We sometimes forget that before the end of World War II and the advent of the G.I. bill, a college education was not considered a universal entitlement in America, nor was it necessarily something that everyone felt they had to have. Hemingway was offered the chance to go to college—his father wanted him to attend Oberlin-but he decided he'd rather go out and get educated in the business of life instead, first as an ambulance driver in the First World War, and then as a reporter on the Kansas City and Toronto *Star* newspapers. In his day you could still do this. Hemingway educated himself in literature not by

attending seminars and writing research papers, but by
reading, and throughout his life he loved to list the authors
he had read or claimed to have read for the commiseration
of the reading public, although he always got very touchy
when anyone dared whisper the word "influence." He had
sufficient perspective to generously acknowledge his
admiration for the "big guns"—his high regard for
Shakespeare and Tolstoy were never alloyed with irony—
but when it came to lesser, or God forbid, *contemporary*
influences, friends and associates had to step carefully
around him. With his enormous ego and extreme
competitiveness, Hemingway was not one to be generous
to colleagues, and the surest way to get him to turn on you,
as Gertrude Stein and Sherwood Anderson learned the hard
way, was to help him out. Hemingway wasn't comfortable
owing anyone anything, especially not any aspect of his
style. Perhaps that's not surprising in view of the way
Hemingway's style co-opted his personality, (or perhaps it
was the other way around.) In any case, identifying the
influences on Hemingway has amounted to a full-time job
for scholars and critics for decades.

Nevertheless, when he began assembling the
sketches for *A Moveable Feast* circa 1957, Hemingway's
need to show the world the breadth of his youthful reading
centered largely around the great Russians—Tolstoy,
Dostoevski and Turgenev chiefly, but also Gogol and
Chekhov. Tolstoy's impact on Hemingway is as hard to
ignore as an iceberg-after all, no one has ever written on
the subject of war with anything like the sweep, depth,
power and drama of Tolstoy, and war was a subject that
Hemingway found endlessly fascinating. Admiration for
Tolstoy was a "natural", for him. Dostoevski, too, seems to
have interested him, if only because he reports himself
wondering aloud to the poet Evan Shipman how Dostoevski
could "write...so unbelievably badly, and make you feel so
deeply." In the Paris sketch in which he describes his first
visit to Sylvia Beach's famous bookstore, Shakespeare and
Company, Hemingway lists Dostoevski's *The Gambler and
Other Stories* as one of the volumes he first borrowed, along
with *War and Peace*, some D.H. Lawrence and *A Sportsman's*

Sketches by Ivan Turgenev.

A less obvious object of Hemingway's admiration was Henry James, whose highly stylized, mannered prose was worlds away from Hemingway's short sentences, and whose world of elegant drawing rooms and upper-class parlors was continents away from Hemingway's world of battlegrounds, bullrings and African hills. And the contrast isn't only in subject matter. James was a practitioner, in fact he was the very apotheosis of the 19th-century's idea of good writing, the highly-polished "polite prose" that Hemingway was trying to get away from.

So was Turgenev. I've bracketed Turgenev and James together because they seem to me similar writers in some ways: although Turgenev wrote in Russian and James in English, both spent much of their adult lives living outside their country of birth, and both wrote in an elegant, highly-polished style that doesn't appeal to everyone. Oscar Wilde once remarked that James wrote prose "as if it were a painful duty," and to this day it is fashionable among bookish Russians to deride Turgenev as "feminine" owing chiefly to the elegance and gracefulness of his style. And because I have heard that term applied to Turgenev more than once, I find it ironic that he should have influenced the macho-obsessed Hemingway, with his laconic tough-guy characters who speak in short sentences. And yet, if you take a look at that very book of Turgenev's that Hemingway reports having borrowed from Sylvia Beach in 1922, *A Sportsman's Sketches,* and then glance through Hemingway's first widely-read book of short fiction, *in our time,* a few of Turgenev's fingerprints do indeed seem to appear on Hemingway's pages. The most powerful influences on the style that Hemingway evolved in the early 1920s may well have been, as has been often pointed out, the Kansas City *Star's* stylebook, with its emphasis on keeping things short, clipped and free of adjectives, and Gertrude Stein, whose mammoth novel *The Making of Americans* Hemingway helped to type and whose "cubistic" approach to prose, repeating phrases over and over with slightly different wordings, doubtlessly influenced Hemingway's sense of prose rhythm. But Turgenev, too, is part of the mix, and Hemingway certainly never made his admiration for Turgenev a secret. In 1925 he told Archibald MacLeish that he thought Turgenev "the greatest writer there ever was," and then added "*War and Peace* is the best book I know, but imagine what a book it would have been if Turgenev had written it."

I suspect that Hemingway's admiration for such writers as Turgenev and Joseph Conrad stemmed to some extent from the personal appeal of their subject matter. Tolstoy had dazzled him by writing dazzlingly about war. Conrad, like Herman Melville, had been a sailor, and many of his tales center around the adventurous and—at least in those days, manly—world of the sea. Turgenev, in *A Sportsman's Sketches*, creates a world—a peculiarly Russian one—around a man who spends all of his time indulging his greatest passion, which also happened to be one of Hemingway's: hunting. I think that, with regard to Turgenev, this was the hook that drew Hemingway in. But once he was there, within Turgenev's world, Hemingway took something else away with him besides the enjoyment of a string of vignettes about a man out hunting.

A Sportsman's Sketches was an unusual book for the middle of the 19th century. Perhaps it could have been written nowhere except Russia, where there actually wasn't much in the way of literary "tradition" circa 1850. At the same time that Dickens, Thackeray and their contemporaries in England were building on the foundations of the great 18th-century English novelists such as Richardson and Fielding, and writers in France like Hugo and Flaubert were doing the same with the traditions of Rousseau, Chateaubriand and Stendhal, Russian writers were still trying to create a tradition for themselves. Russian literature is often said to have begun with Pushkin and Gogol, both of whom flourished in the 1830s. Mikhail Lermontov's highly idiosyncratic novel *A Hero of Our Time* had appeared in 1840, when Pushkin had only been dead three years. Lermontov himself was killed in a duel, (the same fate that had befallen Pushkin) just a year after his novel came out. Russian authors of the 1840s and 50s may have had to contend with the tyranny of the czar's government, but they were working relatively free of the tyranny of a literary tradition.

Turgenev didn't bother writing "stories" in the accepted sense of the word when he wrote *A Sportsman's Sketches* (I'm using the title Hemingway knew; in more recent translations the book has been called *A Sportsman's Notebook*.) There is no conventional "plot" or schematic narrative anywhere to be seen. The stories are snapshots of places, characters, situations. Hemingway's *in our time*, a product of "modernism" written not long after he had been reading Turgenev in Paris, works in much the same way. It was an uncommon technique for a writer of the mid-19th century to be using, to understate rather than overstate, use observation and description rather than rhetoric, and as often as not, to end on a "dying fall" rather than a crashing chord, as at the end of the sketch called "Raspberry Water:"

> "Styopushka started up. The peasant sat down beside us. We fell silent again. On the other bank someone started singing, but such a melancholy song...My poor friend Vlas grew sadder and sadder. Half an hour later, we parted."

Now hear Hemingway at the end of "The Battler:"

> "Nick climbed the embankment and started up the track. He found he had a ham sandwich in his hand and put it in his pocket. Looking back from the mounting grade before the track curved into the hills he could see the firelight in the clearing."

The dying fall, the laconic understatement. Two of Hemingway's trademarks. And yet as I re-read *A Sportsman's Sketches* last summer, I found example after example of the same sort of thing in Turgenev that later made Hemingway's reputation. Listen to this bit of dialogue from "Bezhin Meadow:"

> "Well, Vanya," began Fedya tenderly, "is your sister

Anyutka well?" "Very well," answered Vanya, slightly slurring the "r." "Tell her to come and see us. Why doesn't she come?" "I don't know." "Tell her to come." "I will." "Tell her that I'll give her a present." "And me too?" "Yes, you too."

Take out just one word, "tenderly," and that snatch of dialogue could be Hemingway. Or, perhaps it might be more appropriate to say, the following exchange from *The Sun Also Rises* could be Turgenev:

"What's the matter with the old one?" I asked. "He hasn't got any passport." I offered the guard a cigarette. He took it and thanked me. "What will he do?" I asked. The guard spat in the dust. "Oh, he'll just wade across the stream." "Do you have much smuggling?" "Oh," he said, "they go through."

Yes, between Turgenev and Hemingway came Chekhov, another master of emotional tautness and the restrained phrase. And Hemingway greatly admired Chekhov too. But there can be little doubt that Turgenev's evocation, a generation before Chekhov, of the lovely, vast and brutal Russian countryside and its characters, in prose all the more effective for its restraint, gave Hemingway the cue for some of his own efforts, three-quarters of a century later, to evoke his own landscapes and characters, lovely and brutal, in prose all the more effective for its restraint.

Half a Century and Half a World:
Turgenev's and Hemingway's *The Torrents of Spring*

Judy Henn

> For your information I started out trying to beat
> dead writers that I knew how good they were....I
> tried for Mr. Turgenieff first and it wasn't too hard.
> (Hemingway *Selected Letters* 673).

Ernest Hemingway steeped himself in the novels of Ivan Turgenev. Turgenev (or as Hemingway spelled his name, Turgenieff) first came to Hemingway's attention in Paris in the 1920s; Turgenev's works "account for 13 of the 85 borrowed books" between 1925 and 1929, taken from Sylvia Beach's lending library, which was at the back of her bookshop, Shakespeare and Company (Fitch 166). A few articles and a chapter of a dissertation have been written in the past decade comparing *The Torrents of Spring* by Ivan Turgenev (published in 1872) and *The Torrents of Spring* by Ernest Hemingway (published in 1926); prior to 1988 there are no critical materials examining both texts. The history of the comparison of the two works is thus relatively new, and critical analysis to date has left much ground unexplored. The function of this article is to examine the nature of and extent of Hemingway's utilization of Turgenev's novel, using the theoretical vehicles of parody/satire, intertextuality, and Bakhtinian theories of dialogism, to determine Turgenev's importance to Hemingway's anti-Romantic message.

Although there is no indication in Hemingway's letters or fiction as to the reason for his appropriation of Turgenev's title, it appears that Hemingway adopts and adapts distinct patterns from Turgenev's *The Torrents of Spring* and subverts them to suit his purposes. Some of the highly romanticized aspects of Turgenev's novella, such as the nature of the Byronic hero, the position of the outsider in an unfamiliar setting, the epistemology of nationality, the centrality of fate, the role of nature (in its human and scientific aspects), criticism of cultural institutions, and the importance of art to life, are rendered banal and ridiculous under Hemingway's parodic pen.

Michael Reynolds writes in his book, *Hemingway's Reading, 1910-1940*,

> When Hemingway liked an author, he read him in depth. Roughly twenty percent of the entries fall into this category. Some of the names confirm what we knew: Conrad, Kipling, Turgenev, Stendhal, Dostoevsky"(16).

Hemingway would write thirty years later in his memoir, *A Moveable Feast*, "From the day I had found Sylvia Beach's library I had read all of Turgenev"; Hemingway claimed he learned from him how to write about "the landscape and the roads" (Hemingway *Feast* 133). In *The Sun Also Rises*, whose first draft he had completed a few weeks before writing *The Torrents of Spring*, the drunk Jake Barnes reads "the same two pages over several times....[from] one of the stories in [Turgenev's] "A Sportsman's Sketches," remarking, "I had read it before, but it seemed quite new. The country became very clear" (Hemingway *Sun* 147). Turgenev's rendition of nature seems crucial as a calming effect, both for Jake Barnes, fictional character, and for Ernest Hemingway, author.

Hemingway borrowed Turgenev's *The Torrents of Spring* on October 27th, 1925 from Sylvia Beach's library, and returned it on November 16th (Reynolds *Hemingway's Reading* 194). He had just completed his first draft of *The Sun Also Rises*, yet, inspired by Turgenev's novella, his mind was so full of material, that "for ten solid days he typed steadily, revising little as the draft spun off the rollers...,

[then] unplanned and unedited, *The Torrents of Spring* was ready for the typist" (Reynolds *Hemingway: The Paris Years* 333-4 [hereafter Reynolds *Paris*]). Hemingway decided to contend with the best when he undertook to compete with Turgenev. In a letter to Archibald MacLeish dated December 20th, 1925, just a month after he completed writing *The Torrents of Spring*, Hemingway writes:

> Turgenieff to me is the greatest writer there ever was. Didn't write the greatest books, but was the greatest writer. That's only for me of course....War and Peace is the best book I know but imagine what a book it would have been if Turgenieff had written it....Turgenieff was an artist (Hemingway *Selected Letters* 179).

Hemingway's interest in Turgenev's unique style glances at Tolstoy as another potential rival.

The fairly prevalent consensus to date that *The Torrents of Spring* was written as a parody of Sherwood Anderson's *Dark Laughter*, seems to have created a blind spot in criticism which therefore has not attempted to correlate Hemingway's use of the Turgenev novella. Clearly, reading Turgenev's novella had had a profound effect, and Hemingway's choice to make an explicit link between that work and his own literary effort by recycling the title indicates that Hemingway sought some form of comparative recognition and analysis.

Hemingway's use of Turgenev's title and his engagement of Turgenev's ideas in dialogue can be interpreted as an Oedipal disparagement of a predecessor whom he perceived to be a literary rival to be incorporated, embattled, and then assimilated. According to Myler Wilkinson :

> from his [i.e. Hemingway] earliest beginnings as a serious writer, one notes a melancholy insistence on priority and a truly savage rejection of literary fathers whenever [Hemingway] felt it necessary to clear imaginative space for his own poetic vision

(Wilkinson *Hemingway and Turgenev* 14).

The vehicle chosen by which to criticize Sherwood Anderson is Ivan Sergeyevich Turgenev (1818-1883), who stands out in his generation because of his life of self-imposed exile in the West, which lent a rootlessness and sense of estrangement to his characters. Critics of his novels identify characteristics of displacement in space, time, and logical consequence. Typically, "the narrator or hero travels abroad....[and] chronology and illusion" are combined (Fisher 45, 47). Hemingway was an expatriate in Europe during the 1920s and shared the position of an outsider with Turgenev. It is possible to read similarity in Turgenev's and Hemingway's backgrounds, aligning vantagepoints from which they perceive life and art.

Turgenev became Westernized early in his writing career and was "the first Russian author to be read and admired by Europe" (*Britannica* 585B). He associated with Gustave Flaubert and was admired by Guy de Maupassant, though he was not highly regarded by his Russian compatriots, Tolstoy and Dostoevsky. Turgenev wrote a number of short stories and novellas, and seven novels, the most respected of which is *Fathers and Sons* (a title which Hemingway borrowed for a short story written in the early 1930s).

Turgenev wrote his *The Torrents of Spring* between November 1870 and February 1871 while he lived in London. The novella narrates the memoirs of the fictional Dimitri Pavlovitch Sanin, suddenly recalled in great detail upon Sanin's unexpected discovery of "a little octagonal box of old-fashioned make" (Turgenev 2). Within this box Sanin comes across "under two layers of cotton wool, yellow with age, ... a little garnet cross" (Turgenev 2). The "regret and delight" that this object raises in Sanin, returns his consciousness to a period thirty years earlier, when at the age of twenty-two, he experienced a great love affair (Turgenev 2). The revelation of the treasured object serves as a frame for the embedded story of love and its subsequent betrayal. As Sanin unwraps the cross, the narrator reveals the story.

Vladimir Fisher relates in a note, "for a half-century

Russian criticism has viewed Turgenev's novels as historical criticism of the Russian intelligentsia" (Fisher 63). Turgenev makes frequent allusions to famous European painters, thinkers, and writers, and names great works of literature, music, and art, much as Hemingway inserts names of cultural edifices of his day. Turgenev prefaces his novel with lines "from an Old Ballad," which serve as an epigraph: "'Years of gladness,/ Days of joy,/ Like the torrents of spring/ They hurried away'" (Turgenev 1). The ballad stands as a signpost, hinting at and introducing the idea of fleeting happiness, which is as brief and passing as melting vernal snows.

Wilkinson notes: "Turgenev was a precursor and influence to whom Hemingway looked, particularly in the 1920s, as a model for poetic voice and aesthetic judgment" (Wilkinson *Hemingway and Turgenev* 16). After a fairly steady diet of Turgenev since 1922, by 1925 Hemingway appears to feel ready to engage in dialogue with him. Using Turgenev, Hemingway finds means to project "human emotion into and through a landscape" (Wilkinson *Dark Mirror* 137). The artistic thrust that Hemingway finds in Turgenev becomes focused in the modern encounter with the earlier *The Torrents of Spring*.

Ten years before he wrote *The Torrents of Spring*, Turgenev had published *Fathers and Sons* in 1862, whose hero, Bazarov, was "a Byronic figure in motley," according to Wilkinson (Wilkinson *Hemingway and Turgenev* 19). The protagonist of Turgenev's *The Torrents of Spring*, Dimitri Pavlovitch Sanin, is a parody of that Byronic hero. Turgenev invents the term "superfluous man" to characterize the figure who, according to Wilkinson, "retreats into a private life of egotistical self-analysis, romantic theorizing, futile affairs, meaningless gestures, and ultimately, self-despair," which succinctly describes Sanin (Wilkinson *Hemingway and Turgenev* 18). Sanin speaks and thinks in clichés: when he discovers that the object of his affection, Gemma, "was not very fond of Hoffmann," he explains to himself—"The fantastic, misty northern element in his stories was too remote from her clear, southern nature" (Turgenev 25). Sanin uses Romantic metaphor to characterize himself

and Gemma. Perhaps Turgenev himself could be found to
be parodying one of his precursors, although the space of
this work prevents pursuance of this issue. In general,
however, Turgenev's construct of Sanin plays into the hands
of the larger-than-life, brooding and secretive attributes of
the Byronic hero. Sanin is

> [a] handsome, graceful figure, agreeable, rather
> *unformed* features, kindly bluish eyes, golden hair, a
> clear white and red skin, and, above all, that *peculiar*,
> naively-cheerful, confiding, open, at the first glance,
> *somewhat foolish* expression (emphasis added)
> (Turgenev 28).

There is a duality, which belies what on first glance seems
to be a flattering portrait. The words "unformed," "peculiar,"
and "foolish," call into doubt the later statement that Sanin
"was not stupid" (Turgenev 28).

The novel reveals often lacking in circumspection is
Sanin, and how indecisive he is when he is supposed to be
forthright. The romantic posturings of a Byron are replaced
by Sanin's childish unreliability. Wilkinson sees part of
Hemingway's fascination for Turgenev tied to the former's
interest in Byron, evinced by the presence of two
biographies of Byron dating from 1912 and 1924 in
Hemingway's library (Reynolds *Hemingway's Reading* 158,
163).Wilkinson's definition of the Byronic Bazarov will serve
us in our analysis of Sanin:

> He is the cynic and nihilist who looks with disdain at
> the old order and awaits its collapse; the man who
> believes in nothing but direct sensory impressions,
> who no longer believes in the fine phrases and
> romantic dreamings of the older generation. And yet
> underneath this seemingly impenetrable exterior
> exists a fierce idealism and hope for change
> (Wilkinson *Hemingway and Turgenev* 19).

These inconsistencies – the 'nihilist' who 'hope[s] for
change' – give a hint that Turgenev parodies himself in

creating a character like Sanin, who is a much filtered down version of Bazarov. Sanin is too vapid to be cynical; even in later life when he realizes how his life was ruined due to Maria's manipulations, he dreams of a reconciliation with Gemma after thirty years. Although Sanin may give a thought to ideals – he is appalled at the idea that he must sell his serfs, nevertheless, expediency dictates his moves, more than morality or conscience:

> He remembered that in a conversation with Signora Roselli and her daughter about serfdom, which, in his own words, aroused his deepest indignation, he had repeatedly assured them that never on any account would he sell his peasants, as he regarded such a sale as an immoral act (Turgenev 83).

Sanin, is an incurable romantic when compared to Bazarov: the moment he realizes he is falling in love with Gemma, "he remembered her marble arms, like the arms of Olympian goddesses," and grasping a rose she had given him imagines, "that its half-withered petals exhaled a fragrance of her, more delicate than the ordinary scent of the rose" (Turgenev 47).

Unlike Bazarov, Sanin has no ideals, and indeed, is a Philistine. In spite of the lengthy European tour that Sanin had just completed, little of the cultural delights seem to have affected him. In Frankfort,

> He went in to look at Danneker's Ariadne, which he did not much care for, visited the house of Goethe, of whose works he had, however, only read *Werther*, and that in the French translation (Turgenev 4).

Although he reveals himself (probably to his own surprise) to be capable of acting swiftly to save Gemma's brother Emil from a physical collapse, that is the only positive character trait we see in him. Sanin is hailed "festive[ly]" as a savior for reviving the unconscious youth, little knowing that this impulsive gesture sets in motion a series of events which shape his life (Turgenev 9).

Hemingway breaks down the mock-heroic Sanin by splitting him into two average men of the Mid-West who are trying to live their lives modestly and without undue fuss, while harboring romantic views of women. As the nature of parody is to establish close ties with a previous text, and then to criticize it, Hemingway begins with the most obvious part of the text, the title. Whereas Turgenev creates his fictional characters in the image he wanted, Hemingway demonstrates "his attitude toward the sentiment displayed" in Turgenev, by referring "not literally to the world of action but intertextually to the other ...[text] which it negates" (Scholes and Comley *Text Book* 131). Hemingway does not "close off an argument" with Turgenev — he qualifies through "digression" (Griffin 113). The milieu that produced Turgenev's text does not resemble that of Hemingway's, thus the texts are quite different. In the few cases where the two novellas have been compared, the misunderstanding of Hemingway's text may be precisely because Turgenev's text (among others) is precluded. Nevertheless, the Hemingway text has a direct thematic connection to Turgenev's *The Torrents of Spring*, which will now be examined.

According to Wilkinson, in both Hemingway's and Turgenev's works, "the expatriated man, without home or family, becomes the only kind of man who exists in this world" (Wilkinson *Hemingway and Turgenev* 49). Turgenev's protagonist, Sanin, is a Russian tourist in Germany as are the wealthy Polozovs, whom he meets halfway through the novella. The object of Sanin's infatuation, Gemma, is a member of a family of Italian immigrants living in Germany. Turgenev engages his characters in a challenge to the definition of nationalism by including numerous references to national traits, customs, and idiosyncrasies.

As foreigners in Germany, Sanin and Gemma need to create a haven of harmony far from the anxieties associated with absorption. When Sanin sees himself through Gemma's eyes, as the dashing savior, he impulsively abandons his plans to return home to Russia, and attaches himself to Gemma, all the while, commenting on the curious customs of the Italian family. The idealized love seems perfect, but Sanin swiftly abandons Gemma when a strong physical attraction to his compatriot, the wealthy and ruthless Maria Polozova, who tempts him "to gratify an urge that [he] cannot rationally and morally justify" (Elizabeth Allen 60). His conscience assails him: "A thousand times he mentally asked forgiveness of his pure chaste dove, [Gemma] though he could not really blame himself for anything" (Turgenev 110). The familiar mother tongue is a form of power that Maria wields: "he could not rid himself of her image, could not help hearing her voice, recalling her words, could not help being aware even of the special scent, delicate, fresh and penetrating" (Turgenev 111).

Among contemporary issues common both to Turgenev's revolutionary times, and Hemingway's post World War I era is nationalism, the establishment of national boundaries, and the subsequent sharpening of so-called scientific basis for racial and class characteristics, culminating in developing xenophobic outlooks in both periods. Significantly, both novels engage in repeated examinations of national characteristics and of the consequences of foreignness. Part of the xenophobia in both texts is depicted through characters who are outsiders. Although his narrative is by far more scathing in its depiction of other ethnic groups, Sanin also criticizes his own national identity: "Like every true Russian he was glad to clutch at any excuse that saved him from the necessity of doing anything himself" (Turgenev 19-20).

Near the beginning of the novella, Sanin meets Gemma's German fiancé (Herr Karl Kluber) for the first time, and spares no opportunity to ridicule him. While calling Kluber "handsome, rather severe, excellently brought-up," he casually notes that he is also "superbly washed," and measures Kluber's honesty according to his "stiffly starched collars" (Turgenev 18). Gemma's rejected fiancé is "a little reserved, and stiff...in the English style," and as Sanin prepares himself for a duel to defend Gemma's honor, "he walked up and down the path, listened to the birds singing, watched the dragonflies in their flight, and like the majority of Russians in similar circumstances, tried not to think" (Turgenev 21; 50).

Similarly, the description of the Italian family servant, Pantaleone (whose name echoes one of the characters from the Italian *commedia dell' arte*), is described as having negative attributes ascribed to all Italians: he has "the privilege of sitting down in the presence of the ladies of the house; Italians are not, as a rule, strict in matters of etiquette" (Turgenev 22). The theme of foreign-ness in Turgenev's *The Torrents of Spring* has major proportions. Indeed, the text seems to question the nature of nationality: it speaks of Gemma caressing her mother's forehead, "not like a cat, not in the French manner, but with that special Italian grace in which is always felt the presence of power" (Turgenev 23). Later Sanin is surprised that Gemma does not like the *Tales* of the German Hoffmann, saying she found them "boring! The fantastic, misty northern element in his stories was too remote from her clear, southern nature" (Turgenev 25). The issue of national differences is underscored in these words; Sanin views the northern European peoples, including himself, as having more imagination than the decisive southern Europeans, among which he considers Gemma.

The Germans receive much of Sanin's comic pique: he remarks on a meal,

> Who does not know what a German dinner is like? Watery soup with knobby dumplings and pieces of cinnamon, boiled beef dry as cork, with white fat attached, slimy potatoes, soft beetroot and mashed horseradish, a bluish eel with French capers and vinegar, a roast joint with jam, and the inevitable '*Mehlspeise*', something of the nature of a pudding with sourish red sauce (Turgenev 32).

Turgenev in general does not seem to reserve compliments for any single national group, including his own.

Regarding Turgenev's novels, Vladimir Fisher, an early Russian critic, wrote in 1920 that they have: "vivid social....[and] autobiographical significance" in which "chance rules in life" (Fisher 44, 49). Fisher examines "how an outside force irrupts into a person's life, takes him into his universe," and applies it to Sanin, Gemma, and Maria, the main characters in the romantic plot of Turgenev's *The Torrents of Spring* (Fisher 50). The impossible chance meeting of Sanin and Gemma when he resuscitates her brother, makes him an instant hero, and insinuates him, the young Russian tourist in Germany, into the family of Italian immigrants, who are also foreigners. Their whirlwind love affair leads them to the brink of marriage; Sanin plans to return to Russia to sell his property and serfs in order to move to Germany and his intended life with Gemma. However, Sanin meets a school friend whose wealthy wife, Maria, promises to find a buyer for his estate, but instead, entices him into becoming a member of her entourage, a hanger-on, and thus he loses Gemma, and nearly forfeits his personality. The catastrophic consequence of sexual infatuation is a hinge upon which Turgenev hangs his moral cautionary tale: both women — the innocent Gemma, and the scheming Maria — have the ability to drive Sanin to total distraction, causing him to change the course of his life twice. Woodward refers to this turn of plot as "Turgenev's distinctive treatment of love as a paralyzing and destructive obsession" (Woodward 96). While Turgenev's novella could potentially be seen as a proto-Harlequin romance in its depiction of the exciting adventures between Sanin and a beautiful young Italian woman, such tendencies in the romance abruptly end when Sanin becomes slavishly attached to Maria, the cruel, wealthy, older married woman.

Shortly after meeting Gemma and becoming engaged to her, Sanin finds himself intoxicated by the "enigmatical, uninvited intimacy with a woman, so alien to him!" (Turgenev 110). Maria utilizes her "half-Russian, half-Gypsy woman's body in its full flower and full power" to enthrall Sanin, and to force him to relinquish Gemma for a life of emotional servitude in which he cannot "succeed in concentrating his attention for one instant" on anyone other than Maria (Turgenev 97, 121). Sanin is a weak man who is ruled by his hormones; as a protagonist he functions as a storyteller who only has begun to realize the force of

his own tale. Turgenev seems to be offering Sanin as the
parodic answer to the manly man - when Sanin agonizes
he recalls works of literature in which fictional heroes
provide him with the correct mode of behavior: "He began
saying goodbye to Gemma. For some reason he recalled
Lensky's parting from Olga in *Eugene Onegin*" (Turgenev
60).

In an article published in 1930, Lev Pumpyansky
mentions "the powerful landscape orchestration" in
Turgenev's novels (Pumpyansky 142). Wilkinson echoes
the importance of nature to Hemingway, "a writer whose
own aesthetic concern was always to relate landscape and
terrain to the shifting moods of the human psyche"
(Wilkinson *Dark Mirror* 137). The most apparent example of
Turgenev's use of nature to depict emotion occurs after
Sanin and Gemma have gotten to know each other, but
have not yet revealed their mutual feelings:

> All of a sudden, in the midst of the profound stillness,
> over the perfectly unclouded sky, there blew such a
> violent blast of wind, that the very earth seemed
> shaking underfoot, the delicate starlight seemed
> quivering and trembling, the air went round in a
> whirlwind. The wind, not cold, but hot, almost sultry,
> smote against the trees, the roof of the house, its
> walls, and the street (Turgenev 46).

Turgenev's use of nature is "an effort to convey
emotion rather than describe it" (Wilkinson *Hemingway and
Turgenev* 64). This summer hurricane is a catalyst for
Gemma and Sanin: he "raised his head and saw above him
such an exquisite, scared, excited face, such immense,
large, magnificent eyes – it was such a beautiful creature
he saw, that his heart stood still within him" (Turgenev
46). Much later in the novella, Sanin's first sexual
experience with Maria is preceeded by a horseback ride,
which leads them "into a rather narrow gorge....[featuring]
the smell of heather and bracken, of the resin of the pines,
and the decaying leaves of last year" (Turgenev 129). The
sensuality of nature, with its ripeness and musky odor,

sets the scene for Maria's seduction of Sanin, who feels himself "bewitched...[by] one idea, one desire" (Turgenev 130). In Turgenev and Hemingway, nature has its own causes and rhythms, and human life is often fore-grounded to natural forces: "for both, nature becomes an extended metaphor of man's possible self; terrain becomes a projection of his body, both psychic and physical" (Wilkinson *Hemingway and Turgenev* 37). Nature correlates with humans, giving depth to both novellas.

According to Wilkinson, the late romantics, among whom he counts both Turgenev and Hemingway, share "a cultural vision of a man's life and his progress toward self-definition [that] become[s] a critique of the society in which he lives" (Wilkinson 70). One of the basic differences between the two novellas lies in the period of half a century which separates their writing. Turgenev created in the nineteenth century, and for him, "the possibility of both social and personal reconciliation between the generations is always implicit and often explicit" (Wilkinson *Hemingway and Turgenev* 48). Inasmuch as Turgenev's most impressive work, *Fathers and Sons*, "transmutes the generational, ideological, and social conflicts of the 1860s into clashes of temperament and personality,'" Turgenev's *The Torrents of Spring* can also be seen to engage social historical elements in turmoil (Wilkinson *Hemingway and Turgenev* 19). This is particularly apparent when Sanin decides to sell his estate and peasants in order to finance his marriage to Gemma, thus fixing the date prior to 1861 when the Tsar freed the serfs (Fisher 46). Vladimir Fisher discusses the "socio-historical element" in Turgenev's *The Torrents of Spring*, that "indicates the place of action precisely" (Fisher 46). Fisher attributes this "unprecedented phenomenon" to "a psychological ...necessity[,]...not an artistic" one (Fisher 47). Thus, Fisher asserts,

> Of course the essence of Sanin and Gemma's relations would remain the same in another era as well, but Turgenev wants to see them alive; and for that he needs specifically Frankfurt, specifically 1840, [specifically] Gemma's Italian gestures (Fisher 48).

This interest in historic accuracy is attributed to Turgenev's desire to "fetter a person to a place, fix him in the framework of chronological dates, and observe him in that little corner...that is Turgenev's artistic mission" (Fisher 48).

Turgenev's men can be grouped under the category of 'other' too; just as different ethnic groups are distanced and even demonized, so women remain entirely outside the male definition of the species. It is not a great gap for Turgenev to breach to see stereotyped women as either Madonnas or whores, however, the ironic overtone in both novels reveal that the women may be less to blame than the men who enforce those standards. He sets up a typically romantic situation and then undermines it by having a woman responsible for creating a sinister conclusion to Sanin's romance with Gemma. The wicked temptress, Countess Maria Nikolayevna Polozova, possesses eyes with near magical potency: "When she screwed up her eyes, there was a very caressing and a slightly ironic look in them; but when she opened them wide, something evil, something menacing, came into their bright, almost cold brilliance" (Turgenev 136).

In both novellas the development of masculine identity is frequently attached to that of a feminine counterpart. Neither Turgenev's Sanin, nor Hemingway's Scripps or Yogi can live with women, or without them, and they flail about for some anchors to help them form self-identities. Perhaps in an attempt to expand their consciousnesses, characters in both novellas turn to art to express for them what they find difficult to say or feel.

Art in Turgenev's work gains great importance, but only to mock Sanin, who cannot really appreciate any of these great works whose names he drops. Turgenev's text parades a list of cultural icons such as Correggio (10), Pushkin (12), Rossini (14), La Fountaine (14), Rafael (21), Don Juan (54), The Barber of Seville (79), The Marriage of Figaro (115), The Aeneid (116) and Liszt (118), all of which are remarked upon in Sanin's attempt to find the tools to describe experience. At the end of Turgenev's novella,

Sanin remarks "For such feelings there is no satisfactory expression: they are too deep and too strong and too vague for any word" (Turgenev 138).

However, rather than art being a cultural force in the novel, it remains tagged on and foreign, much as it is to the bourgeois Sanin and the working class Gemma. Maria Pozolova, however, utilizes occasions of the display of art, such as attending the opera, to provide an impressive setting for her charms and to create the correct atmosphere for her romantic conquests. An early reference to art is Sanin's recollection of Gemma's beauty:

> Her nose was rather large, but handsome, aquiline-shaped; her upper lip was shaded by alight down; but then the colour of her face, smooth, uniform, like ivory or very pale milky amber, the wavering shimmer of her hair, like that of the Judith of Allorio in the Palazzo-Pitti; and above all, her eyes, dark grey, with a black ring round the pupils, splendid, triumphant eyes (Turgenev 7).

In this case, life is like art, fashioned by rules, and not random or spontaneous as the natural state of affairs is. Sanin searches for metaphors to arrange his thoughts about Gemma while she and her mother sing:

> It was not Gemma's voice – it was herself Sanin was admiring. He was sitting a little behind and on one side of her and kept thinking to himself that no palm-tree, even in the poems of Benediktov – the poet in fashion in those days – could rival the slender grace of her figure (Turgenev 13).

Indeed, Sanin frequently allows art to mediate between him and the world; the day following the first dramatic meeting of Gemma and Sanin, he returns to their home and observes her again:

> Sanin was especially struck that day by the exquisite beauty of her hands; when she smoothed and put back her dark, glossy tresses he could not take his eyes

off her long supple fingers, held slightly apart from
one another like the hand of Raphael's Fornarina
(Turgenev 21).

The moment at which Sanin realizes he has fallen in love
with Gemma is described by him as being present at the
creation of a work of art:

He too sank into a kind of dream, and sat motionless
as though spell-bound, while all his faculties were
absorbed in admiring the picture presented him by
the half-dark room, here and there spotted with
patches of light crimson, where fresh, luxuriant roses
stood in the old-fashioned green glasses...and the
young, keenly-alert and also kind, clever, pure, and
unspeakably beautiful creature with such black,
deep, overshadowed, yet shining eyes....What was it?
A dream? A fairy tale? And how came *he* to be in it?
(Turgenev 23).

By making Gemma into a work of art, he keeps her on a
pedestal, and, although he dotes upon her, there is no depth
in the relationship, foreshadowing Sanin's precipitous
abandonment of her, which is as impulsive as the beginning
of their whirlwind romance was. Gemma's mother is
distressed that her daughter has abandoned her wealthy
German fiancé for the sake of the Russian, causing Sanin
to think of the force of his love: "those emotions were of
the sincerest, those intentions were of the purest, like
Almaviva's in *The Barber of Seville*" (Turgenev 79).
    An Italian woman and a Russian man in a German
city undertake the courtship; there are vastly different
customs surrounding such intimate rituals. Gemma's
mother "asked him to describe the ceremony of marriage
as performed by the ritual of the Russian Church, and was
in raptures already at Gemma in a white dress, with a gold
crown on her head" (Turgenev 83). In a gesture, Gemma
embraces, like the Biblical Ruth, a new faith:

'do you remember, the difference of our religion – see
here! ...'She snatched the garnet cross that hung
round her neck on a thin cord, gave it a violent tug,

snapped the cord, and handed him the cross. 'If I am yours, your faith is my faith!' (Turgenev 84).

Sanin freely accepts Gemma's pledge of belief and love, only to sacrifice her on the altar of Mammon and lust in the body of a fellow countrywoman, the "enchantingly beautiful" Maria (Turgenev 103).Maria declares her penchant for Russian culture, as she spins a web about Sanin and captivates him. She enquires:

> 'Are you fond of art? of pictures? or more of music?'
> 'I am fond of art....I like everything beautiful.'
> 'And music?"
> 'I like music too.'

'Well, I don't at all. I don't care for anything but Russian songs' (Turgenev 105).

During the course of a few days, Maria shares with Sanin "how sick she was of Germans, how stupid they were when they tried to be clever, and how inappropriately clever sometimes when they were stupid" and totally captivates Sanin with her "rare gift" of telling "Russian stor[ies]" (Turgenev 112-13). Sanin is taunted by Maria – "you're a Russian, and yet mean to marry an Italian. Well, that's your sorrow," until he is bewitched into agreeing with her (Turgenev 127).

Maria seduces Sanin in order to win a bet with her husband; Sanin no longer thinks of his foreign betrothed, Gemma, and obediently follows Maria and her husband to Paris where he becomes "her bondslave....[until he] is cast aside at last, like a worn-out garment" (Turgenev 133). What had previously been enchanting – the foreignness of the Italian Gemma and her family in the German city – is forgotten for years till the embedded story reaches it end when Sanin, thirty years later, finds himself in "his own country, the poisoned, the devastated life, the petty interest and petty cares, bitter and fruitless regret" (Turgenev 133). The nature of the exile is to forever long for that which he cannot have, and Gemma is once again seen by Sanin to be an undiscovered country, especially after he journeys back to Frankfort in an attempt to find what happened to her. Only after the long thirty years journey through life does Sanin allow himself to acknowledge the loss and to mourn the past. The capricious final sentence of the novellas calls the basis for the entire previous text into question, dissembling and potentially leaving the reader shamed into recognizing the degree to which he or she had cooperated in believing the possibility of romantic fulfillment. The narrative voice, in an apparent aside to the reader, remarks: "It is rumoured that he [i.e. Sanin] is selling his estates and is about to leave for America" (Turgenev 188). The sentence reveals just how vain and vapid Sanin is, how unreliable he was 30 years earlier when he met Gemma and Maria, and to what extent he imagines he will arrive as conquering hero in the New World to see his lost love, Gemma, once again. The use of an aside steps out of the frame of the story to slap the reader back into reality; the entire story is clearly marked as a fiction and, as the grammatical use of the present progressive tense indicates, the narrative cycle of romance continually feeds into the end-product a funnel of blunt modern materialism. What seemed earlier to be authorial assent to Sanin's path in life is now clearly colored by a parodic hue. Whereas in Turgenev's *Fathers and Sons* "pathos is borne out of the contradictions which exist between a yearning for self-definition and the realization of its social impossibility", in his *The Torrents of Spring* Sanin never reaches self-awareness (Wilkinson *Hemingway and Turgenev* 69).

Hemingway's attempt at parody at this point in his writing career may be due to what Allen identifies in language as "an on-going dialogic clash of ideologies, world-views, opinions and interpretations" (Allen 28). Hemingway may have thought that he was aiding in the interpretation of predecessors, even if that were in the form of parodic critique (suggested by Allen 59). Allen's interpretation of Harold Bloom's theory of misprision claims that new writers "must rewrite the precursor's [works], and in that very act they must defend themselves against the knowledge that they are merely involved in the process of rewriting" (Allen 135). Hemingway does not appear to expend much energy to promote *The Torrents of Spring*, once some critics (and friends) saw it as a nasty poke at Anderson, without delving further into its myriad other meanings and derivations. In the end, Hemingway abandoned the novella by not referring to it further after the early 1930s.

Reading Turgenev provided Hemingway with a valuable role model; ten years later Hemingway would write in one of his monthly "letters" to *Esquire* magazine that a writer should read (among a list of seventeen writers) "all of Turgenev" (Hemingway *By-Line* 232). Hemingway continues to say that the reason a writer must undertake his own education is to "know what he has to beat" (Hemingway *By-Line* 232). Tellingly, Hemingway adds,

> there is no use writing anything that has been written before unless you can beat it. What a writer in our time has to do is write what hasn't been written before or beat dead men at what they have done (Hemingway *By-Line* 232).

Hemingway attempts to take a step beyond the Russian master, "whose own aesthetic concern was always to relate landscape and terrain to the shifting moods of the human psyche," according to Myler Wilkinson (Wilkinson *Dark Mirror* 137).

In her book *Parody/Meta-Fiction*, Margaret Rose examines how parody and metafiction are both characterized by affinity with a prior text. This essay examines "the attitude of the parodist [ie. Hemingway] to the work parodied [ie. Turgenev's *The Torrents of Spring*]," seeking to locate how Hemingway's explicit reference to a prior text serves to underscore his handling of particular subjects and themes (Rose *P/M-F* 17). As in the case of his use of quotes from Henry Fielding's Preface to *Joseph Andrews*, Hemingway appears to be "motivated by sympathy with text" although he occasionally mocks it too (Rose *P/M-F* 28).

Hemingway's Scripps and Yogi are gripped by obsessions over women, though the former cannot settle upon stability with a woman, and the latter fears all connections to women. The theme — "how an outside force irrupts into a person's life," developed in Turgenev's Sanir reemerges in Hemingway's Yogi and Scripps (Fisher 50). However, unlike Sanin, who "remains in the company of the temptress, enduing all the humiliation of his false position" Yogi and Scripps are able to extricate themselves and to indulge themselves further (Fisher 59).

Turgenev's ironic use of the Russian intelligencia is mirrored by Hemingway's sarcasm in handling the American intellectuals of the 1920s. The *Encyclopedia of Contemporary Literary Theory* defines parody as "a conscious ironic or sardonic evocation of another artistic model," which undermines the original form, that becomes implicated in satire "by targeting poor literary performances" (Makaryk 603, 604). This definition is then correlated to Mikhail Bakhtin's theories of dialogism: "For Bakhtin, parody ... is implicitly transgressive and subversive of conventional ideology" (Makaryk 604). Hemingway's *The Torrents of Spring* appears to be an experiment aimed at enlarging the canon while censuring the premises upon which literature is judged. His chosen method to carry out his criticism of the current state of arts and letters in the United States is parody. Margaret Rose defines the function of parody:

> to expand the corpus of fiction, contributing to progress in literary history, while also presenting critiques of the epistemological processes, structural problems, and social assumptions involved in the writing and reception of literary texts (Rose *Parody/Meta-Fiction* 13-14 [hereafter *P/M-F*]).

Much in the way that Bakhtin demonstrates classical cases of parody "to provide a mirror to ... [one's] own world," Hemingway utilizes the parody of Turgenev to criticize contemporary culture (Rose *P/M-F* 168). Parody, as Rose most importantly points out, "has been put to work in the cause of subverting established canons – of literary, political, and ideological kinds" (Rose *P/M-F* 169). Based on my reading of the text, Hemingway's unwritten goal in writing *The Torrents of Spring* seems to be a modernist manifesto, upsetting the literary consensus. Hemingway mixes and matches elements of plot, characterization, and theme, to attempt to demonstrate his ability to better Turgenev, in addition to galvanizing writers to abandon post-romantic tendencies at the end of the nineteenth century.

Hemingway's *The Torrents of Spring* can be seen as dialogically engaged with its Russian prior text, its "meaning and logic dependent upon what has previously been said" (Allen 19). In Hemingway's text, the doubled protagonist (Scripps and Yogi) is a deflated version of the upper-class Sanin. They are the American version of the culture hero - working men. One, Yogi Johnson, sacrifices his potency after defending his country in World War I, and the other, Scripps O'Neil, attempts to be a writer, though he tries his hand at any manual trade, in imitation of some of the great creators of the past, while searching for a cure for his writer's block. The text counters prejudice with a chapter title that disparages white mistrust of Native Americans — "The Passing of a Great Race and the Making and Marring of Americans" (Hemingway 71). Hemingway's *The Torrents of Spring* has this chapter title for a dual purpose; while it castigates whites for decimating the Native Americans, it also alludes to the demise of the nineteenth century writer and the alleged ruin of American literature by the generation which came of age after World War I. Scripps attempts to establish his origins – his mother is an Italian immigrant and his father a general in the forces of the north in the American Civil War. Yogi innocently identifies with Native Americans, but when they discover his family came from Sweden their reaction is fierce:

> Yogi felt the barrel of an automatic pushed hard against his stomach. "You'll go quietly through the club-room, get your coat and hat and leave as though nothing had happened.... And never come back. Get that, you Swede" (Hemingway *TOS* 66).

The women in Hemingway's *The Torrents of Spring* are similarly powerful; Lucy O'Neil keeps her husband by drinking together with him, and by having his child. When

Scripps 'loses' her, "everything was dark" (TOS 18). Scripps O'Neil, a slave to his hormones, cannot exist more than a few days without female companionship. He hastens to make ties with the elderly waitress, Diana, who is obviously unsuited for him. He melodramatically "reached forward to take the elderly waitress's hand, and with quiet dignity she laid it within his own. 'You are my woman,' he said. Tears came into her eyes, too" (Hemingway TOS 33). Scripps is swift to imbue the female characters with magical qualities; their hold over him is great. Even the male sense of identity comes under question; male attributes as well as those of the female gender, are being parodied in these texts. The protagonists in Hemingway's The Torrents of Spring, Scripps and Yogi, are plagued by indecision and self-examination. As heroes, they function as both opposites and dualities.

According to Owen Miller, the relationship between two texts can be best understood by thinking "of it metaphorically as a form of citation in which a fragment of discourse is accommodated or assimilated by the focused text" (Miller 21). In this framework, one can approach Myler Wilkinson's book, The Dark Mirror: American Literary Response to Russia [1996], which devotes ten pages to a discussion of the importance of Russian literature to Hemingway in the 1920s, and especially focuses on Turgenev, the writer "who held Hemingway's critical attention first and longest" (Wilkinson Dark Mirror 136). Wilkinson's depiction of Hemingway's fascination with Russian writers in general and with Turgenev in specific substantiates a need to view Hemingway's novella as an intertextual construction which "foregrounds notions of relationality, interconnectedness and interdependence" (Allen 5).

"I think you should learn about writing from everybody who has ever written that has anything to teach you" (Ernest Hemingway in a to F. Scott Fitzgerald, 15 December 1925).

While seemingly ridiculing his predecessor to establish himself, Hemingway exposes the liability of his own inheritance. In parodying Turgenev, Hemingway parodies himself as well: his concerns are found first in Turgenev. By using Turgenev, Hemingway demonstrates the need to return to Romanticism as a theme and then to dismantle it textually. While Hemingway appears to ridicule Turgenev, it can also be seen that Turgenev himself does not ascribe to the very "politics" he presents. Therefore, it can be argued that Hemingway's use of parody itself is also affected by the dramatic build-up and let-down of expectations that Turgenev develops in his novella. To verify this analysis, one would to well to engage the translation version which Hemingway is ascribed by Sylvia Beach's library cards to have read. Therefore, Constance Garnett's translation of Turgenev is examined and compared to Hemingway's work.

This is a pattern of male behavior in Turgenev's character which is repeated in Hemingway's text: Scripps O'Neil reacts with "dumb terror" when he realizes his wife Lucy has left him (Hemingway *Torrents* 7). However, with his relocation to Petoskey, and after swiftly marrying Diana, the elderly waitress, he suddenly notices "the relief waitress. She was a buxom, jolly-looking girl, and she wore a white apron" (Hemingway *Torrents* 35). He is easily misguided in his "expectation of future gratification" much as Turgenev's Sanin is (Elizabeth Allen 92).While Turgenev disparages foreign cookery, Hemingway glories in it. Hemingway appears to make sarcastic use of prejudices and the limitations of national identities. The reader will recognize Turgenev's impishness in Hemingway's version:

> We lunched on rollmops, Sole Meuniere, Civet de Lievre a la Chez Cocotte, marmelade de pommes, and washed it all down, as we used to say (eh, reader?) with a bottle of Montrachet 1919, with the sole, and bottle of Hospice de Beaune 1919 apiece with the jugged hare. Mr. Dos Passos, I believe, shared a bottle of Chambertin with me over the marmelade de pommes (Hemingway *The Torrents of Spring* 68).

From Turgenev Hemingway takes "a stylistic approach, and a stance in relation to nature" which serve him well in *The Torrents of Spring*. Throughout Hemingway's novel, one can sense the anxiety he was to express over twenty years later in a letter to his publisher, Charles Scribner: "I started out trying to beat dead writers that I knew how good they were (Excuse vernacular) I tried for Mr. Turgenieff first and it wasn't too hard" (Hemingway *Selected Letters* 673). Notwithstanding Hemingway's later bravado, he keeps a close eye on Turgenev's "sense of place [and] ... feeling of having lived in a country, which Turgenev had achieved in his work" (Wilkinson *Hemingway and Turgenev* 22).

NOTES & REFERENCES

Allen, Elizabeth Cheresh. *Beyond Realism: Turgenev's Poetics of Secular Salvation.* Stanford: Stanford UP, 1992.

Allen, Graham. *Intertextuality.* London: Routledge, 2000.

Bloom, Harold. *The Anxiety of Influence: A Theory of Poetry.* 2nd ed. New York: Oxford UP, 1997.

Chapple, Richard. "Ivan Turgenev, Sherwood Anderson, and Ernest Hemingway: The

Torrents of Spring All." New Comparison 5 (Summer 1988): 136-49.

Coltrane, Robert. "Hemingway and Turgenev: *The Torrents of Spring.*" *Hemingway's Neglected Short Fiction: New Perspectives.* Ed. Susan Beegel. Tuscaloosa: U Alabama P, 1989: 149-61.

Costlow, Jane T. "Dido, Turgenev and the Journey toward Bedlam." *Russian Literature* 29 (1991): 395-408.

Encyclopaedia Britannica. Vol. 22. Chicago: Encyclopaedia Britannica, 1958.

Encyclopedia of Contemporary Literary Theory: Approaches, Scholars, Terms. Ed. Irena R. Makaryk. Toronto: University of Toronto P, 1993.

Fisher, Vladimir. "Story and Novel in Turgenev's Work." *Critical*

Essays on IvanTurgenev. Ed. David A. Lowe. Boston: G. K. Hall, 1989: 43-63.

Fitch, Noel."Ernest Hemingway - c/o Shakespeare and Company." *Fitzgerald/Hemingway Annual 1977*: 157-81.

Griffin, Dustin. *Satire: A Critical Reintroduction.* Lexington: UP of Kentucky, 1994.

Hemingway, Ernest. *By-Line: Selected Articles and Dispatches of Four Decades.* Ed. William White. London: Grafton, 1989.

————. *Ernest Hemingway: Selected Letters 1917- 1961.* New York: Scribner's, 1989. *A Movable Feast.* New York: Scribner's, 1964.

————. *The Sun Also Rises.* New York: Macmillan, 1926. 1986.

————. *The Torrents of Spring: A Romantic Novel in Honour of the Passing of a Great Race.* Intro. David Garnett. London: Collins, 1977.

Junkins, Donald. "'Oh, Give the Bird a Chance': Nature and Vilification in Hemingway's *The Torrents of Spring.*" *North Dakota Quarterly* 63.3 (1996): 65-80.

Miller, Owen. "Intertextual Identity." *Identity of the Literary Text.* Eds. Mario J. Valdes and Owen Miller. Toronto: U Toronto P, 1985: 19-40.

Pumpyansky, Lev. "Turgenev's Novels and the Novel *On the Eve.*" *Critical Essays on Ivan* Turgenev. Ed. David A. Lowe. Boston: G. K. Hall, 1989: 124-44.

Reynolds, Michael. *Hemingway: The Paris Years.* New York: W. W. Norton, 1989.

Hemingway's Reading, 1910-1940: An Inventory. Princeton: Princeton UP, 1981.

Rose, Margaret A. *Parody/ Meta-Fiction.* London: Croom Helm, 1979.

Scholes, Robert, Nancy R. Comley and Gregor L. Ulmer. *Text Book: An Introduction to Literary Language.* 2nd ed. New York: St. Martin's, 1995: 130-32.

Turgenev, Ivan. *The Torrents of Spring* with *First Love* and *Mumu.* Trans. Constance Garnett. London: Heinemann, 1897. 1970.

Wilkinson, Myler. *The Dark Mirror: American Literary Response to Russia.* New York: Peter Lang, 1996.

————. *Hemingway and Turgenev: The Nature of Literary Influence.* Ann Arbor: UMI Research Press, 1984. 1986.

Woodward, James B. "Typical Images in the Later Tale of Turgenev." *Critical Essays on Ivan Turgenev.* Ed. David A. Lowe. Boston: G. K. Hall, 1989: 87-101.

Humor in *The Sun Also Rises*

Scott Donaldson

Ernest Hemingway started out trying to be funny. On the evidence of his high school compositions, a classmate recalled, "one might have predicted that he would be a writer of humor."[1] In the *Trapeze*, the Oak Park and River Forest Township high school weekly newspaper, he made fun of himself, his sister, his friends, and the school itself. Some of these pieces were fashioned after the epistolary subliteracy of Ring Lardner's *You Know Me, Al* (1916). "Well Sue as you are the editor this week I thot as how I would write and tell you about how successful I was with my editorials so you would be cheered up and fell how great a responsibility you have in swaying the public opinions." He had written "a hot editorial" on "Support the Swimming Team" and expected at least 500 people at the next meet, "and do you know how many guys there was there? Only one, and he "never read no editorials."[2] Parody also figured in contributions to the *Trapeze*; from the beginning, Hemingway understood how to take an elevated, formal pattern and bring it crashing to earth.

> Lives of football men remind us,
> We can dive and kick and slug.
> And departing leave behind us,
> Hoof prints on another's mug.[3]

In his juvenile fiction, too, he was working for laughs. One of his three published high school stories," A Matter of Colour," does nothing but build up to a punch line delivered by and somewhat at the expense of a stolid Swede.[4]

After brief tours with the Kansas City *Star* and the

ambulance service on the Italian front during World War I, Hemingway came back to Chicago, landed a job writing booster copy for the *Cooperative Commonwealth*, and in his spare time experimented with humor. He fired off satirical rewrites of world news to *Vanity Fair*, which fired them right back. He also concocted mock advertising campaigns to entertain his friends. One involved bottling stockyard blood as "Bull Gore for Bigger Babies." Another, rather less surprising today than in 1920, ridiculed the "current Interchurch World campaign to sell Christianity in paid-for space."[5] Together with Bill Horne and Y.K. Smith, he put together thirteen verses of the doggerel "Battle of Copenhagen," its humor aimed at ethnic groups.

> Ten tribes of red Pawnees
> Were sulking behind trees
> at the battle of Copenhagen.

> Three greasy Greeks
> Arrayed in leathern breeks
> And smelling strongly of leeks
> at the Battle of Copenhagen.

> A half million Jews
> Ran back to tell the news
> of the Battle of Copenhagen.[6]

Jewish jokes, especially, were part of Hemingway's heritage. At school he was called Hemingstein, apparently because he was careful in money matters, and rather enjoyed the nickname.

When he caught on with the Toronto *Daily Star* and *Star Weekly*, first as a freelancer in 1920 and then as a regular feature writer and correspondent from early 1921 until the end of 1923, Hemingway found a commercial outlet for his brand of comedy. As *Star Weekly* editor J. Herbert Cranston put it, "Hemingway. ...could write in good, plain Anglo-Saxon, and had a certain much prized gift of humor."[7] His earliest pieces for the paper dealt with such subjects as a shaky-kneed visit to a barber college for a free shave,

a politician totally ignorant of the sport who appeared at
prizefights to curry favor with the voters, and the disastrous
consequences of believing the promotional copy issued by
summer vacation resorts. Later, during nearly two years
as a roving European correspondent based in Paris,
Hemingway derided the empty life of do-nothing expatriates
and refused to be impressed by the supposedly great men
he encountered at conferences in Lausanne and Genoa.
The watchword was "irreverence," the target all received
wisdom. The attitude most commonly struck was that of
the "wise guy," and as Delmore Schwartz pointed out, it
was in this role that Hemingway first made an impression.
"To be a wise guy," Schwartz wrote, "is to present an
impudent, aggressive, knowing, and self-possessed face or
'front' to the world. The most obvious mark of the wise guy
is his sense of humor which expresses his scorn and his
sense of independence; he exercises it as one of the best
ways of controlling a situation and of demonstrating his
super to all situations."[8]

That description well suits the Hemingway feature
for the *Star Weekly* entitled "Our Confidential Vacation
Guide," with descriptions such as this:

> Beautiful Lake Flyblow nestles like a plague spot in
> the heart of the great north woods. All around it rise
> the majestic hills. Above it towers the majestic sky.
> On every side of it is the majestic shore.. The shore
> is lined with majestic dead fish—dead of loneliness.[9]

The wise guy pose also pervades "Condensing the
Classics," an August 1921 venture into Shrinklits that
reduced great novels and poems to a headline and a lead
paragraph. Among the headlines were "Crazed Knight in
Weird Tilt," "Big Cat in Flames," "Albatross Slayer Flays
Prohibition," and "Slays His White Bride—Society Girl, Wed
to African War-Hero, Found Strangled in Bed."[10] And it
explains the irreverence with which Hemingway dismissed
Benito Mussolini as the biggest bluff in Europe and the
Russian foreign minister Tchitcherin as a homosexual
dandy. Sometimes his journalistic humor was good-natured

or high-spirited; more often it was satirical, with a target firmly in mind. As that satirical bent was translated into Hemingway's fiction it became clear that no target was sacrosanct. His first fictional publication as a professional writer, the May 1922 two-page fable for *The Double Dealer* called "A Divine Gesture,"[11] employed irony and dark humor in depicting an indifferent God and trivial human beings.

When Hemingway left the newspaper business at the end of 1923, had been turning out amusing copy for so long that he naturally tended think of himself as a humorist.[12] The wise guy strain of that humor led directly to *The Torrents of Spring*, the satiric novella he dashed off between drafts of *The Sun Also Rises* in November 1925. Like much of Hemingway's juvenilia, *Torrents* was a parody. Its victim was Sherwood Anderson, and particularly Anderson's novel *Dark Laughter*, which had appeared earlier in the year. In that book, Anderson celebrated the wisdom and virtue of the unlettered primitive and indulged in a good deal of obtrusive philosophic musing. Anderson had earlier helped to introduce Hemingway to the literary world of Paris, but in *Torrents* the young writer relentlessly exposed the failings of his benefactor, while also making sport of expiration, literature with a capital L, Scott Fitzgerald, and Gertrude Stein.

Individual passages are very funny indeed. Scripps O'Neil, a Harvard graduate and would-be writer with two wives and minimal brain power, masquerades as the hero. He comes to a railway depot bearing the sign PETOSKEY in large letters. "Scripps read the sign again. Could this be Petoskey?" He comes across another sign advertising BROWN'S BEANERY THE BEST BY TEST. "Was this after all, Brown's Beanery?" he wonders. He goes to a pump factory to get a job. "Could this really be a pump factory?" He walks up to a door with "a sign on it: KEEP OUT, THIS MEANS YOU. Can this mean me? Scripps wondered."[13] But the whole of *The Torrents of Spring* adds up to less than the sum of its sometimes hilarious parts. The humor is almost always at someone's expense; the characters are insignificant, the plot fantastic, the theme invisible. *Torrents* runs to only about one hundred pages, and could profitably have been cut to half that length.

Thirty years later, when his own work became the butt of various parodies, Hemingway renounced the genre. "Parodies," he told A. E. Hotchner, "are what you write when you are associate editor of the Harvard *Lampoon.....*The step up from writing parodies is writing on the wall above the urinal."[14] The step he himself took in late 1925 and early 1926 was to rewrite the novel that most successfully incorporates his gift for humor. The epigraph to The *Torrents of Spring*, from Fielding, declares that "the only source of the true Ridiculous (as it appears to me) is affectation." When Hemingway finished *Torrents* to take up *The Sun Also Rises* again, he was keenly aware of the affected and the pretentious in all their forms, but he subordinated the wise guy, satiric vein in his novel. In its place Hemingway achieved in *Sun* "a delicate balance of ridicule and affection"[16] that contributes to character development and underscores the theme. The humor turns bitter as the novel progresses, but it does not start that way and the bitterness is earned, not gratuitous.

II

Hemingway announced *The Sun Also Rises* with an inside joke. The two epigraphs—one from "GERTRUDE STEIN *in conversation*, the other from Ecclesiastes—are linked together rhetorically. "You are all a lost generation," Stein said, and in the Bible the preacher said, "One generation passeth away, and another generation cometh; but the earth abideth forever... The sun also ariseth." Once one knows the provenance of Stein's remark, it is impossible to take it seriously as the biblical passage In *A Moveable Feast*, written thirty years later, Hemingway told the story as he remembered it. Stein had had some trouble with her Ford, and the young garage man who tried to repair it did not do a good job. Chastising him, the garage owner said, " You are all a generation perdue," and Stein appropriated his comment in talking to Hemingway. "That's what you all are," she told him, referring to the young people who had served in the war. "You have no respect for anything. You drink yourselves to death ....You're all a lost generation, just exactly as the garage keeper said." When wrote his first novel, Hemingway added, he "tried to balance Miss Stein's quotation from the garage keeper with one from Ecclesiastes," but he did not agree with her about the particular lostness of his generation: "all generations were lost by something and always had been and always would be."[17]

It is not surprising that Hemingway, in writing *A Moveable Feast*, recalled the anecdote rather differently than he did on September 27, 1925, when he set it down as a foreword to the novel-in-progress he then intended to call *The Lost Generation*. The scene is the garage once again, but as it happens, the young mechanic who fixes Stein's car does an excellent job and she asks the garage owner where he finds boys to work so well. She heard that one couldn't get them to work anymore. He has no trouble with the young boys of 1925, the garageman says. He's taken and trained them himself. "It is the ones between twenty-two and thirty that are no good. *C'est un generation perdu.* [Hemingway uses the feminine form in his preface to *The Sun Also Rises* and this form in *A Moveable Feast.*] No one wants them. They are no good. They were spoiled. The young ones, the new ones are all right again." There are two very different things in this earlier version of the "lost generation" story. First, Stein does not generalize from the garageman's remark. Second and more important, instead of denying the uniqueness of his generation, Hemingway goes on to insist upon it: "this generation that is lost has nothing to do with any Younger generation about whose outcome much literary speculation occurred in times past. This is not a question of what kind of mothers will flappers make or where is bobbed hair leading us [the sort of subjects addressed by the Fitzgeralds in magazine articles]. This is about something that is already finished. For whatever is going to happen to the generation of which I am a part has already happened." No matter what future entanglements or complications or promised salvations occur, "none of it will matter particularly to this generation because to them the things that are given to people to happen have already happened."[18]

This foreword of Hemingway's was later cut, of course, and Stein's remark stands on the page without elaboration, unless you happen to read *A Moveable Feast* or Item 202c in the Hemingway Archive at the Kennedy Library in Boston. But the private joke—that Stein's aphorism came originally from the lips of a French garage owner and that it is his voice, not that of the pontifical Stein, that is juxtaposed to the eternal Word—could not have escaped Hemingway's consciousness as he was working on *The Sun Also Rises*. In fact, the dual epigraphs suggest the complicated nature of the book's tone, an intricate mixture of humorous and serious elements. This tone shifts according to which character is speaking. *The Sun Also Rises* runs heavily to dialogue, and the characters reveal themselves largely through what they do and say, with only occasional interpretive suggestions from the narrator. Most of these characters are capable of producing merriment in others, whether or not they intend to do so. But what is remarkable is how different their kinds of humor are and how they are distinguished from each other in this way.

Hemingway had an excellent ear for talk, and much that is funny in *The Sun Also Rises* depends on that gift. Consider, for instance, the pidgin English of Count Mippipopolous, which features the rugged Anglo-Saxon verb "got," does not discriminate between tenses, and shows a knack for choosing almost the right word. "You got class all over you," he tells Brett. "You got the most class of anybody I ever seen." "Nice of you," she responds. "Mummy would be pleased." As for himself, he gets more value for his money in old brandy, he says "that in any other antiquities." "Got many antiquities?" Brett inquires. "I got a houseful." Though hardly a native speaker of English, the count is perceptive enough to note Brett's clipped manner of speech. "When you talk to me, you never finish your sentences at all," he complains. Jake also notices this linguistic trait: "The English spoken language—the upper classes, any way —must have fewer words than the Eskimo," and this is amply illustrated in the conversation of Lady Ashley and

Mike Campbell (58,62,149).

This early conversation delineates Brett's rather wry manner and the count's serious attention (he never "jokes" anyone, he insists) to enjoying the best things in life: beautiful women and objects, good food. and drink. Moreover, the discussion foreshadows certain questions that the novel eventually confronts. What constitutes "class" in human behavior? Do the count's "values" suffice? And, of course, it does these things in the context of humor deriving from the gulf between the subjects under examination—rare antiques, social position, ethical standards—and the count's tough, unlettered speech.

Belaboring the origins of humor is notoriously unrewarding. There used to be a course in comedy at Yale that the undergraduates critiqued, quite rightly, as "English 63. Comedy. 63 dollars worth of books and not a laugh in the course." Still, it needs to be observed that Hemingway's humor in *The Sun Also Rises*, like that in the Count Mippopopolous -Brett Ashley exchange, usually depends on what the philosopher Paul Morreall calls "incongruity of presentation."[19] "Hemingway's primary technique of humor," as Sheldon Grebstein observed in his fine treatment of the subject, "is that of incongruous juxtaposition," among other things the juxtaposition of "highbrow speech against the vulgate."[20] Working with word play—verbal slips, puns, double entendre—James Hinkle recently located some sixty jokes embedded in the novel'[21]. But there is more to it than word play, for Hemingway plays with ideas as well as words, adopting an incongruous point of view, confusing categories, violating logical principles, and so forth. The precise technique varies from character to character, and some characters are a good deal funnier than others.

Jake Barnes tells the story of *The Sun Also Rises* so unobtrusively and convincingly that it never occurs to us to challenge his view of events, as for instance we tend to do with that of Fredric Henry in *A Farewell to Arms*. Jake deserves sympathy because of his wound. But he wins our trust primarily because of his capacity to assess human behavior with objectivity. Like the prototypical newspaperman he has few illusions about anyone, including himself. So he adopts a posture of irony, one that moves from a good-natured sarcasm at the beginning of the novel to a biting, bitterly sardonic strain at the end.

In Chapter III Jake picks up a streetwalker and takes her to dinner "because of a vague sentimental idea that it would be nice to eat with someone." But the girl objects to the place he takes her. "This is no great thing of a restaurant." "No," Jake admits. "Maybe you would rather go to Foyot's. Why don't you keep the cab and go on?" (16). He takes a rather cynical view of the political and journalistic professions as well:

> At eleven o'clock I went over to the Quai d'Orsay in a taxi and went in and sat with about a dozen correspondents, while the foreign-office mouthpiece, a young Nouvelle Revue Francaise diplomat in horn-rimmed spectacles, talked and answered questions for half an hour. ....Several people asked questions to hear themselves talk and there were a couple of questions asked by news service men who wanted to know the answers. There was no news. (p.36)

His concierge has social pretensions and wants to make sure that all of Jake's guests measure up to her standards. If they do not, she sends them away. It gets to the point where one friend, "an extremely underfed-looking painter," writes Jake a letter asking for "a pass to get by the concierge"(53).

Where his war wound is concerned, Jake obviously does not think it funny himself, but he is capable of seeing the humor in the way others react to it. He is particularly amused by the "wonderful speech" of the Italian liaison colonel who came to see him in the Ospedale Maggiore in Milano:

> "You, a foreigner, an Englishman" (any foreigner was an Englishman) "have given more than your life." What a speech! I would like to have it illuminated to hang in the office. He never laughed. He was putting himself in my place, I guess. "Che mala fortuna! Che

mala fortuna!" (p.31)
In conversation, the subject is taboo. He's "sick," Jake tells his poule (15- 16). "Well, let's shut up about it," he tells Brett (26-7). When the count proposes that Jake and Brett get married, they collaborate on an evasive reply, "We want to lead our own lives," Jake says. "We have our careers," Brett chimes in (61). Twice Bill Gorton hovers on the brink of the forbidden subject. Why, he wonders, did Brett go to San Sebastian with Cohn? "Why didn't she go off with some of her own people? Or you?—he slurred that over—or me? Why not me?" Then, to break the awkwardness, Bill delivers a soliloquy on his own face in the shaving mirror. The next day, while they are fishing the Irati, Bill refers to the wound again in the course of satirizing the conventional stateside view of expatriation. According to this view, he tells Jake, expatriates like himself "don't work. One group claims women support you. Another group claims you're impotent."

"No," Jake responds forthrightly, "I just had an accident. "But Bill shuns the topic. "Never mention that," he tells Jake. "That's the sort of thing... ..: ought to work up into a mystery. Like Henry's bicycle." The reference is to a rumored childhood injury that compromised the masculinity of Henry James and it caused a good deal of consternation at Scribners before they allowed, it to stand, stripped of the identifying surname. But in context, it allows Jake and Bill to guide their conversation in a related but less personally sensitive direction. The important thing to note is Jake's capacity to put himself in Bill's place here. Bill has been doing splendidly but then, Jake thinks, "I was afraid he thought he had hurt me with that crack about being impotent." So Jake takes the cue from Henry's bicycle to launch into an inane discussion of whether it was on two wheels or three, on a horse or in an airplane, that the master suffered his injury. This leads to joysticks, though, and eventually Bill can only clear the air by telling Jake how fond he is of him (115-16).

It is not talk about his injury that most distresses Jake, of course, but the way it impairs his relationship with Brett. At the fiesta the high spirits of the fishing trip dissipate as Brett transforms the men around her into steers or swine. Cohn adopts an annoying air of superiority, then an equally annoying pose of suffering. Mike Campbell rides him unmercifully in attacks Jake despises himself for enjoying. Brett further compromises his integrity by persuading him to take her to Pedro Romero. Eventually, Jake's sardonic bent assumes a bitterness that inhibits rather than encourages laughter. "It seemed they were all such nice people," he reflects at mid-fiesta (146). On the last evening in Pamplona, after Brett has run off with Romero, Jake feels "low as hell" and drinks absinthe in an attempt to brighten his mood "Well," Bill says, "it was a swell fiesta." "Yes," Jake answers, "something doing all the time"(222).

By the time he and Bill and Mike have parted, Jake Barnes is in the grip of a thoroughgoing cynicism. A few weeks earlier, he had rather enjoyed the count's unabashed cultivation of material pleasures:

> We dined at a restaurant in the Bois. It was a good dinner. Food had an excellent place in the count's values. So did wine. The count was in fine form during the meal. So was Brett. It was a good party. (p.61)

During the fiesta, however, he learns how devastating it can be to be stay on at a party with Brett. And he is reminded repeatedly by Cohn, by Campbell, and by Romero of his own incapacity to make love to the woman he loves. Food and drink and friendship are the pleasures left to him, but the first two have lost their savor, and it sometimes seems that all three must be purchased. Dining alone in Bayonne, he reflects witheringly on the materialism of the French:

> Everything is on such a clear financial basis in France. It is the simplest country to live in. No one makes things complicated by becoming your friend for any obscure reason. If you want people to like you you have only to spend a little money. I spent a little money and the waiter liked me. He appreciated my valuable qualities. He would be glad to see me back. I would dine there again some time and he would be

glad to see me, and would want me at his table. It would be a sincere liking because it would have a sound basis. I was back in France. (p.233)

From that point to the end of the novel, Jake cannot enjoy human transactions. There is some healing benefit to be derived from diving into the ocean off San Sebastian, but at the hotel, the corrupt bike riders are arranging who will win the following day and then the two wires from Lady Ashley arrive:

COULD YOU COME HOTEL MONTANA MADRID AM RATHER IN TROUBLE BRETT.(pp.238-9)

And Jake must answer the call.

In Madrid, things go badly. Jake is nervous about leaving his bags downstairs at the somewhat seedy Hotel Montana. Perhaps it is true that the "personages" of the establishment are "rigidly selectioned," but nonetheless he "would welcome the upbringal" of his bags. As for Brett, she keeps insisting that she doesn't want to talk about her time with Romero, but she cannot resist going on about it. Jake becomes increasingly monosyllabic in response: "Yes." "Really?" "Good." "No." "Good." "Dear Brett." Then he proceeds to get drunk. At the Palace Hotel bar downtown, they each have three martinis before lunch. Aside from Romero, there is nothing to talk about. "Isn't it a nice bar?" Brett asks. "They're all nice bars," Jake answers. They have lunch at Botin's, where Jake eats "a very big meal" of roast young suckling pig and drinks three bottles of *rioja alta* (or is it five?) with little assistance from Brett. "Don't get drunk," she implores him. "Jake, don't get drunk." But there is not much else to be done and it does not help when they take a ride and sit close to each other and Brett says, "Oh, Jake, we could have had such a damned good time together." The mounted policeman ahead raises his baton and the taxi slows suddenly, pressing Brett against him. "Yes," Jake says. "Isn't it pretty to think so?" (pp.241- 7). Hemingway tried that closing line in two other ways—"It's

nice as hell to think so" and "Isn't it nice to think so"—
before settling on the bitter adjective "pretty" that exactly
communicates Jake's despair.[22] Brett is going back to Mike,
but for Jake there is no one, and no hope, and no humor.

At certain places in the first draft of the novel,
Hemingway interchanged "I" and "Jake" tellingly; in fact,
the parallels between author and character are marked
enough for readers to suppose that for the most part Jake
Barnes thinks and talks very much like Ernest Hemingway
himself. Jake is a repository *of* those same ethnic and
nationalistic prejudices, for instance that often cropped up
in Hemingway's juvenilia and journalism. Mrs. Braddocks,
loud and rude, "was a Canadian and had all their easy social
graces" (17). The German maitre d'hotel at. Montoya's, nosy
and knowing is satisfactorily put in his place by Bill Gorton
(209-11). The American, ambassador and his circle exploit
others for their amusement and are stupid into the bargain
(171-2, 215).[23] The French are grasping (233). The Spanish
on the other hand, generously share their food, wine, and
companionship (103-4, 156-7). Spanish peasants,
significantly, cross the language barrier to express their
good humor. The Basques who accompany Bill and Jake
on the bus ride to Burguete offer them a drink from their
big leather winebag. As Jake tips up the wineskin, one of
the Basques imitates the sound of a klaxon motor horn so
suddenly and surprisingly that Jake spills some of the wine.
A few minutes later, he fools Jake with klaxon again, and
everyone laughs (103-4, 156-7).

Most of the ethnic humor in the book, however, is
less good-natured and depends upon linguistic nuance.
Robert Cohn is the butt of most of it. Some of the jibes
against him are made by relatively minor characters.
Harvey Stone and Jake are having a drink at the Select
when Cohn comes up. "Hello, Robert," Stone says, "I was
just telling Jake here that you're a moron" (43-4).
Immediately thereafter Frances Clyne devastates Cohn at
greater length, also in the presence of Jake. Frances
satirically unveils Cohn's narcissism, his self-pity, his
habit of buying himself out of entanglements, and his
stinginess in doing so. "I do not know," Jake thinks, "how

people could say such terrible things to Robert Cohn... Here it was, all going on right before me, and I did not even feel an impulse to try and stop it. And this was friendly joking to what went on later" (48-50). What went on later, at its worst, came in the form of Mike Campbell's increasingly unfunny insults at Pamplona. But the primary source of information about Cohn and the group's attitude toward him, is Jake himself.

Jake artfully belittles Cohn throughout, but especially in the opening chapter. "Robert Cohn was once middleweight boxing champion of Princeton," the novel begins, and the depreciation follows at once. "Do not think that I am very much impressed by that as a boxing title, but it meant a lot to Cohn." A "very shy and thoroughly nice boy," Cohn did not use his skill to knock down any of those who were snooty to him, as a Jew, at Princeton. In the gym itself, however, he was overmatched once and "got his nose permanently flattened. This... ..gave him a certain satisfaction of some strange sort, and it certainly improved his nose." Jake never met anyone in Cohn's class at Princeton who remembered him. Having disposed of his college career, Barnes continues his demeaning account.

Though Robert Cohn was "a nice boy, a friendly boy, and very shy," Jake acknowledges, his experience at Princeton embittered him; he came out of it "with painful self-consciousness and the flattened nose, and was married by the first girl who was nice to him." Married by, not to. After siring three children in five years and losing most of the fifty thousand dollars his father had left him, Cohn had just made up his mind to leave his wife when she left him instead, running off "with a miniature painter." A *miniature*-painter! Next, Cohn goes to California and buys his way into the editorship of a literary magazine, but it becomes too expensive and he has to give it up. Meanwhile, he has "been taken in hand by a lady who hoped to rise with the magazine. She was very forceful, and Cohn never had a chance of not being taken in hand." This is Frances, who does not love Cohn but wants to "get what there was to get while there was still something available" and then to marry him. She brings him to Europe, where she had been

educated, though he "would rather have been in America."
Cohn then produces a novel that was "not really such a bad
novel as the critics later called it," and for the first time
begins to think of himself as attractive to women and able
to assert himself with them. It is at this dangerous stage
of his continuing adolescence that Cohn meets Brett
Ashley, with her curves like the hull of a racing yacht.
Gazing at her, Jake comments, he "looked a great deal as
his compatriot must have looked when he saw the promised
land. Cohn, of course, was much younger. But he had that
look of eager, deserving expectation" (3-7,22). The mode is
obviously ridicule, and Cohn's subsequent behavior—
particularly his romanticization of *his* affair with Brett, his
air of superiority toward Jake and Bill on that score, and
his excessive barbering—well merits ridicule. Still, the
opening salvo pretty much settles his hash.

To his credit, at one stage in Pamplona it appears
that Cohn may be achieving a new maturity. He has
foolishly proclaimed that he might be bored at the bullfights.
Afterward Bill and Mike kid him about that, and Cohn is
able to laugh at himself. "No, I wasn't bored. I wish you'd
forgive me that." Bill forgives him, but not the rivalrous
Mike (165-6). He continues baiting Cohn until even Brett
tells him to "shove it along" (165-6). From this stage on,
and despite Cohn's outbreak of pugilistic violence, Mike
supplants him as the villain of the piece. Moreover, Mike's
descent can be accurate calibrated on the scale of humor.

On first introduction, Mike Campbell seems an
engaging ne' er-do-well. He is more than a little drunk on
arrival in Paris and Brett accurately introduces him to Bill
Gorton as "an undischarged bankrupt," but he is so excited
about seeing Brett again and so eagerly anticipatory about
the night ahead that these shortcomings appear
unimportant. "I say, Brett," he thrice tells her, "You *are* a
lovely piece." And he asks Jake and Bill twice, "Isn't she a
lovely piece?" To taunt him, Bill asks Mike to go along to
the prizefight but he and Brett have a date in mind. "I'm
sorry I can't go," Mike says, and Brett laughs (79-80). When
the group reassembles in Pamplona, Mike again works his
vein of humorous repetition. Brett suggests that he tell

the story of the time his horse bolted down Piccadilly, but Mike refuses. "I'll not tell that story. It reflects discredit on me." Well, she suggests, tell them about the medals. "I'll not. That story reflects great discredit upon me." Brett could easily tell it, he supposes. "She tells all the stories that reflect discredit on me." In the end, he tells the story himself, and it does indeed place him in an unfavorable light, for he had gotten drunk and given away someone else's war medals to some girls in a nightclub. "They thought I was hell's own shakes of a soldier" (135-6).

Once started, Mike persists in his self-depreciation. He went bankrupt, he says, two ways - "gradually and then suddenly." What brought it on, he observes in sentence fragments, were "Friends... .-1 had a lot of friends. False friends. Then I had creditors, too. Probably had more creditors than anybody in England" (136). Soon thereafter there is the one successful dinner at the fiesta, where both Bill and Mike were "very funny.... They were good together"(146). Mike's bantering becomes progressively more strident however, as the drinking increases. Cohn continues to hang about in pursuit of his lady love (Mike's fiancée), and Brett herself becomes infatuated with Romero. Mike ventilates his outrage in a vicious assault on Cohn. "Why do you follow Brett around like a poor bloody steer? Don't you know you're not wanted? I know when I'm not wanted. Why don't you know when you're not wanted? You came down to San Sebastian where you weren't wanted, and followed Brett around like a bloody steer." Once started, Mike's invective is hard to stop. None of their friends at San Sebastian "would invite you" to come along, he tells Cohn. "You can't blame them hardly. Can you? I asked them to. They wouldn't do it. You can't blame them, now. Can you? Now answer me. Can you blame them?...1 can't blame them. Can you blame them? Why do you follow Brett around?"(142). Here, Mike's talent for repetition is used to abuse another human being, and there is nothing funny about such scorn.

Similarly, his habit of *self*-disparagement also palls as his financial irresponsibility becomes more manifest. "Who cares if he is a damn bankrupt?" Bill objects after they are ejected from a Pamplona bar by some people Mike owes money to (189). The answer, finally, is that everyone cares. Mike's technique is to disarm criticism by accusing himself before others do so, but that does not always amuse. He won't go into the bullring for the morning *encierro* at Pamplona, he tells Edna, because it "wouldn't be fair to my creditors" (200). At the last meeting with Bill and Jake in Biarritz, when it turns out that Mike is broke and cannot pay for the drinks he's gambled for at poker dice, and has spent all of Brett's money as well. Mike again touches the wound, but less amusingly this time. Bill proposes another drink. "Damned good idea." Mike says. "One never gets anywhere by discussing finances." Then, since they've rented a car for the day, Mike suggests that they "take a drive. It might do my credit good." They decide to drive down to Hendaye, though Mike remarks he hasn't "any credit along the coast" (230). Under the circumstances, Mike's attempts at humor invite contempt. It has been ethically dubious of him to savage Cohn. And, as Morreall points out, "it can also be morally inappropriate to laugh about one's own situation, if by doing so we are detaching ourselves from our own moral responsibilities."[24]

In a less blameworthy fashion, Brett makes fun of her own drunkenness and promiscuity. The count advices her to drink the Mumm's champagne slowly, and later she can get drunk. "Drunk? Drunk?" she replies (59). When Jake brings his poule to the balmusette, Brett is amused by the supposed disrespect for her status as a pure woman. "It's an insult to all of us," she laughs. "It's in restraint of trade," she laughs again (22). Laughing at herself in this way serves, of course, to forestall any change in her reckless style of life. In this sense it is fitting that she goes back to Mike, who is "so damned nice" and "so awful" and so much her "sort of thing"(243).

III

The most consistently funny character in *The Sun Also Rises* is Bill Gorton. Gorton is clearly modeled on the humorist Donald Ogden Stewart who did in fact go to Pamplona in 1925 with the Hemingways, Harold Loeb, Bill

Smith, Pat Guthrie, and Lady Duff Twysden. Stewart later characterized Hemingway's novel as almost reportorial in its fidelity to the events of the fiesta. He may have come to that judgment, which undervalues the book's artistry, largely as a consequence of recognizing so much of his own sometimes "crazy humor" (as he called it) in Bill Gorton's material. In fact Don Stewart, like Bill Gorton, was almost constitutionally incapable of not amusing people.[25] As Scott Fitzgerald said of him, he "could turn a Sunday school picnic into a public holiday."[26]

It was very much in character, then, for Hemingway to make Bill Gorton—Don Stewart the source of humor in the two most high-spirited chapters of the novel. These are Chapters VIII, where Bill and Jake go out to dinner in Paris, and Chapter XII, where they go fishing along the Irati. In the Paris chapter, Bill has only recently come to Europe and has just returned from a trip to Austria and Hungary. Gorton is described as "very happy". His last book has sold well. He's excited about the new crop of young light-heavyweights. He knows how to have a good time. He finds people and places wonderful. "The States were wonderful," he tells Jake. "New York was wonderful." Vienna was wonderful, he writes "Then a card from Budapest: 'Jake, Budapest is wonderful' ". Then he returns to Paris, where Jake greets him:

> "Well," [Jake] said, "I hear you had a wonderful trip."
> "Wonderful," he said, "Budapest is absolutely wonderful."
> "How about Vienna?"
> "Not so good, Jake. Not so good. It seemed better than it was."(p.70)

A few days later, Jake and Bill meet an American family on the train to Pamplona, and the father asks if they're having a good trip. "Wonderful," Bill says (85).
This sort of highly repetitive nonsense is much funnier when spoken than on the page, as Jackson Benson has pointed out.[27] So is the famous stuffed dog discussion on the way to dinner. Jake and Bill walk by a taxidermist's

and Bill asks, "Want to buy anything? Nice stuffed dog?"

> "Come on," I said. "You're pie-eyed."
> "Pretty nice stuffed dogs," Bill said. "Certainly brighten
> up your flat."
> "Come on."
> "Just one stuffed dog. I can take' em or leave' em alone.
> But listen Jake. Just one stuffed dog."
> "Come on."
> "Mean everything in the world after you bought it. Simple
> exchange of values. You give them money. They give
> you a stuffed dog."
> "We'll get one on the way back."
> "All right. Have it your own way. Road to hell paved with
> unbought stuffed dogs. Not my fault.
> We went on.
> "How'd you feel that way about dogs so sudden?"
> "Always felt that way about dogs. Always been a great
> lover of stuffed animals." (pp.72-3)

Then they are off on the subject of not being daunted, but
Bill understands the humorous potential of the echo. "See
that horse-cab?" he asks Jake. "Going to have that horse-
cab stuffed for you for Christmas. Going to give all my friends
stuffed animals." Brett comes along in a taxi ("Beautiful
lady," said Bill. "Going to kidnap us"[74]), and they hit it off
beautifully. It is too bad, Bill thinks, that she's engaged to
Michael. Still: "What'll I send them? Think they'd like a
couple of stuffed race-horses?" (76)

Liquor obviously plays an important role in Bill's
comedy. "Don [crossed out] Bill was the best of the lot,"
Hemingway wrote in a discarded first draft, "and he was on
a hilarious drunk and thought everybody else was and
became angry if they were not.[28] Alcohol not only fuels his
tomfoolery, it also provides him with a potent source of the
topical humor that runs through Chapter XII. "Direct
action... beats legislation," Bill remarks when Jake doctors
their rum punches at the inn in Pamplona (123). Bill's voice
predominates in this Burguete section that in the first draft

Hemingway tried switching to him as the first-person narrator.[29] Later he went back to Jake as narrator and straight man for Bill's repartee. Among other things Bill makes fun of the cliches of literary criticism, Bible Belt morality, H.L. Mencken, and —— especially—the Scopes trial and William Jennings Bryan's rhetoric in attacking the theory of evolution. Putting aside a hard-boiled egg and unwrapping a drumstick, Bill reverses the order: "For Bryan's sake. As a tribute to the Great Commoner. First the chicken; then the egg."

> "Wonder what day God created the chicken?"
> "Oh," said Bill... .., "how should we know? We should not question. Our stay on earth is not for long. Let us rejoice and believe and give thanks."

"Let us not doubt, brother," he adds. "Let us not pry into the holy mysteries of the hen-coop with simian fingers." Instead, "Let us utilize the fowls of the air. Let us utilize the product of the vine. Will you utilize a little, brother?" (121-2). Jake will, and so will Bill, and so will the genial Englishman named Wilson Harris they play three-handed bridge with in the evening.

As almost every commentator on the novel has noticed, the interlude at Burguete stands in idyllic counterpoint to the sophisticated pretentiousness of Paris and the destructive passions of Pamplona. In the first draft, Hemingway let Jake and Bill confess how they felt about their lives on that fishing trip. No one can believe that he's happy, Bill remarks, but "honest to God," he is. So is Jake, he admits, "ninety percent of the time," although they're both a little embarrassed to confess it.[30] Geography has little to do with this. After their dinner at Madame Lecomte's and a long walk back to Montparnasse, Bill feels so good that he doesn't need a drink. In fact, Jake and Bill are almost always in good spirits when together, either alone or with other male companions. Don Stewart himself blamed the trouble at Pamplona in 1925 on that old "devil sex." The previous year, when he, Ernest, Hadley, John Dos Passos, Bill Bird, and Bob McAlmon had gone to

Pamplona for the bullfights, the trip had been a great success.

    The Sun Also Rises is the great book it is partly because of Bill Gorton's humor that directs its jibes at ideas and institutions, not human beings. In this way, Gorton provides a model of behavior that—unlike the code of the intrepid Romero—it is possible to emulate. "I did not care that it was all about," Jake reflects in one of his interior monologues. "All I wanted to know was how to live in it"(148). Gorton seems to have discovered how: without Jake's bitter sarcasm, without Mike's and Brett's disingenuous self-depreciation, without Robert's self-pity, with the best will in the world.

    Not everyone, it might be objected, is temperamentally suited to enjoy life as much as Gorton, just as very few could be expected to entertain one's companions as well as he. Yet in the very subject matter of his humor, Hemingway conveys an attitude toward existence available to all. It is easiest to understand, through negation, which attitudes are invalid. The religious preach brotherhood and arrange for special privileges. The do-gooding of the Prohibitionists does no good. The know-nothingism of what are currently called "creationists" is ridiculous, and so is the catchword pedantry of the literati: "Irony and Pity." More positively, at least one basic value emerges in the subtext of such ventures into comedy as the twelve shoeshines Bill buys Mike Campbell, and his persistent sales pitch for stuffed dogs.

    The shoeshine scene represents Bill's humor for once gone off the rails under the tensions of Pamplona. When bootblack after bootblack polishes Mike's shoes to a higher gloss, the repetition becomes more awkward than amusing. As Mike sardonically observes, "Bill's a yell of laughter" (173). By contrast, not even a taxidermist would be likely to find the stuffed dog passage unfunny. Whether successful in inducing laughter or not, however, both scenes have a bearing on the theme of compensation in the novel.[31] Rather casually dropped into the stuffed dog dialogue is Bill's comment about "Simple exchange of values. You give them money. They give you a stuffed dog." This seemingly

innoeent observation underscores Hemingway's theme that
the good things in life—not exclusively limited to hedonistic
pleasure—have to be earned through effort and experience.
It is for this reason, in part, that the shoeshine episode
fails flat, since Bill's jesting contradicts that message by
demeaning the low but honest trade of the bootlblacks.

    In his autobiography, Donald Ogden Stewart chastised
himself for having produced so much of the "crazy humor"
characteristic of Bill Gorton and pervasive in such Stewart
books of the period as *A Parody Outline of History* (1921),
Perfect Behavior, a 1922 takeoff on Emily Post, *Aunt Polly's
Story of Mankind* (1923), *Mr. and Mrs. Haddock Abroad* (1924)
The Crazy Fool (1925), and *Mr. and Mrs. Haddock in Paris,
France* (1926). As his political beliefs swung to the left,
Stewart came to believe that he should have used his gift
for humor less to amuse his readers than alert them to
the ills of American society. And he seems never to have
recognized the accomplishment of his friend Hemingway,
whom he thought an indifferent humorist, in incorporating
certain strains of humor, including his own nonsensical
and topical predilections, within the framework of a novel
that has an ethical, if not a political, statement to make.
    Hemingway's early humor consisted mostly of
parodies and pieces that mocked others and tacitly asserted
his superiority. Later in his career humor became
increasingly dark, as in the macabre "A Natural History of
the Dead" (1932). In the course of writing an unpublished
tale along similar grisly lines, Hemingway took issue with
the claim of Henry Seidel Canby that there was "no humor
in American writing... .no humor in the way we write nor
in the things we write about. I always thought there was
but perhaps it was not clear enough; it needed a label so
that they [the critics would know it was funny when they
read it."[32] *The Sun Also Rises does* not carry such a label,
nor does it need to. In this novel alone, Hemingway used
humor brilliantly to assess character and underline theme
without descending to parody or black comedy. *The Sun Also
Rises* stands as proof that Hemingway was "above all a
magnificent craftsman, and among his prime virtues was

the ability to laugh."[33]

NOTES AND REFERENCES

1. Charles A. Fenton, *The Apprenticeship of Ernest Hemingway:The Early Years* (New York: Viking, 1958), p.12.

2. Ernest Hemingway, "Ring Lardner, Jr., Discourses on-Editorials," Oak Park *Trapeze* 16 (February 1917):3.

3. Ernest Hemingway, "Dedicated to F. W.," Oak Park *Trapeze* 24 (November 1916):4.

4. The plot of "A Matter of Colour" is summarized in Carlos Baker, *Ernest Hemingway: A Life Story* (New York: Scribner's, 1969), pp.22-3.

5. Donald M. Wright, "A Mid-Western Ad Man Remembers," *Advertising & Selling* 28 (March 25, 1937): 54.

6. "The Battle of Copenhagen" is reprinted in *Ernest Hemingway: 88 Poems*, ed. Nicholas Gerogiannis (New York: Harcourt Brace Jovanovich! Broccoli Clark, 1979), pp.22-4.

7. Quoted in Fenton, *Apprenticeship*, p.32.

8. Delmore Schwartz, "The Fiction of Ernest Hemingway," *Perspectives U.S.A.* no. 13 (Autumn 1955): 71.

9. "Our Confidential Vacation Guide" appears in *Hemingway: The Wild Years*, ed. Gene Z. Hanrahan (New York: Dell, 1962), pp.38-41.

10. Condensing the Classics," Toronto *Star Weekly*, August 20,1921, p. 22, quoted in Robert O. Stephens, *Hemingway's Nonfiction: The Public Voice* (Chapel Hill: University of North Carolina Press, 1968), pp.110-11.

11. Ernest Hemingway, "A Divine Gesture," *Double Dealer* 3 (May 1922): 267—8.

12. Fenton, *Apprenticeship*, p.260.

13. Ernest Hemingway, *The Torrents of Spring* (New York: Scribners, 1926), pp. 32, 35-6,42. Thomas N. Hagood draws attention to this pattern In "Elements of Humor in Ernest Hemingway," his 1968 Ph.D. dissertation at Louisiana State University.

14. A.E. Hotchner, *Papa Hemingway* (New York: Random House, 1966), p.70.

15. Epigraph to *Torrents*, p. 16.

16. See Lloyd Frankenburg, "Themes and Characters in Hemingway's Latest Period," *Southern Review* 7 (Spring 1942): 787-8.

17. Ernest Hemingway, *A Moveable Feast* (New York: Scribners, 1964) pp.29-31.

18. Ernest Hemingway, Item 202c, Hemmgway Archive, Kennedy Library Boston. I am indebted to Michael S. Reynolds for letting me consult his notes on this manuscript.

19. Paul Morreal, *Taking Laughter Seriously* (Albany: State University of New York Press, 1983). The section on incongruity of presentation is on pp.69-84.

20. Sheldon Norman Grebstein, *Hemingway's Craft* (Carbondale: Southern Illinois University Press, 1973), p.172. Grebstein's chapter on Hemingway's humor remains the best discussion of the subject.

21. James Hinkle, "What's Funny in *The Sun Also Rises,*" *Proceedings of the First National Conference of the Hemingway Society.* Traverse City, Michigan, October 20-3, 1983, pp.62-71.

22. The alternative endings are cited in Baker, *Hemingway,* p.155.

23. In his first draft, Hemingway explicitly associates the women in this coterie with sexual adventurism involving handsome young men like Romero. Item 202c, Hemingway Archive, Kennedy Library Boston.

24. Morreall, *Taking Laughter Seriously*, pp.112-13.

25. See Stewart's autobiography, *By a Stroke of Luck* (London: Paddington Press, 1975).

26. F. Scott Fitzgerald, "Reminiscences of Donald Stewart," St. Paul *Daily News,* December 11, 1921, City Life section, p.6, in *F. Scott Fitzgerald in His Own Time: A Miscellany.* Ed. Matthew Bruccoli and Jackson R. Bryer (Kent, Ohio: Ohio State University Press, 1971)pp 231-2.

27. Jackson J. Benson, *Hemingway: The Writer's Art of Self-*

Defense (Minneapolis: University of Minnesota Press, 1969), pp.68-9.

28. Item 202c, Hemingway Archive, Kennedy Library, Boston.

29. This experiment in shifting points of view was noted by Frederic Joseph Svoboda, *Hemingway and The Sun Also Rises: The Crafting of a Style* (Lawrence: University Press of Kansas, 1983), p.42

30. Item 202c, Hemingway Archive, Kennedy Library, Boston.

31. For a fuller discussion of this theme, see Scott Donaldson, "The Morality of Compensation," in *By Force of Will: The Life and Art of Ernest Hemingway* (New York: Viking, 1977), pp.21-33.

32. Item 636, Hemingway Archive. Kennedy Library, Boston.

33. Grebstein, *Hemingway's Craft.* p.201.

The Alternate Titles of *The Sun Also Rises*

Chidananda Bhattacharya

The Sun Also Rises of 1926 reappeared in Britain as *Fiesta* in 1927. This was not all; as Carlos Baker, Hemingway's authorized biographer informs us, "Ernest listed some alternate titles inside the back cover of one of his *cahiers*: "River to the Sea," "Two Lie Together," "The Old Leaven," "The Sun Also Rises." He rejected them all except the last, a quotation from *Ecclesiastes...*"(155). These tentations and vacillations about naming the novel are seen to be loaded with meanings and I have gained some conviction that a meaningful decoding of the novel's content as well as the artist's gradual arrival at some intent can be done when one uses some of these titles as the stairs, keeping the biography in mind. This is an imperative, especially because critical disagreements, if not outright confusions any longer, still stick around the exact significations that the work should suggest, now as it had been at the time of its first critical reception. Allen Tate's review in the *Nation* (123:15 December, 1926; 642,644) showed his frustration in this regard:

> With great skill he reversed the usual and most general formula of prose fiction: instead of selecting the details of physical background and of human behavior for the intensification of a dramatic situation, he employed the minimum of drama for the greatest possible intensification of the observed object. The reference of emphasis for the observed object was therefore not the action; rather, the reference of the action was the object, and the action

could be impure or incomplete without risk of detection. It could be mixed or incoherent......

In *The Sun Also Rises*, a full-length novel, Mr. Hemingway could not escape such leading situations, and he had besides to approach them with a kind of seriousness. He fails. It is not that Hemingway is, in the term which he uses in fine contempt for the big word, hardboiled; it is that he is not hard-boiled enough, in the artistic sense. No one can dispute with a writer the significance he derives from the subject matter; one can only point out that the significance he derives is mixed or incomplete. Brett is a nymphomaniac; Robert Cohn, a most offensive cad; both are puppets. For the emphasis is false; Hemingway doesn't fill out his characters and let them stand for themselves; he isolates one or two chief traits, which reduce them to caricature. His perception of the physical object is direct and accurate, his vision of character singularly oblique. And he actually betrays the interior machinery of his hard-boiled attitude: 'It is awfully easy to be hard-boiled about everything in the day-time, but at night it is another thing,' says Jake, the sexually impotent, musing on the futile acceptability of Brett. The history of his sentimentality is thus complete. (*Hemingway: The Critical Heritage*, 94-5)

Surely, as one can see it plainly, Tate has the nose only for a clear-cut unit of significance and he little suspected that it could as well be synthetic in nature and inhere subliminally the conscious understatement that the narrative offered. About the same sense of bafflement and a consequent impatience comes to surface in the criticism of Edwin Muir as he wrote in *Nation and Athenaeum* (41: 2 July 1927:450, 452):

There is, however, a curious inequality among his characters. Brett, the heroine, might have stepped out of 'The Green Hat' (a novel written by Michael Arlen in 1925, which became phenomenally popular

because of its combination of sexual farce and
melodrama, she is the sentimentally regarded
daredevil, and she never becomes real. But most of
the other characters, the majority of them American
Bohemians living in Paris, are graphically drawn. The
original merits of the book are striking; its fault,
equally apparent after one's first pleasure, is a lack
of artistic significance. We see the lives of a group of
people laid bare, and we feel that it does not matter
to us. Mr. Hemingway tells us a great deal about those
people, but he tells us nothing of importance about
human life. He tells us nothing, indeed, which any of
his characters might not tell us; he writes with
honesty, but as a member of the group he describes;
and, accordingly, his narrative lacks proportion,
which is the same thing as significance. (*Hemingway:
The Critical Heritage*, 96)

Muir finds Brett and other characters not successfully
growing from the matrix of the narrative, in short, not
sufficiently and spiritually contextualized. It is curious to
hear Muir complain of the lack of artistic significance in
the same breath with his admission of "one's first pleasure."
The novel definitely had pleased him as an uncritical
reader, and it was only in the aftermath of a re-run as
critic that he fell out with Hemingway.

The very opposite extreme in terms of critical views
was also not wanting. Contrary to Muir's accusation, Conrad
Aiken's insertion in the *New York Herald Tribune Books*
(31 Oct. 1926,4) commended the very profundity of
Hemingway's vision:

If one thing is striking about it, furthermore, it is its
extraordinary individuality of style...one has the
feeling that he is a little afraid of being caught with
any sort of purple on his palette, whether it be of
rhetoric or of poetry. The action, he seems to say,
must speak wholly for itself.

This results, as might be expected, in a quite
extraordinary effect of honesty and reality. The half

dozen characters, all of whom belong to the curious
and sad little world of disillusioned and aimless
expatriates who make what home they can in the
cafés of Paris, are seen perfectly and unsentimentally
by Mr. Hemingway and are put before us with
maximum of economy. In the case of the hero,
through whose mind we meet the event, and again
in the cases of Brett, the heroine, and Robert Cohn,
the sub-hero, Mr. Hemingway accomplishes more
than this – he achieves an understanding and
revelation of character, which approaches the
profound. When one reflects on the unattractiveness,
not to say the sordidness, of the scene, and the (on
the whole) gracelessness of the people, one is all the
more astonished at the fact that Mr. Hemingway
should have made them so moving. These folks exist,
that is all; and if their story is sordid, it is also, by
virtue of the author's dignity and detachment in the
telling, intensely tragic. (*Hemingway: The Critical
Heritage*, 90-1)

Aiken and Muir differ in one point from each other, and
that is important. Muir charges Hemingway for having
written as one of those men described within the novel,
while Aiken fetes him for his "author's dignity and
detachment" which heightens the novel's significance to
a tragic intensity. So it becomes obvious that criticism of
the novel was still uncertain of a comprehensive and
acceptable approach to reading the text and the alternate
titles of the novel were still more or less held to have been
mutually exclusive. I have tried to ignore here this mutual
exclusivism among the diverse facets warranted apparently
by these projected or realized titles, for they seem very
cogently to enter one into the other. And while the total
truth about the experience and its significance offered in
the novel cannot be accommodated in any one of those
facets, together, that is as collocations and simultaneities,
they signify an immensely meaningful passage out of the
rut into a healthy realization about existence as being of
an abiding value. My method, therefore, will not be so much

a prerogation of any one title/facet before the others, but to keep passing from the one into the other in a bid for progressive revelation of the total resonance of meaning, if any.

Perhaps it would be too late by way of information that the First World War had darkened the mind of Hemingway and made him long pathetically for some subterfuge in the pristine and primordial countryside that still may have been unspoilt by the horrible infusions of man's decadent civilization. Many of his short stories betray in their titles Hemingway's overwhelming preference for trees, rivers, mountains and idyllic landscapes where sports and fishing only should keep the day. The two alternate titles: "River to the Sea" and "The Old Leaven" live up to this sentiment of the young writer who found Spain to be the most wonderful and old country, second in beauty only to his own Michigan where he had spent many of his boyish summers. The last chapter of *Death in the Afternoon* was originally meant to have a long section that Hemingway had to cut out finally at the suggestion of John Dos Passos, and in this excised part Hemingway had made explicit his sentimental givenness to the three peninsulas – Michigan, Italy and Spain. His love for Michigan had started early when as a boy he had spent summers there. But he had to witness with increasing pains each year the progressive deforestation that made the forest shrink, together with the pollution of the crystalline streams and ruining of fishing prospects. Roads newly built not only scarred the primitive landscape but also conducted in tourists who ravaged the quiet and the beauty of the location. In place of the ruined northern Michigan, Hemingway entertained dreams of northern Italy, a new good country in an old country. But Mussolini and his men had, in the meantime, turned it into a nightmare. So, Hemingway's emotional axis brought him to Spain (via Paris) where he found things being practiced he believed in. "The Old Leaven" which stands for as much had been no more in America and Hemingway was sore on this score:

Our people went to America because that was the

place for them to go then. It had been a good country
and we had made a bloody mess of it ....Let the others
come to America who did not know that they had
come too late. Our people had seen it at its best and
fought for it when it was well worth fighting for. Now
I would go somewhere else. [*Green Hills of Africa*, 285]

This somewhere else had to have a fresh river that has
not been sullied and choked at its mouth but meets the
sea in an idyllic aspiration. Hemingway's romanticism
about some fresh land of primitive unboundedness, free
from modern travesties, makes him a kin in this particular
facet of another modern romantic – W.B. Yeats in his urge
for going down to The Lake Isle of Innisfree. Alfred Kazin
picked up this excerpt from *Green Hills of Africa* and made
it an epigraph for the chapter on Hemingway in his book
An American Procession. In the book he tells us how "at
every stage of his life ...[Hemingway] found himself a
frontier appropriate to his fresh needs as a sportsman and
his ceremonial needs as a writer."(357)

Hemingway's letters between 1923 and 1925
reiterate his faith in Spain being his destined 'frontier'
because it had as yet remained unspoiled: "Spain is the
very country of all. It's unspoiled and unbelievably
wonderful," (written to James Gamble, Dec. 1923: *Letters*
107); again, as he confided in his old friend and fishing
mate Howell Jenkins in 1924, "There is swell fishing. Like
the Black when we first hit it." He was effusive over
Pamplona; it happened to be "the greatest country you ever
saw and right on the edge of the only trout fishing that
hasn't been ruined by motor cars or railroads....The people
have any people in the world skinned....You can only live
once, Carper, and this is as good as the best of the days we
ever had on the Black and Sturgeon....But Spain is the
only country left that hasn't been shot to pieces. They treat
you like shit in Italy now. All post war fascisti, bad food and
hysterics. Spain is the real old stuff" (*Letters* 130-1).

However, much as "The River to the Sea" may explain
Hemingway's emotional axis, the title quite justifiably could
have been found by him to be wanting in the much-desired

human significance. It would have been ideal if the novel had lain within the tout confines of a topography novel. About the same tardiness serves to constrict the other projection, "The Old Leaven"; it balks the human material which is so important and which makes the novel. Although, however, Hemingway's conscious declining of reference in the phrase "the old leaven" has its due appropriateness, for it accentuates the moral axis to some extent in Hemingway. It does so by implying Hemingway's preference for an old world with the old leaven of ancient codes and values about living, and living it in the pristine lap of nature. In his "Toreo: The Moral Axis of *The Sun Also Rises*" Allen Josephs excerpts from one of his earlier articles [on *Death In the Afternoon* in *The Hemingway Review*] in his attempt to explain how the "explanation and exaltation of the pristine savagery of the *plaza de toros* was tantamount to Hemingway's embracing an ancient mystery and iconoclastically rejecting much of what passed for modern western values" (16). Against the depressing scenario of the World War I and the rot of modern existence Hemingway's search for a 'home' with real, unfailing heroic values finds a deeper meaning.

"The Old Leaven" thus leads us, as it did Hemingway, to his *Fiesta*. In his letter to Scott Fitzgerald, written from Burguete in 1925, he related his experience of fishing in that "wonderful country" and, as he was making his way to Pamplona in order to witness and participate in the fiesta he would immortalize in his novel, he made a comment that goes far to explain the nature of the subject treated in *The Sun Also Rises*: "To me heaven would be a big bull ring with holding two barrera seats and a trout stream outside that no one else was allowed to fish in...."(*Letters* 165). It is significant how the title *Fiesta* came to Hemingway's mind not only out of his deliberations to transcribe the contemporary events in his life into fiction but also by way of an aesthetic countering of the sham of war and of the debased Montparnassian 'lost generationism'. Hemingway protests 'toreo' and 'torero'/'toreador' and 'ferier' (Hemingway's uses respectively for 'bull-fight', 'bull-fighter' and the 'tournament' part in the fiesta) as his model for the hero and the artist if he is to fall back on some ritual against the *nada* and the biological trap of meaningless suffering and despair, and ultimately, death in his life. Hemingway's equation of the *toreros* (bull-fighters) with the most admirable artists is suggestive as he tells Ezra Pound:

> The Plaza is the only remaining place where valor and art can combine for success. In all the other arts the more measly and shitty the guy, i.e. Joyce, the greater the success in his art. There is absolutely no comparison in art between Joyce and Maera – Maera by a mile... (*Letters* 119)

The *toreros* appeared to be the right kind of people and he wrote to Edward J.O'Brien:

> Do you remember me talking one night....about the necessity of finding some people that by their actual physical conduct gave you a real feeling of admiration like the sealers, and the men off the banks [George Bank] up in your country [Boston]? Well I have got a hold of it in bullfighting. Jesus Christ yes. (*Letters* 117)

War was simply brutal and negative; it did not bring out the real manliness of a man; it bred meaninglessness through wastage just as the derivative and sickly Parnassus existence on the left banks of Paris left humanity distorted. Against this post-lapsarianisms bullfight stood as an unfailing saga of man's perfect heroism. After his debuting as an *aficionado* in Pamplona in 1923 Hemingway went effusive about bullfighting because it seemed to give him his much-sought Code, the bulwark against the fear of erasement. In his letter to his roommate and old associate, William D. Horn, he wrote:

> .....just got back from the best week I have had since the Section.....
> You'd be crazy about a really good bullfight, Bill. It isn't just brutal like they always told us. It's a great tragedy

and the most beautiful thing I've ever seen and takes
more guts and skill and guts than anything possibly
could. (*Letters* 87-8)

Hemingway's choice of *Fiesta* as the title found its
motivation from multiple perspectives some of which are
literary and aesthetic while others biographical. I mean to
bring out its resonance more fully by pitting it against the
'lost generationism' against which 'fiesta' provides the
counterpoint. In the meantime let me quickly provide, in
a nutshell, the externals that led him to this choice. Kitty
Cannell, a friend and well-wishing mentor of Ernest had
been advising him for quite some time to write stories
based on real experience and having real plots in place of
the *contes* which according to her were strung together by
simple emotions. Carlos Baker in *Ernest Hemingway: A Life
Story* refers to the incident at the farewell dinner (possibly
early September, 1925), which Kitty arranged for the
Hemingways at the Negre de Toulouse:

> She invited Hadley and Ernest and they all walked to
> the restaurant. Hadley strode on ahead with Bill and
> Harold while Ernest followed with Kitty..."Hey, Kitty,"
> said Ernest, "I'm taking your advice. I'm writing a
> novel full of plot and drama." He gestured ahead
> towards Harold and Bill. "I'm tearing those bastards
> apart," he said. "I'm putting everyone in it and that
> kike Loeb is the villain." (154)

The Pamplona fiesta of 1925 which Hemingway, Hadley and
their friends and associates like Harold Loeb, Bill Smith,
Lady Duff Twysden and Pat Guthrie went down to see not
only put up the creditable performances of Cayetano
Ordonez – the nineteen-year old real for *Nino de la Palma*,
or the historical prototype of *guerrita* in Romero – but it also
led to a foul distemper and falling out which turned
everything to gall at Pamplona, St. Jean-de-Luz and
Burguete. The clandestine tensions and sex-jealousies
prevailing among the males (including, one is afraid,
Ernest), centered on Lady Duff Twysden. The pristine fiesta

thus came to take on unwarranted doses of the Parnassian strains and, judged in this light, Hemingway's 'fiesta' as a title no longer remains a pretty and uncritical choice; it takes on an ironic marginalia: 'fiesta' as the members of the 'lost generation' made of it!

Only the bullfight fiesta does not cover the entire range of significations in the novel for all these reasons. It is not a Spanish fiesta meant solely for the Spaniards; it is a Spanish fiesta for the Americans in the novel. Hence the bruised psyche of these American expatriates in the France of the post-war twenties needs a timely excavation. Hemingway, quite reasonably, brooded on the possibility of 'The Lost Generation' perspective in his novel and we may well review the how and the why of it.

Late in September 1926 the manuscript came ready. But the dithering of Hemingway remained, mainly about what title to give it. So far he had called it *Fiesta*, but as Carlos Baker informs us, he "did not want to use a foreign word." While in Chartres he was contemplating to designate it as *The Lost Generation* and Baker gives the background of it:

> He wrote out a foreword to explain where it came from. That summer Gertrude Stein had stopped at a garage in a village in the Department of Ain. One of the valves in her Ford was stuck and a very young mechanic fixed it quickly and efficiently. Gertrude asked the owner of the garage where he got such good workers. He said that he had trained them himself: these young ones learned fast. It was those in the age group twenty-two to thirty who could not be taught. "*C'est une generation perdue*," the owner said. (155)

Our knowledge of this incident does qualify to some considerable extent any flat equation that Hemingway must have given a simple, ingénue rendering of the expatriate 'lost generation' in their values and lifestyle. Or that he wrote sympathetically as being one of those 'lost' crew. The pitch has been queered by Hemingway's shifting responses in turns on this issue. The 'lost generation' qualifier was suffered to remain face to face with the epigraph – "The Sun Also Rises" – on the facing page, and Hemingway's literary pals like Fitzgerald and others loudly proclaimed the novel's 'lost' ardor. Yet, somewhat ironically, Hemingway later scornfully rejected this identity for himself and protested that his insistence in this novel was not the lostness of man in a world embroiled in war as well as mental and moral anarchy, but rather on the note that "the earth abideth forever" which the Ecclesiastes proclaims. This bodes trouble for us, for like Carlos Baker in *Hemingway: The Writer as Artist* we should then have to subscribe to Hemingway's own emphatic denial of his having any spiritual nexus with the 'Lost Generation' and also endorse the assumption of Baker that with an aesthetic impersonality and artistic detachment Hemingway gave only dramatized renderings of the 'lost 'ethos through the trio – Robert Cohn, Brett Ashley, and Mike Campbell – while "it ought to have been plain to discerning readers that Jake Barnes, Bill Gorton, and Pedro Romero were solid – if slightly beat-up—citizens of the republic. They were not lost."(*The Writer as Artist*: 81)

With all my reverence for Hemingway I yet cannot resist the temptation of wondering as to whether the artist can always precisely and unerringly reclaim post eventum an exact memory of what drove him while at the forge. Hemingway the artist may well have eluded Hemingway the man during his off hours. Something very close to it must have happened because there is so much there in the novel which otherwise refuses to get explained or elucidated. The recurrent coming close and the recurrent fiasco in the relation of Jake Barnes and Brett Ashley do not only bespeak the fatal spell of the *femme fatale* on the hero, neither does it warrant only the 'emasculation' of a man injured at the front. The biography of Hemingway shows more than that. Hemingway's own injury at Fossalta, not to speak of his sense of hurt at the rejection by the comely Polish nurse of Milan, Agnes Von Kurowski, did not leave him impotent literally. Barnes's literal impotency, therefore, masquerades Hemingway's psychological

retardation of sorts when in the company of Lady Duff
Twysden at the Spanish fiesta. Hemingway did come very
near to being 'lost' under the fatal spell of Lady Twysden
and that he did not finally go under or 'fall' was not the
least because he was impotent physically but because
something within him, some inhibition of sorts, told him
that he could not stoop to it. It needed him a stoic courage
to tell himself that stooping to a physical relation would
make him one of those 'lost' fellows – Bill Smith, Harold
Loeb and the rest. This inhibition looks to the Bible,
wherefore the *Ecclesiastes*. Otherwise the Sun would never
have risen, and the novel would be a meaningless
assortment of chaotic elements disobliging any
transcendence to meaning.

My observation looks sudden and cryptic unless it is
backed up with reference. Let me refer to Carlos Baker's
reconstruction of the Pamplona days, specially the run up
to the crisis:

> The "devil sex" was also apparent. Don sensed that
> something was afoot between Ernest and Duff. Ernest
> seemed angry that she had spent a week with Loeb
> at St. Jean-de-luz. Had Duff fallen for Ernest? Don
> "was not sure".....
> Bill Smith was also aware of the distemper. Harold
> Loeb, whom he both liked and pitied, seemed at a
> very low ebb throughout the fiesta, an object of scorn
> to Hemingway and Guthrie. It was clear to Bill that
> Duff was "wild about Ernest" even though he did not
> believe they had established an overt sexual
> connection. Ernest's behavior was that of a dog in
> the manger. He could not or would not have Duff, yet
> he made no secret of his resentment over Loeb's
> temporary success with her during their romance in
> June.
> The abscess broke after dinner on Saturday night.
> The evening before, Harold and Duff had slipped away
> from the others for a drink in one of the cafés.....She
> refused to leave and Harold was obliged to return to

the hotel alone. She appeared for lunch with a black
eye and a contusion on her forehead. When Harold
asked about it, Ernest cut him short by saying that
she had fallen against a railing. "Pat was sour, ugly.
Hadley had lost her smile. Don tried a quip that went
lame. Bill looked grim." Over the brandy that night,
Guthrie suddenly told Harold to get out: he was not
wanted. Harold turned to Duff who said at once that
she did not want him to go. Ernest exploded in manly
wrath. "You lousy bastard," he shouted at Loeb,
"running to a woman." He meant using Duff as a shield
against Guthrie's boorishness instead of hitting him,
as he no doubt deserved. (*A Life Story* :150-1)

Naturally, after this, the fiesta became a fiasco for all of
them and "they all dispersed in different directions"(151).
Cohn's cowardice within the novel gets explained, one
hopes, in Loeb's flunking. Yet, what is of greater
consequence is that Hemingway's secret passion, for Duff
Twysden, as a married (to Hadley) man did not seem for
his friends to stoop to sexual intercourse. That it was
emotionally intense, and the Lady knew and appreciated
it as love. Hemingway noted down in one of his little cahiers
seven fragments of Duff's intimate remarks, made to him,
and he meant to put them in the mouth of Brett Ashley.
Some of these statements are remarkably revealing:

1) It is like living with fourteen men so no one will know
   there is someone you love.
2) We can't do it. You can't hurt people. It's what we
   believe in in place of God.
3) I have to have it and I can't have what I want with
   you so I'm going to take this other thing.

Sure enough, Ernest loved her but never let her have him.
Baker's reading supports this:

Her behavior in Pamplona convinced both Don Stewart
and Bill Smith that something was afoot between Duff
and Ernest. His explosion against Harold Loeb hinted
at something like sexual jealousy. Yet the evidence
indicates that if the topic of sexual intercourse arose,
as it probably did, Ernest was able to resist temptation.

Something of this got into *The Sun Also Rises* in disguised form. Jake Barnes's war wound left him capable of sexual desire but incapable of fulfilling it. The situation between Barnes and Brett Ashley, as Ernest imagined it, could very well be a projection of his own inhibitions about sleeping with Duff. (*A Life Story* : 157)

Hemingway's deliberations on the possible title "Two Lie Together" are thus seen to have a powerful base underneath. Lying without committing? Or, are their love for each other nothing but a lie – they must have been *lying* then in the sense of telling lies—since they do not lie themselves down to bed? However, Hemingway's insistence in the novel was on the act of 'rising' by facing the truth and outfacing the 'lie', i.e., the debased, illusory and very transient ephemera of the loose Montparnassian living; hence the lost generationism of 'lying together' was neither allowed in his real life, nor in his fiction. The novel was an act of exorcism for its author, and very moral for that. The continence and concentration of a bull-fighter is needed to hold the 'toreo' of libido by the horns, and one must learn and perfect the art of confronting it and pierce the shot with a 'recibiendo'. Patience and fortitude are needed; Jake shows it by his passive holding out; Gordon and Pedro Romero also exhibit their honest powers for holding out actively. Cohn and Campbell find it beyond their vision, hence also beyond their powers. Brett has been physically in the mess, but she is not unqualifiedly 'lost'. She has been there just because there is none to lift her out of the morass. And in a world, which seems at this hour to be infested with 'lost crews' the Jakes are always a rarity, an underling forming a depressed minority. So, in this special sense, Jake is 'impotent'; first because his philosophy and attitude to life have no prevalence; secondly, 'potency' for these members of a dissipated coterie has a special libidinous connotation against which Hemingway's envisioned manliness and continent rectitude must appear 'impotent'. The novel thus warrants a deeper reading with probity.

Thus, in *The Sun Also Rises* Hemingway announced his exit from the allegedly "lost generation" members of which fluttered around Montparnasse as artistic scum with aimless revelries; with the novel's appearance on October 22, 1926, Hemingway seemed to have started rising at length from the morass of personal trauma and disillusion which now he seemed set to exploit artistically to some constructive end. There has to be a way out of the impasse created by the War and the Montparnassian anarchy, he tried to reassure himself. The novel was the testing ground where he would like to try and validate his thesis of an exercise of strong and controlled will against the raging anarchy in the ambience. Against the 'nada' of despair and the biological trap of suffering and death the 'fiesta' of ritualized 'agon' was to be Hemingway's answer. The true grit and honorability of the hero-fighter would lend meaning and tragic sublimity to his existential fight. Anarchy with its spiritual darkness would give way to light. War and moral perversion are temporary distortions, made by man, of life that is destined to curl back to its proper shape after the subsidence of such special and localized phases. The hero knows this or comes to pick up this truth through his patent and grilling ordeal. That is why he does not get 'lost'. For this reason, the paradigm latent in the novel was to be like this: War (with its concomitant decadence) in its aftermath provides the intrusion of an unlovely counterpoint against which the pronouncement in the *Ecclesiastes* provides the inherent and abiding point; the two visions, namely, wasteland as the aftermath of war, dissolution and death vis-à-vis "this earth abideth for ever.....the sun also riseth" came to a conflict in the novel leading to a temporary stalemating from which only disciplined action can retrieve the case in favor of "this earth abideth for ever."

Jake Barnes's emasculation not only "relives" (with modifications, though, of Philip Young's "reliving of the wound" theory) Hemingway's own wound, it also metaphorically projects the wounded age itself with its potential for crippling everything that came under it. And yet Barnes's detached persistence and observation without

participation in the debased Montparnassian variation of
life must not be misconstrued as a cripple's inaction. It is
action gestatory, because his standing off aloof with an
unrelentingly cool but controlled reserve of mental strength
shows his resolute (never mind if incipient as yet) non-
conformity to the ethos that was reigning there – at the
Paris cafés, Boulevard of Montparnasse and Pamplona.
Hemingway means us to read in Barnes's reticence not a
sheepish surrender but a continuance within his mind of
an 'agon' against war, anarchy and death; his
endorsements of Barnes's code of values are obvious and
positive when seen against the false and 'romantic' view
of Cohn who gloats on sexual potency as the *sine qua non* of
masculinity and heroism. Cohn lacks in experience of war
and by so much he conjures in him, for the reader, a
historically past position with regard to war. His wordiness
exposes the hollowness and the cowardice within him
while it also serves to accentuate by contrast Jake's
unperturbed reticence. It is not in one's sexual virility,
Hemingway would communicate to us, but in the undiluted
gutsiness to give the dare to the reality without
sentimentalizing that true heroism consists. Jake's
continuous observation of life is by no means an empty or
negatively charged disposition therefore; in his observation
lies his endurance – ability to "abide" (like the unspoilt
"earth" in Spain) – and dissent emphatically from the
"lostness" of one aberrant generation. Spain with her fiesta
did not fail him in his apprenticeship. Jake thus comes to
be like "Will," in Langley's *Piers Plowman,* witnessing the
mundane spectacle of the Malvern Hill with its deep
dungeon below – typified in the Parnassian scene of Paris
– and looking up to the Tower of Truth at the mountain top:
Burguete, in this instance, with its rich implications of
purity and wholesomeness of the mother earth.

   Bill Gorton and Pedro Romero are extensions in two
different but positive lines of the 'Code Hero' ethics. The
courageous but sympathetic assertion on Gorton's part and
his instinctive intuition of a spiritual kin in Jake Barnes
bring out the real message in the novel: heroism consists
in the raw courage and not in libidinousness. Equally,

Romero's plucky instinct for holding out against opposition through dogged fighting – typical of a bull-fighter – is preferred to Cohn's boxing for an identical reason. Romero as the matador needs the friendly presence of an *aficionado* which Barnes unfailingly provides him. The bull-fight image is the central image in the story which works out the model for taking out against life's adversities. Little is "lost" if a man's sex-power is lost. Life has more than just sex. Hence Barnes accepts his emasculation in war with calm, grit and a becoming nobility, just as his ability to retain his ground against Brett Ashley's fatal charm shows honor in him, what though in defeat. Romero's showdown with Cohn is an implicit criticism of the "lost" part of the universe typified in Robert Cohn, Mike Campbell and, with a subtle volatility, in Brett Ashley. Barnes was threatened for a time by the overwhelming pressure of this *counterpoint*, but like a quester-knight he shows little deflection and remains unswerving in his composure and integrity. So, he has his reward too in the end. Brett does not quite get him as at the end of the novel they are talking to each other in a taxi riding down the Gran Via. "Oh Jake," Brett said, "we could have had such a damned good time together." Jake's answer, which formed the closing sentence of the novel, showed Hemingway's vacillations about the exact phrasing. As Baker points it out, Hemingway had first drafted the sentence like this: "It's nice as hell to think so." Hemingway subsequently changed the line to a question; in one edition it is "Isn't it nice to think so?"; still another has got it as "Isn't it pretty to think so?" The reader is free to discern an irony on Jake's part in "nice as hell to think so." "Isn't it nice/pretty," equally, is a polite indifference! The sun already has risen for Barnes!

NOTES AND REFERENCES

Baker, Carlos.   *Hemingway: The Writer as Artist.* Princeton:
                        Princeton UP, 1963.

————.Ed.   *Ernest Hemingway: Selected Letters, 1917-
                        1961.*New York: Charles Scribners' Sons,
                        1981.

————.   *Ernest Hemingway: A Life Story.* New York:
                        Scribner's, 1969: 147-160.

Hemingway, Ernest.   *Green Hills of Africa.* New York: Scribner's,
                        1935.

————.   *Fiesta: The Sun Also Rises.*London,
                        Toronto, Sydney & New York: Granada/
                        Panther Books, 1984.

Josephs, Allen.   "Toreo: The Moral Axis of *The Sun Also
                        Rises*." *The Hemingway Review* 6.1 (Fall
                        1986):88-91.

————.   "*Death in the Afternoon*: A Reconsideration."
                        The Hemingway Review 2.1 (Fall:1982):2-
                        16.

Kazin, Alfred.   *An American Procession.* New York: Random
                        House, 1984.

Meyers, Jeffrey. Ed.   *Hemingway: The Critical Heritage.* London:
                        Routledge & Kegan Paul, 1982: 88-100.

Yeats, W.B.   "The Lake Isle of Innisfree."*W.B. Yeats:
                        Selected Poetry.* Ed. A.Norman Jeffares.
                        London: Pan Books, 1974. 16.

Young, Philip.   *Ernest Hemingway: A Reconsideration.*
                        University Park: Pennsylvania UP, 1966
                        [1952].

Opening of Hemingway's *A Farewell to Arms*

Amitabha Sinha

As I open, not Hemingway's novel[1], I ought to say, but this article, mine, overlaps with yet another one on the same novel, not totally, yet perhaps, overlaps, which has been printed already, and will further be – perhaps – printed (this has been hinted by some relevant persons). Following my preliminary apology – assuming you all are allowing my personal ontology (?) – now allow me to begin, open. One of my ideas is, I insist – whatever any forthgone (my jargon) or forthcoming (easy English) critic and/or theorist will/would opine (old-fashioned English mine) —, terse, simple language never was often seen within Hemingway's age. Yet, within such simplicity, you find – if you are careful—there exist (I insist) yet plenty, plenty, yes frequently, subtlety, further your (could be perhaps mine, but I am never sure, too) favored phrase, yes, ambiguity, further, (I accept New Critical jargons, one or two) tension I believe, with certainty, that nevertheless, these all contribute to a frisson. I shall, within my rather small article, try (as much as I can), to exhibit one rather small, well, particle, of the play/ploy of frisson, tension, within, yes, our business (? No, I have no liking for this expression but what can I use? Suggestion, any, for this? I believe 'no' suggestion exists), yes, fiction. Yes, further, obviously within works of fiction, I mean, of Hemingway, focusing on the – at last I come to our business (?) – opening of this novel, a welcome novel (inversion mine, but no subversion (!); I hope you receive what I believe, yes about, on what so fervently I mean obviously about, on Hemingway. We shall begin, or open the actual opening, now, following our 'opening' opening now looking on to the novel's Chapter One.

Prior to that, nevertheless, one ought to remind oneself that this novel's total <u>arrangement</u> – you and I often say, an <u>organization</u> – is, well, say, metaphorical like the way – wonders! – Henry James's Ambassador's end-to-beginning totalization (i.e. Strether-<u>Strether</u> emblematic of American-in-European idea) yes, artistic, yes, no antic). As for this novel, tropes and figures I will explicate in Chapter One, perhaps indicate, exist (I insist!) fully in my mentioned organization, yes, of end-to-beginning, totally swinging between <u>rain-to-rain</u> (see ending, see beginning) like your aforesaid way of Strether – <u>Strether</u> moving on and back all the way (that, surely, is something we would like to welcome, <u>rain! rain!</u> pleasure, yes pleasure, alas! Functions in some binary (!) way, as I see, you too will see, you and we!). Our function will be now, reverting to idea of say, metaphor, language or trope (I hope, you will receive, yes, what I believe).

I find subtle repetitions, even sense of rhymes, further syllabic (syllablewise, God forbid! Yes, no <u>syllabus involved</u> !) –cum- say, numerological methods, ways, for example, <u>dust</u> and <u>road</u> each thrice repeats, craftily, itself in paragraph one of 129 (1+2+9=12=1+2=3, this author's favorite often-used number <u>three</u>) words; 43:1 proportion becomes total, 21:50:1 to each and one or two single expressions help, like <u>dry, sun;</u> yes, naturally this becomes, <u>naturally</u> (nature involved) protometaphor (my jargon), of unbearable <u>heat</u> – proto-etc of theme of, you know, <u>war,</u> of this novel, offering a contrast, too, yes, <u>water</u> and <u>river</u> (together repeated thrice; 43:1! Once again ! and you remember <u>rain,</u> won't you?); now these become one yet <u>proto-etc.</u> of, a counter-theme of the novel, <u>farewell</u> to <u>arms,</u> isn't (ironically, actually) welcome somewhat might we say, yes, somewhat yes, ambiguously, obviously, but nevertheless, <u>welcome</u> idea of a cold, rainy, refreshing (you find some sort of inversion, <u>subversion</u> (?) obviously through a twist, ironical, as I said), cold, emblem, sort of token, yes of peace, of ours novel; that's naturally a way of yours, ours, Hemingway.

Further, see now the sense of rhyme/rhythm; for example, "late summer of the year" (// — + — — / ; dactylic

+ anapaestic) along with the half rhyme <u>summer</u> / <u>year</u>
;....<u>dusty and</u> ... <u>fell early</u> – half rhyme once again ; "...<u>the
soldiers marching and afterwards</u> ...."

(iambic + iambic + iamb-doubles, yet how they totally
provide us with effects trochaic, yet how artistic, never any
antic!). Further, too, syllables – 108 monosyllables with 21
(20 + 1 = 2 (0) + 1 + 3 ; <u>three</u>! favourite of Hemingway
!) within all those 129 words. Yet, I said for this reason,
terse and simple yet subtle language, crafty, though
something like hefty is sometimes often thought about
Hemingway. (my emphasis throughout)

That sort of features can easily be plucked off the
second paragraph, but <u>phonological effects</u> not quite always
as in the first paragraph (opening !) might be found in the
<u>alliterative aspects</u> of the <u>third</u> (significant,
numerologically, somehow always in Hemingway); <u>troops,
traffic, trucks, tractors, trees,</u> such as it is called,
phoneme/allophoneme (tr) keep crowding loudly, as it were,
giving us the sense of sounds of gun-fire, reflecting,
redounding on the novel's theme (war), such an oblique,
obvious, effective phoneme. While the following paragraph
is somewhat ironical, the final one gives us the ironical
crux; the <u>rain</u> comes there (how welcome! <u>binary</u> (!) to
farewell), but is coupled with cholera yet an obvious idea,
in conjunction with mud ; nevertheless see further irony
with "<u>only seven thousand died</u>" (looks rather like a cheque
or draft, but that is beside the point), but <u>only seven
thousand</u> who <u>die</u> ; would a few more thousands be
sufficient? nevertheless, cannot you and I find, in the
narration of this incident, an experiment ? redounding,
resounding, yet concealed, artistically revealed, providing
the sense of <u>war</u>, making one emphatically aware of what
this novel conveys. See, now? the way of our Hemingway
in this novel.

Now this is, within a nutshell, the way Hemingway
opens his novel remarkably well, one should say, reflecting,
refracting, the theme. Yet, however, one should note the
technique – artistic – of what you call <u>inversion</u> ; that <u>rain</u>,
repeated time and again, is bidden <u>farewell</u> by the <u>arms</u>
(heat of gun, artillery) while such <u>water</u> is welcome,

whenever will come; how come? This what you and I call ambiguousness, whose name in such a context, respect, totally, is <u>inversion.</u> Within a nutshell (I repeat) yes, metaphorically this simply <u>rebounds</u> on war, a well-known, well, idea, a theme, whatever.

Yet, however, incidentally, one extraneous idea redounds, rebounds, on, off (respectively, respectfully) the novel's opening. <u>Arms</u> repel the sense of tranquility, call <u>peace,</u> yet you find one further sense of <u>ambiguity.</u>[2] For whose <u>arms</u>? Whose? One becomes rather tempted, rather, to say/ask; yes of guns, artillery, but there is one <u>binary</u> (!) ; yes, I mean <u>love</u> [3], Catherine-Frederick (I repeat, certainly artistic); surely, certainly the <u>arms</u> belong to that lady, and that love is propelled by <u>these</u> (her) <u>arms,</u> yet repelled by those (war's) <u>arms.</u> Yes, obviously now you guess, this your <u>opening</u> never accommodates those arms. Now, two interpretations become probable, of this; either, this opening is faulty, self-contradictory, for love-<u>arms</u>-trope seems ignored; or this becomes true and correct opening, for war-<u>arms</u> shuts off love, bids, so to say, <u>farewell</u> to love. I side with obviously the latter, for war becomes, is, bidden <u>farewell,</u> while, while love is <u>welcome,</u> is certainly, not, never allowed to be welcome (fate of that woman).

Yes, this is the way I <u>end</u> my idea on the <u>beginning</u> of this novel; I, indeed, fervently hope, that this, yes, ambiguousness (mine) leads, nevertheless, away, to some new avenue, some fresh <u>beginning,</u> opening of a window, on Hemingway and his way. I, certainly, hope, too, that this is <u>welcome.</u>

NOTES

1. I should mention that Edward Waggeneght, in *The Cavalcade of the American Novel* (1958; Oxford & IBH, 1969) gives some succinct ideas on Hemingway.

2.   " ....inconsistencies and ruptures...", writes Margot Norris in "The Novel as Was: Lies and Truth in Hemingway's

A *Farewell to Arms*" (*Modern Fiction Studies*, Vol. 40, number
4, Winter 1994, p. 693); I like this idea, in spite of the
jargon <u>capture</u> !

3. H.R. Stoneback's title of his article, "Lovers, Sonnets
    (et.al; my abbreviations)...Love in *A Farewell to Arms*" (my
    ellipses, too) (*The Hemingway Review*, Fall 1989) is
    sufficient commentary on this feature.

A Reader's Guide to Pilar's Bullfighters:
Untold Histories in *For Whom The Bell Tolls*

Miriam B. Mandel

In *For Whom the Bell Tolls*, his most extended fictional foray into Spain and Spanish issues, Hemingway set himself the difficult task of refracting the action through the consciousness of a foreigner. To circumvent Robert Jordan's necessary limitations, Hemingway turned to secondary characters: political theory, for example, is presented to us by professionals like Karkov and Golz, and the complexity of Spanish society is suggested by the presence of such varied minor characters as a gypsy, a peasant, a mayor, a priest, and an aspiring bullfighter. By means of their embedded narratives—Karkov's military and political reports, Rafael's dramatic description of the blowing of the train, Joaquin's painful family history, Maria's and Pilar's stories of rape and murder—Hemingway is able to enlarge the novel beyond the tight restrictions he has imposed in terms of time (three days), place (Guadarrama Mountains), action (one military operation, one love affair), and protagonist (romantic outsider). Many of these second-level narratives mention contemporary personalities, including the military and political leaders of the Spanish conflict. Hemingway does not tell us who these people are, but not a few critics and biographers have resurrected them for us.

Just as access to the novel's political background enriches our reading of it, so can knowledge of the cultural figures who dominated pre-Civil War Spain help us

understand the characters shaped by those figures.
Spanish culture enters the novel through Pilar's stories,
in which she mentions famous singers, dancers,
musicians, and most importantly, bullfighters—the cultural
icons of the peacetime Spain in which she grew up.[1] These
figures are not explicated in the text because they would
have been familiar to the Spaniards who comprise the
intratextual audience. Distanced by place, those artists
were unfamiliar to most of Hemingway's contemporary
readers. And with the passage of more than half a century,
during much of which Franco's Spain was inaccessible to
Americans, their names have become doubly unfamiliar.
The following short biographies should fill that gap, making
some of that lost Spanish world accessible to Hemingway's
English-speaking audiences.

Two of Pilar's narratives, her definition of the smell
of death and her description of the party given in Finito's
honor, are particularly rich in cultural references. When
Pilar discusses the smell of death (Chapter Nineteen), she
mentions not less than seven bullfighters. The most
famous of them all is identified only by his first name (José,
Joselito) and the place of his death (Talavera)-sufficient
detail for Pilar's primary narratees to identify José Gómez
Ortega, who for many years and by many critics was
considered the best matador of the twentieth century.

JOSÉ GÓMEZ ORTEGA
(1895-1920)

Born into a bullfighting family, this virtuoso showed great
talent as a boy and had a large following years before his
promotion to full *matador de toros* in 1912, by which time
he was already ranked first among the nation's matadors.
In 1913, Joselito appeared 80 times; it was an extraordinary
season both because of the number and the quality of his
performances. He had to cancel some contracts in 1914,
due to illness and some gorings, but even so fought in 75
corridas. In 1915, 1916, and 1917 he continued to dominate
the ring, appearing in over 100 *corridas* each year, many of
them *mano a mano* (the six bulls being fought by two instead

of three matadors) with Belemonte and not a few solo (fighting all six bulls by himself). Illness at wounds cut the 1918 season to 81 appearances (he had contracted for 105) and the 1919 season to 91 (one serious wound early in the season caused him to miss eighteen fights). His performances in the bullring were almost consistently magnificent; he mastered all aspects of bullfighting and fought with grace, gallantry, and art. Joselito and Juan Belemonte (the aging bullfighter in The *Sun Also Rises*) dominated the bullring, defining the 1910s as a golden age of bullfighting. Joselito's death at the horns of the bull Bailaor in Talavera de la Reina, on 26 May 1920, shocked the public which had, for years, considered him invincible, able to master any bull.[2]

MANUEL (MANOLO) GRANERO VALLS
(1902 -1922)

Pilar claims that she witnessed the killing of another famous young bullfighter, Granero. Born in Valencia, Manuel Granero was a talented violin student when, as an adolescent, he became infatuated with bullfighting. As a *novillero* (the rank or degree preceding the top rank of *matador de toros*), Granero acquired a large following. He became a full *matador de toros* in Seville on 28 September 1920, under the auspices of Rafael Gómez Ortega (el Gallo, the older brother of Joselito), this *alternativa* (investiture, the awarding of the top rank in the profession) being confirmed, as tradition requires, in Madrid (22 April 1921; Granero's promotion was confirmed by Chicuelo, whom Pilar also mentions). In1921, his first full season as matador, Granero was lightly gored four times. Even so, he managed almost a hundred appearances that season, an extraordinarily large number of contracts to obtain and fulfill, more than twice the number needed to mark a successful season. He shared top billing with other great matadors like Juan Belemonte and Ignatio Sánchez Mejias and was hailed as a fine, elegant fighter, a fit successor to Joselito. His 1922 season began triumphantly but ended

after thirteen *corridas*. Granero was' fatally gored by
Pocapena, the fifth bull fought in Madrid on the afternoon
of 7 May 1922, and the second fought by Granero. Pilar's
narrative is accurate: when Pocapena charged, veering to
the right, he gored Granero in the thigh, flung him to the
ground, pushed him up against the *barrera*, and crushed
his head against the wood. (The fatal goring is recreated
with life-size figures in Madrid's Wax Museum, at the Plaza
de Colón.) Granero died minutes after reaching the plaza's
infirmary.[3]
Pilar also mentions the two bullfighters who shared the
bill with Granero that fatal afternoon: Juan Luis de la Rosa
and Marcial Lalanda.

JUAN LUIS DE LA ROSA DE LA GARQUÉN (1901-1938)

Born in Cadiz, Juan Luis de la Rosa may have been
descended from gypsies. Pilar insists that, like Blanquet
and herself, Juan Luis de la Rosa was able to smell death
(251-53). This bullfighter was invested as a *matador de toros*
in 1919 by Joselito and his *alternativa* confirmed in Madrid
by Belmonte in 1920. His first full season as a fully-
accredited matador (1920) was disappointing, his sword-
work being severely criticized, but his next two seasons
were impressive. On the day Granero suffered his fatal
wounds, de la Rosa had also been gored; he was in the
infirmary when Granero was brought in. That year, 1922,
was his last good year: he fought 38 *corridas*. In 1924 he
had only seven *corridas*, and from then on he performed
more and more often in Venezuela, not appearing in
Spanish bullrings after 1927 except for an embarrassing
performance in Barcelona in 1936.[4] Juan Luis de la Rosa
was consistently impressive with the cape and often
spectacular with the muleta (especially in the *pase natural)*)
but his sword work was deficient from the beginning of his
career to the end and, like his friend Chicuelo, he lacked
the commitment and discipline that bullfighting requires
(Cossio III 834-36; Tapia 390-91).

MARCIAL LALANDA DEL PINO

(1903 -1990)

Unlike Joselito, Granero, and de la Rosa, Marcial Lalanda lived to an old age. Like many great matadors before him, Lalanda was a child prodigy. He was granted the degree of *matador de toros* in September 1921, just a few days after his eighteenth birthday; his investiture was confirmed in Madrid on 7 May 1922, on the afternoon when Granero was killed and de la Rosa injured. It was Lalanda who distracted the bull Pocapena from the fatally injured Granero. While Granero was being rushed to the infirmary, Lalanda killed Pocapena—a dramatic beginning to a long, impressive career. This urbane matador improved steadily from season to season. Two serious gorings in 1927 seemed only to increase his courage, and the next few years established him as one of the all-time masters of the art. His 1929 season was brilliant; in 1930 he fought in an impressive 87 engagements, in 1931 the taurine critics, never given to understatement, were hard put to describe his performances. Lalanda's success and stature allowed him to charge enormous fees, and he consequently reduced the number of his appearances to 35 in 1933, 41 in 1934, and 43 in 1935. He performed in 48 bullfights during the three years of the Civil War, in support of the Nationalist cause. After the war he returned to his more usual schedule of between 40 and 50 fights a year until his retirement in 1942.[5] Unlike Blanquet, de la Rosa, and Pilar, Marcial Lalanda was unable to "smell death" (251-52), perhaps because he was born and lived all his life in Madrid, far from gypsy influence.

MANUEL JIMÉNEZ MORENO (CHICUELO)

(1902 -1967)

In spite of his gypsy connections, Manuel Jiménez Moreno, better known as Chicuelo, lacked the olfactory talent Pilar is discussing. The son and nephew of bullfighters, he was born in the Triana section of Seville and was a talented, carefully educated matador who excelled in all aspects of the fight. He had *"una gran técnica, una gran facilidad en today las suertes, incluso en la de matar"* (a great technique, a great facility in all maneuvers, including that of the kill. Cossio III 464). A contemporary of Granero and de la Rosa he had a much longer career, retiring in 1951. The 1920s were his triumphant decade, even though in 1922 and 1927 he turned down many contracts (as he did throughout the 1930s), mostly due to frequent bouts of illness and a seeming lack of ambition or, some say, of character. Since his appearances were generally praised—in 1928 he went *"de triunfo en triunfo"* for 81 dazzling *corridas* in all the great plazas of Spain—he was able to maintain his following in spite of the occasional reduced season. A Nationalist supporter, he continued to perform during and after the Spanish Civil War, though infrequently.[6] Chicuelo may have been in Madrid on the day Granero was gored, but he did not share the bill with him as Pilar claims (251): the three matadors featured that afternoon were Granero, Lalanda, and de la Rosa.

ENRIQUE BERENGUET SOLER (BLANQUET)
(1881—1926)

Enrique Berenguet Soler, known as Blanquet for all his long professional life, was also a familiar personality in the bullrings Pilar visited during the 1910s and 1920s. An excellent *banderillero* and cape handler, he worked with the outstanding matadors of his time. But in spite of his intelligence and skill, he was unable to rescue the matadors José Gómez Ortega (Joselito), Manuel Granero, or Manuel Báez (Litri), all of whom were killed in fights at which Blanquet was serving as *banderillero*. Pilar claims that although he was not a gypsy, Blanquet had the gypsy's ability to smell death on a person about to die (252-53).

IGNACIO SÁNCHEZ MEJÍAS
(1891—1934)

Pilar ends her dissertation on the smell of death with a reference to "the last season of Ignatio Sánchez Mejias"(253), who was badly gored on 11 August 1934 and died two days later. Sánchez Mejias, the only bullfighter about whom Jordan appears knowledgeable, was an unconventional matador, attracted both by the active and the literary life. Because his well- to-do family opposed his taurine ambitions, he ran away from home at the age of 18, stowing away in a boat and ending up in the home of his older brother in Mexico. His training in the art of bullfighting was deliberately slow: having made a name for himself at the rank of *novillero*, he chose to work in the *cuadrillas* (the matador's crew or team) of Juan Belemonte and Rafael Gómez Ortega (el Gallo) instead of moving on quickly to the final rank. His investiture as *matador de toros* came only at the end of the 1919 season, when he was 28; it was confirmed in Madrid in 1920. In both those years he enjoyed triumphant seasons, giving polished performances in Spain and in Mexico. In 1921 he missed part of the season due to illness, but even so he fought more than forty *corridas* that year. In 1922, having established his reputation and amassed a fortune, he retired. He returned to the ring late in the 1924 season, immediately resuming his position at the top of the profession. In 1925 he fought 61 *corridas.*

Ignacio's preoccupation with literature distracted him from the bullring. In 1926 he worked on a novel (which he never finished), wrote for a bullfighting magazine, and was active in the theatre. In 1927, he chose to perform in only three *corridas,* announcing his retirement at the third one. In 1928 his plays *Sinrazón* and *Zayas* (a taurine comedy) were successfully produced; other plays were less successful. He befriended and encouraged other writers, and dedicated himself to literary life until 1934, when at the age of 42, he returned to the ring. His skills, his bravery, and his disregard for danger remained unchanged; he

appeared on the same bills with the best fighters of the
1930s and performed with distinction. But, as Jordan points
out, he was heavy and his reflexes were slow, and he was
fatally wounded in his fifth fight of that season. Federico
Garcia Lorca's "Llanto por Ignacio Sánchez Mejias" is only
the most famous of several laments for his death.[7]

Pilar's first name-cluster, then, introduces seven very
different bullfighters into the novel. They suggest the rich
variety of personalities attracted to the bullring: the
temperamental Southern· gypsies, the polished urbanite,
the sober older craftsman, the dashing young heroes, the
writer, the musician, the poor, the middle-class, and the
rich. Their careers cover the quarter century of bullfighting
preceding the action of For Whom the Bell Tolls, from
Joselito's entry into the arena in the early 1910s until the
death of Sánchez Mejias in 1934; a few were still performing
at the time of the action. Superstars all, they were familiar
names to the characters in the novel, part of the shared
cultural heritage of the generation of Spaniards who fought
in the Civil War.

Hemingway expands this gallery of taurine portraits
by having Pilar mention two more names: Rafael el Gallo
and Retana. They are two of the five historical personages
mentioned at the party celebrating Finito's triumphs in
the bullring (186-87). The other three are flamenco
musicians and dancers, best known by their professional
names: la Niña de los Peines (Pastora Pavón Cruz, 1890—
1969), Pastora Imperio (Pastora Rojas Monje, 1889—1979),
and el Niño Ricardo (Manuel Serrapi Sánchez, 1905—1972).

RAFAEL GÓMEZ ORTEGA (EL GALLO)
(1882—1960)

Rafael Gómez Ortega (el Gallo) was a dramatic
personality, remarkable even among bullfighters. The son
of the bullfighter Fernando Gómez (also known as el Gallo
in his day) and the older brother of José Gómez Ortega
(Joselito, also known as Gallito), he was an exaggeratedly
superstitious gypsy, haunted by fears and fantasies. During
his best years, 1910 -1914, he was a picturesque improviser,

capable of graceful artistry but also of embarrassing cowardice. He retired in 1918, possibly under pressure from Joselito, but, true to his erratic nature, came out of retirement the next year. He spent the next several seasons fighting mostly in Latin America, but was still active in the profession in 1935. He is remembered not only for his enormous talent but also for his flamboyance, both in and out of the ring.[8] Pilar's narrative illustrates his eccentric behavior: having decided to abandon his manager, Rafael showers him with praise, kisses, and jewelry. Because he knows his client, the manager is able to interpret Rafael's effusive professions of loyalty correctly: the wily bullfighter intends to defect to another manager (187). In *The Sun Also Rises*, Rafael el Gallo is described as "crazy" (172).

MANUEL RETANA

Rafael's former manager mentions another icon of the Spanish bullring: Retana. Known to Hemingway's readers from his appearance as the curt, mean manager in the story "The Undefeated," Retana was an important historical figure, the administrative head of Madrid's bullfighting industry from about 1907 until late 1926. With its long history of tough audiences and influential taurine critics, the Madrid bullring was and is the place where reputations are made. A matador who alienates or disappoints the Madrid audience will have to rebuild his reputation in the provinces before being contracted to reappear in the country's premier bullring. In addition, a matador's seniority is determined by his Madrid *alternativa*. For nineteen years, Retana controlled the *gran plaza* of Madrid.

Early in his career, in 1908, Retana and the bullfighting management were challenged by a group of matadors who demanded higher wages and the right-of-refusal for *corridas* featuring Miura bulls. The bullfighters contended that the fierceness of the Miuras justified their demands. Rafael Gonzáles Madrid (Machaquito, 1880-1955), who had been forced to cancel many performances due to serious gorings from Miuras, was the chief instigator of the movement; he was joined by the eminent Ricardo Torres Reina (Bombita, 1879-1936). The controversy raged in Madrid, where Miuras were often fought, and in other bullrings, as matadors, usually fiercely independent, banded together in this common cause and refused engagements with Miuras. Attacking the protestors as cowardly and money-hungry, Rafael Gómez Ortega (el Gallo) and Vincente Pastor Gómez ostentatiously took on Miura bulls and thus advanced their careers rapidly.[9] Together with other rising young stars, they enabled the Madrid management, led by Indalecio Mosquera and the newly appointed Manuel Retana, to vanquish the anti-Miura faction. Thereafter, Retana maintained strict control of the Madrid ring, making life difficult for those bullfighters who had opposed him. By the 1920s not a few taurine critics complained that he abused his power, willfully excluding fine bullfighters from Madrid and favoring the matador Nicanor Villalta, whose *apoderado* (agent) was Manuel Retana's own brother Matias. In March 1924, a long, angry editorial against Manuel Retana accused him of favoritism, profiteering, and manipulation of the press—in short, of destroying the art of bullfighting.[10] The Retana who is mentioned in Pilar's story could be this powerful Manuel (nicknamed Manolo) or his brother Matias. It makes no difference: Retana was such a big name that any bullfight agent wishing to impress his auditors could do so by indicating his acquaintance with any member of the Retana family. And of course, Rafael el Gallo was such a riveting personality that his name would naturally crop up whenever *aficionados* gathered.

Hemingway deliberately draws our attention to Pilar's two bullfighting-related narratives. Not only are the stories themselves carefully introduced, long, and memorably dramatized, but Hemingway had carefully established their teller as an authority on bullfighting (Pilar has lived with several bullfighters, including five years with Finito de Palencia) and in story-telling ("God, how she could tell a story. She's better than Quevedo"[134]). Hemingway enjoins the reader to pay attention to Pilar's narratives because it is mostly through them that he is able to perform the necessary task of introducing the cultural landscape of peacetime Spain into the novel. The bullfighters' names, and the personal histories and cultural contexts they allow us to retrieve, indicate not only Hemingway's own familiarity with *toreo*, but his understanding that this shared experience shapes the Spanish cultural scene.[11]

It may be true, as Arturo Baera, Allen Josephs, and other critics have documented, that *For Whom the Bell Tolls* sometimes falters when its author attempts to render the local idiom into English. But in rendering the local culture Hemingway displayed his skill: he wisely chose to abandon his point-of-view character and turn Pilar into a narrator. The decision has two happy effects: it draws us into the novel by turning us into narratees like Fernando, Jordan, and Maria; and it permits the graceful introduction of historical material for which Jordan would have been an awkward vehicle. When we recontextualize the bullfighters Pilar mentions we can recover some of the Spain described so poetically in Hemingway's other "Spanish" book, his neglected masterpiece, *Death in the Afternoon* (1932).

NOTES & REFERENCES

1. In spite of his many objections to Hemingway's novel, Arturo Baera praised Pilar's "admirable descriptions of the people of the bull ring a quarter of a century ago" (200-201).

2. While researching the bullfighters mentioned by Pilar, I have relied heavily on Cossio's eleven-volume taurine encyclopedia, *Los toros-tratado historico...* particularly Vols. III and IV. Tapia's *Historia del toreo* is less detailed. For Joselito, see also Silva Aramburu 266-70; and "Jose Gomez Ortega," Martinez 193-94. Hemingway discusses most of these bullfighters in *Death in the Afternoon;* many of them appear in other Hemingway's works as well.

3. Hemingway's own account of Granero is accurate (*DIA* 44-45). Granero's fame has not faded in the 70 years since his death; see, for example, "Manuel Granero, gran figura valenciana," *ABC* 22 July 1992: 90- 91. Juan Belemonte was supposed to officiate at Granero's *alternativa*, but was unable to attend.

4. He was killed in that same city in the Civil War.

5. See "Lalanda del Pino, Marcial", Cossio III 475-80 and IV
    523-24; "Marcial Lalanda," "Silva Aramburu 277; "Lalanda,
    Marcial," Rubio Cabeza 456-57; "El matador de toros
    Marcial Lalanda muere en Madrid a la edad de 87 anos"
    and "El mas grande," both articles published in the daily
    newspaper *El pais* (26 October 1990): 41. Hemingway's
    assessment of Lalanda is accurate *(DIA* 215).

6. His *alternativa* took place in 1919 and was confirmed in
    June 1920 by Rafael Gómez Ortega (el Gallo). See "Jimenez
    Moreno (Manuel) Chicuelo," Cossio III 462-65 and IV 515.

7. "Ignatio Sanchez Mejias," Silva Aramburu 273-74 and
    Cossio III 875- 80. Sanchez Mejias was accorded the honor
    of being buried in Joselito's crypt; they were brothers-in-
    law.

8. "Gomez Ortega, Rafael," Cossio ill 384-90; "Rafael Gomez,
    'el Gallo'," Silva Aramburu 262-63. See also "Gomez Ortega,
    Jose" Cossio III 364-79; "Joselito," Cossio IV 959-63;
    "Gomez Ortega, Joselito," Silva Aramburu 267-68; "Jose
    Gomez Ortega," Martinez 193-94.

9. For the great Miura controversy, see Cossio III 403 and
    952-53; and "El pleito de los Muras," Silva Aramburu 260-
    62. Silva Aramburu's date 1808 (top 262) is a typographical
    error, the correct date being 1908.

10. See *Sol y sombra*'s double issue, 20 and 27 March 1924,
    p.14. Matias Retana represented only one or two other
    bullfighters in addition to his main client, Nicanor Villalta.
    A powerful contemporary *apoderado* was Manuel Rodriguez
    Vazquez, whose clients in the 1920s included, among
    others, such famous men as Diego Mazquiaran (Fortuna).
    Ricardo Anllo (Nacional), Juan Anllo (Nacional II), and
    Rodolfo Gaona; this *apoderado* was according to *Toreros y
    toros,* one of several people angling for Manuel Retana's
    job (issue of 10 June, 1923; 10:3). *Toreros y toros*
    campaigned against Retana all through 1923 and 1924, as
    evidenced by articles and editorials in the issues
    Hemingway read and saved (Hemingway Collection, JFK).
    In "The Undefeated," the waiters discuss Retana's
    interference in the careers of several matadors.

11. Several of the novel's characters reveal their interest in
    the bullfight. Before the Civil War, Pablo had been
    tangentially involved with the bullring by his profession

(menial and much despised in *Death in the Afternoon*) as assistant horse contractor; Joaquin wanted to be a matador but he never made it; and Andres dreaded but participated in his hometown's amateur *capeas*. Hemingway carefully establishes that several other characters follow the bullfights, among them Primitivo, Andres' brother Eladio Lopez (133- 34, 182-85), and Jordan himself. The massacre which Pablo organizes is compared to and organized like a bullfight. And one of the murdered men, don Faustino Rivero, was an amateur bullfighter (not a good one, 112).

WORKS CITED

ABC, 22 July 1992.

Barea, Arturo. "Not Spain But Hemingway." In *The Literary Reputation of Hemingway in Europe*. Ed. Roger Asselineau. New York: New York UP, 1965.197-210.

Cossio y Maetinez de Fortun, Jose Maria de. *Los toros: Tratado tecnico e historico*. 11 vols. Madrid:Espasa-Calpe, 1943—.

Hemingway, Ernest. *Death in the Afternoon*. 1932. New York: Scribner's, 1960.

.... *For Whom the Bell Tolls*. 1940 . New York: Scibner's, 1968.

.... *The Sun Also Rises*. 1926. New York: Scribner's, 1970.

Joseph F. Allen. "Hemingway's Poor Spanish: Chauvinism and Loss of Credulity in *For Whom the Bell Tolls*." *Hemingway: A Revaluation*. Ed. Donald R. Noble. Troy, NY: Whitston, 1983.205-223.

Martinez Salvatierra, Jose. *Los toros, la fiesta nacional espanola*. Barcelona: Ediciones Savma, 1961.

El pais. 26 October 1990.

Rubio Cabeza, Manuel. *Diccionario de la Guerra civil espanola*. 2 vols. Barcelona: Planeta, 1987.

Silva, Aramburu, Jose (Pepe Alegrias). *Enciclopedia taurina*. Barceloa:Editorial de Gasso. 11 nos., 1961.

Sol y sombra 20 and 27 March 1924 (double issue)

Tapia, Daniel. *Historia de toreo*. Vol.1: *De Pedro Romero a Manolete*. Madrid: Allianza Editorial, 1992.

Toreros y toros. 10 June 1923 and 30 March 1924.

Intertextualities : *The Old Man And The Sea* and *Islands in The Stream*

Sobha Chattopadhyay

The Old Man and the Sea came out in 1952, towards the fag end of Hemingway's career as a novelist, in fact, nine years before he died in July 1961. No other novel brought Hemingway such instant acclaim from reviewers and critics. Since then this short novel has lent itself to various readings. Philip Young saw it as a metaphor for life as a fight and man as a fighter. Carlos Baker saw analogies between Santiago and Christ on the cross. If the former stressed the central image of the killer, the latter stressed that of the sufferer. The novel is open to different readings on different levels. It is not merely an 'old man catching fish', 'it is also a great artist in the act of mastering his subject' 'actually writing about the struggle'[1]. It has also been read as a classical tragedy on the Greek mould. Santiago tries to surpass the limits of human possibility, goes too far out and thus brings catastrophe on himself. It has been read as a tragedy of 'hubris' in the sense of overreaching. He transgresses the physical order of the universe and ultimately achieves inner victory through outer defeat. More recent critics have emphasized the need to relate the novel to Spanish and Cuban historical and cultural contexts. Then there has been a controversy as to whether Manolin is a child, somewhere between ten to fourteen, or actually a young man of twenty two. There are critics who 'read the baseball allusions more carefully'[2] analysing symbolic parallels between Santiago and Joe DiMaggio relating to popular culture, presented as a subtext.

One approach that has been so far overlooked is to consider *The Old Man and the Sea* as one of Hemingway's last novels, related to the much longer *Islands in the Stream* (posthumously published in 1970). *The Old Man*, a shorter novel was originally a part of it. In Hemingway's letters between 1946 and 1952 there are confusing references to 'the Land, Sea and Air Book' – a post-war novel which never got completed and remained a dream. 'The Land' section which was about the war in Europe got incorporated into the novel *Across the River And Into the Trees*. 'The Sea Book' became *Islands in the Stream*. *Islands* originally had four sections. The first section 'The Sea When Young' ('Bimini' in *Islands*) was written in the last few months of 1945 and the second section 'The Sea When Absent' ('Cuba' in *Islands*) in the first three weeks of December 1950. Shortly after he wrote 'The Sea in Being' and 'The Sea Chase' intended to be third and fourth part of the novel. Soon he made 'The Sea Chase' the third section of *Islands* ('At Sea'), shifted 'The Sea in Being' to the fourth section, ultimately severing it from the rest and publishing it separately as *The Old Man and the Sea*. The fact remains that Hemingway never himself published *Islands*. His wife did after his death.

At the start one must admit that *Islands* is an unequal book, sprawling and loose and the Caribbean setting and the main protagonist Hudson are the only binding factors. It is often difficult to relate certain incidents and characters. But the book is brilliant in sections e.g. the early scene of fishing or the one where the shark attacks David. Hemingway felt that the book needed to be revised and rewritten. Was it that he did not want to damage the reputation he had earned with *The Old Man* by publishing an admittedly inferior product? Could it be that it was too autobiographical? According to Wirt Williams 'No other persona is so close to Hemingway the writer as Thomas Hudson the painter, down to wives, sons, experiences, work, and grief [3]. His former wife, a prominent figure in the novel is much like Hadley, Hemingway's first wife and his eldest son, young Tom, who dies half-way through the novel resembles Bumby. Anyway, Hemingway did decide to offer *The Old Man* for publication separating it from 'The Sea

Book where, as Rose Marie Burwell says, 'it has never seemed to belong'[4]. Today, as it stands, it is difficult to put *The Old Man* back to its place in *Islands* (after the Cuba section). It is hard to fit it in. But then Hemingway originally had decided that *The Old Man* would be a part of it.

A close study of the two novels reveals striking resemblances and links in themes, motifs, symbols and images. They share some characteristic themes like love, the need for reciprocal human relationships, creativity and the artist's concern for craft, the theme of life as a struggle for existence and a preoccupation with death. The symbols of the sea, fish and shark make them a close kin to each other. Today they stand as separate, independent novels, but they do share a unity. A study of one illuminates the other.

The first item that comes to one's mind is the function of the 'Sea' in both the novels comprising the Sea Book. The sea is there not just as the background, the Gulf Stream, the means of livelihood of the entire fishing community in the Caribbean. It is the sea of life which man has to negotiate. Not only are there evocative passages, eloquent descriptions of the sea through concrete sensuality of the characters, Santiago's primitive response and a creative artist's sensitive response in the case of Hudson and his friend Roger contributing to rich poetry. Here are two descriptions of the sea and fine weather between storms in the hurricane months of autumn:

> But now they were in hurricane months and, when there are no hurricanes, the weather of hurricane months is the best of all the year[5].   (*The Old Man and the Sea*)

> Hurricanes, too, might come in September and October and even in early November and there could be freak tropical storms any time from June on. But the true hurricane months have fine weather when there are no storms[6].   (*Islands In the Stream*)

The hues of the sea are differentiated, often richly contrasted with sand and sky. But side-by-side we have the other aspect of the sea - the inexorable quality that evokes awe and fear, the dangers it stands for. Reflections on the caprice of the sea are reflections on the caprice of Nature, of the Universe in general. Both the noble and beautiful marlin and the destructive sharks belong to the sea. It combines benevolence, malice and violence. To Santiago the sea is not merely a place or an enemy but *la mar-* a woman to be loved however cruel. Like Santiago Hudson in 'At Sea' of *Islands* views the sea as a woman but a treacherous one who hides Hudson's enemies, the Germans, in ambush. The sea stands for the insurmountable obstacle against which the tragic hero Santiago or Hudson must assert his manhood. One thinks of the sea as a symbol in Conrad (in *An Outcast of the Islands, Lord Jim* or *Nostromo*). In Synge's *Riders to the Sea* the sea acts like some superpower, inevitably devouring all of Maurya's sons.

As pointed out earlier, the real impact of the *Islands* stems from some of its powerful, dramatic action scenes. Possibly the best of these scenes is the fishing sequence which is an obvious parallel, 'pre-figuration' or 'miniature' of *The Old Man and the Sea*. In 'Bimini' David, the second son of Hudson catches a huge sword-fish, fights it all day, brings it to the edge of the boat but loses it while trying to get the hook off. It is almost a mini-tragedy, an acting out of man's fate suggesting Santiago's heroic battle. As Eddy, the cook comments, the fish nearly tows David's boat just as Santiago's boat is towed by the fish. Though David's hands are bleeding, cut by the line and the straps, he refuses to give up. His father does not panic either 'That's the way a fisherman's hands and feet are supposed to get and next time they'll be tougher'(IS 133). His earlier comment is even more significant: 'If David catches this fish he'll have something inside him for all his life and it will make everything else easier' (IS 131). Thus this fishing passage (almost a subtext running for forty pages) ties *The*

Old Man to 'Bimini'. The action is similar; so is the sensitive evocation of the thrills of fishing. An overall symbolism pervades both novels. The same trend is noticed in the use of specific images. The details are quite rich and dense.

> I don't care if he kills me, the big son of a bitch,' David said. 'Oh hell. I don't hate him. I love him.' (IS 134)

David's cry echoes Santiago's words :

> You are killing me, fish, the old man thought. But you have a right to. Never have I seen a greater, or more beautiful, or a calmer or more noble thing than you brother. Come on and kill me. I do not care who kills who. (OMS 92)

Later, as the ordeal continues, David tells Roger 'I began to love him more than anything on earth'. This is because he feels a certain kinship with it almost merging his identity with that of the fish: ' I couldn't tell which was him and which was me'. (IS 142) Thus *Islands* harps on a theme, close to Hemingway's heart, explicitly taken up and expanded in *The Old Man* – the theme of the close tie between Man and Nature (and the animal world) and the theme of universal brotherhood. In his closeness to the marlin, the flying fish and the birds Santiago has even closer ties with other Hemingway characters like Juan Belmonte (at the bull ring) Manuel Garcia, Anselmo and the other old man at the bridge. In the 'Cuba' section we have Hudson's friendship with Boise, the cat (who has outlived his boy) offering him fresh, chilled slices of mango every morning 'I don't know how many people and animals have been in love before' (IS 212). Of course, this is autobiographical.

In fact, deeply reciprocal human relationship is a characteristic theme of Hemingway. It is developed in *Islands*. Both Hudson and his friend Roger Davis have had troubled relationships with women in the past (two of them, Audrey Bruce and Tom's mother reappear in the first and second sections). However, it is the father-child relationship that lies at the heart of the novel. Hudson's life seems to glow and become meaningful in the company of his three sons. He dreads the loneliness and the emptiness when they move out. Yet he is a father who stays aloof, working at his painting, enjoying their activities from a distance. Roger almost acts as a father substitute constantly giving them company and encouragement. He plays the father to them feeling Hudson's children to be his own ' I'm fond of them like they're my boys and I worry the hell about them' (IS 81). He has a particularly strong bond with David who reminds him of his own dead brother David. Thus Roger relates to Santiago who' has a beloved son-figure in Manolin, but no wife and child of his own. Perhaps the void left by the death of his sons explains Hudson's barren and dissipated life in 'Cuba'. Estranged from his three wives (he has some attachment to his first wife but even that relationship has gone wrong somewhere) he takes up the call of duty and plunges into dangerous action, engages with a superior enemy at the risk of his life ' your boy you lose. Love you lose. Honor has been gone for a long time. Duty you do.' (IS 326) The novel ends with Hudson on his deathbed fatally wounded in his chase of German submarines. In the end his predicament is similar to Santiago's foreshadowing the desperate voyage of the old fishermen and the sharks. Does the novel suggest Hudson's inability to develop and sustain human relationships? The theme of comradeship between the hunter and the hunted (man and fish) developed in *The Old Man* is foreshadowed in the third part of *Islands* when Hudson's men discover a dying German soldier, suffering from gangrene. Though an enemy, they speak to him lovingly and offer him morphine to reduce his pain.

'At Sea' the third part of *Islands* relates well to *The Old Man*. Hudson's struggle parallels Santiago's. Like Santiago and most tragic heroes, Hudson understands the relative insignificance of his search for the escaped German submarines, yet he heroically accepts his duty and the risk involved. Transcendence signifies inner victory through outer defeat: 'A man can be destroyed but not defeated' (OMS 103). Santiago and Hudson know that

they are often fighting with their back to the wall. The
heroism lies in the struggle, the resistance and the fighting
that they put up. Santiago remembers a triumphant arm-
wrestling match with a muscular Negro. Hemingway
believes in life as a sport. It is not victory or defeat that
matters but the struggle itself. Though old, he has inner
youth. Like Tennyson's Ulysses he might well have for
motto 'To strive, to seek, to find, and not to yield'[7]. After the
death of his son Hudson leaves painting and moves from
creation to destruction. One remembers Hemingway's
advice to Lavalle after the death of his daughter Wendy in
'a Japanese internment camp' to join the Marine Corps,
'where he will be able to fight against the people he hates
most'. 'It is a great happiness to kill those we hate'[8]. In
life's game one has to play the destroyer also and kill the
enemy. For Hudson it is the Germans. The shark is one
such enemy in The Old Man. Incidentally David's near
disaster with the shark in 'Bimini', another powerful
extract, relates obviously to the scene in The Old Man where
the sharks attack Santiago and mutilate the fish.
Ostensibly as sea creatures they have a beauty of their
own:

> He was a very big Mako shark built to swim as fast as
> the fastest fish in the sea and everything about him
> was beautiful except his jaws. His back was as blue
> as a swordfish's and his belly was silver and his hide
> was smooth and handsome. (OMS 100)

> The biggest hammerhead he had ever seen rose
> white-bellied out of the sea and began to plane off
> over the water crazily, throwing water like an
> aquaplane. His belly was shining an obscene white,
> his yard-wide mouth like a turned-up grin. (IS 86)

Its appearance is deceptive. The 'jaws' and 'obscene white
belly' are ominous. The shark attacks David as he is goggle-
fishing and he is narrowly saved when Eddy kills it with a
machine gun and like Santiago David says he went out too
far. The shark is a menace, a symbol of evil seeking its

adversary. Santiago's battle with the murderous sharks is long and tiring. Ultimately they win and destroy the marlin. They stand for the destructive elements in the universe prowling around waiting to strike any moment. They are Nemesis too.

If the shark stands for evil, David, who is almost hit by it stands for good, in contrast. His symbolic role, suggested in the scene, is fully developed in the subsequent scene of battle with the giant fish. There he almost becomes like Santiago a miniature Christ figure, undergoing a crucifixion ordeal. David's 'bloody' hands and 'oozing' feet recall Santiago's wounded hands and Christ. David's elder brother young Tom tells his father 'David's a saint and a martyr.(IS 125) After the terrific battle as David lies face down on the bunk he recalls Santiago's posture when he falls asleep after returning home face down with his arms out straight. In 'At Sea' immediately after Hudson is wounded Willie says 'Jesus Christ'.(IS 458) The three hours David spends fighting with the fish recalls Santiago's three days to be related to the three days of crucifixion drama and the Holy Trinity. The leap of David's fish in 'Bimini' is an ascension image as in *The Old Man*. In fact the whole network of Christian symbols relates to *The Old Man* and the central idea that a man who dies and suffers for his commitment has something of Christ in him.

Another motif that runs like a strand through much of Hemingway's fiction is the issue of creativity. The Old Man catching a fish has been seen as a great artist mastering his subject. Santiago, talking about the 'many tricks' he knows, recalls the artist who is a craftsman too. To him nothing is more important than his craft. In *Islands* the theme of creativity is given a much fuller and explicit treatment. Both the central characters, the two friends Hudson and Roger are artists. Hudson is a well-established successful painter, divorced and lonely finding fulfillment in his devotion to art. Roger Davis on the other hand is a failed novelist, a double (in the manner of Conrad's Secret Sharer) given to drinking, brawling and women. His work has been affected by his inability to bring the personal forces into a balance or harmony. There are scattered discussions on creativity, common problems faced in writing and painting, the interconnection of all arts and the unitary origin of creativity. Some critics would go so far as to detect writing as a subtext within the novel. After personal loss Hudson gives up painting for the anti-submarine work. Again all this is autobiographical and one wonders how conscious were Hudson, Roger and Hemingway of the erosion of their creativity. In the later phase of his life Hemingway was constantly badgered by the disparity between his universal fame and fading powers and a fear as to whether he would be able to repeat his past performance.

This brings me to my last point, the preoccupation with death which runs like a strand throughout Hemingway's work. 'Much has been made of Hemingway's interest in death ... labeled in various ways: the cult of death, a death wish, an obsession with death and the like. H.E.Bates goes so far as to assert that "in reality Hemingway has only one theme – death" '[9]. It has been there right from the beginning. It is fear of darkness that is almost synonymous with the fear of death that makes the wounded Nick Adams to 'keep near the street lights' as he walks home in a cold night in Milan. It is fear of death that keeps the old man haunting the 'clean well-lighted place'. For the later Hemingway heroes the fear of death recedes to the background as they learn to live with it, acknowledge the darkness, the nothingness and the void and struggle ceaselessly to overcome it. Romero's fifteen-minute encounter with death in the bullring is similar to Santiago's deep sea-fishing and there is hardly any glamour of love, war and death. As one moves to Hemingway's later novels and the last phase of his life one notices a slight difference in his thinking about age and death. The lonely old fisherman Santiago's stoic acceptance of ironic failure seems very different from the energetic death of the earlier fighters and hunters (e.g. Robert Jordan's death in *For Whom the Bell Tolls* or Francis Macomber's death in "The Short Happy Life of Francis Macomber"). And death looms large in *Islands*. The death of his two young sons David and Andy and their mother in an accident is a blow that stuns

Hudson, makes him give up painting and lose all interest in life. The death of his remaining son Tom, who bears his father's name, destroys the last link between the past and the present and makes him choose a life of destruction: 'Why don't you care anything about anything? .... Why do you just pound and pound on after it like a riderless horse that is still in the race?' (IS 356). Just as Hudson had foreseen Tom's death after his brothers were killed in 'Bimini', Tom's mother anticipates Hudson's death at the end of 'Cuba'. Hudson regrets that he will never paint the beautiful lagoon his boat approaches just before he dies. It is not just that. The book abounds in detailed references to deaths and suicides. In 'Cuba' Hudson tells Lil of his boyhood brush with death when he was trapped beneath the logs 'I drowned'. A very large number of suicides by various means are mentioned. Sometimes the anecdotes are little to the point. There is the pig that swam out to sea ' I am sorry your pig committed such suicide'. 'We all have our small problems'(IS 354). There is Roger's girl-friend who killed herself 'She was headed for it all the time'. 'You wouldn't do it because it would be hell of an example (IS 156). Then there is that gentleman called 'Suicides'. And finally there is Honest Lil's whole inventory to Hudson about the different techniques of committing suicide popular among Cubans- 'by eating phosphorous from the heads of matches', by drinking 'rapid ink', a dye or 'setting themselves on fire by pouring alcohol' (IS 281). Somehow all this suggests obsession and morbidity. It is impossible to read *Islands* without thinking of Hemingway's suicide.

Now to look back to *The Old Man* from this perspective, where does the short novel stand? Looking at the ending of the novel one wonders if there are hints for the old man approaching death. In the closing scenes Manolin is crying each time he withdraws from Santiago's bedside. It could be remorse too, for contributing to his suffering. He should have accompanied him and now it is too late. A man's excellent performance does not compensate for his failure. Does Santiago lie dying at the end? Of course the novel ends with the old man sleeping and dreaming of the lions. Most readers feel that it ends on a note of hope, new strength and vitality. But the very spectacle of the old man at that age challenging Nature with a total disregard of safety (he does confess he went too far out) and his address to the fish 'come on and kill me. I do not care who kills who' (OMS 92) seem to hint at a forced stoicism, should we say, a recklessness almost suicidal.

All this is particularly relevant in the context of Hemingway's suicide a few years later, after years of deep depression, paranoid tendencies and several earlier attempts at suicide (somehow Lillian Ross's recent theory that his death was an accident does not seem convincing). It all goes back to his brush with death in January 1954 when he survived two plane crashes on safari in Africa suffering most drastic injuries from which he never really recovered. His injuries included 'a full scale concussion', 'a ruptured liver, spleen, and kidney, temporary loss of vision in the left eye, loss of hearing in the left ear, a crushed vertebra, a sprained right arm and shoulder, a sprained left leg, paralysis of the sphincter and first degree burns on his face, arms and head'[10]. After that in the last few years his body was deteriorating his energy and strength were ebbing away and he could not write as he once could. He was paying the penalty for taking too high risks throughout his life. The lure of adventure, love of risk and may be a sense of boredom after surfeit of action in the crisis-ridden 'thirties provide a rationale for his own repeated confrontations with danger. And Philip Young virtually predicted self-destruction as an aftermath of the traumatic experience in 1954.

NOTES AND REFERENCES

1. Carlos Baker, *Hemingway: The Writer As Artist* (Princeton, New Jersey: Princeton University Press, 1963), p.322.

2. Bickford Sylvester, 'The Cuban Context Of *The Old Man and the Sea*' in *The Cambridge Companion to Ernest Hemingway*. ed. Scott Donaldson (Cambridge University Press, 1996), p. 251.

3. Wirt Williams, *The Tragic Art of Ernest Hemingway* (Baton Rouge: Louisiana State Univ. Press, 1981), p.199.

4. Rose Marie Burwell, *Hemingway: The Postwar Years and the Posthumous Novels* (Cambridge University Press, 1996), p.57.

5. Ernest Hemingway, *The Old Man and the Sea.* (London: Jonathan Cape, 1952 reprinted 1955), p. 59. Henceforth the abbreviation used is OMS.

6. Ernest Hemingway, *Islands in the Stream* (New York, 1970), p.4. Henceforth the abbreviation used is IS.

7. Alfred Tennyson, 'Ulysses' in *The Penguin Book of English Poetry* ed. G.B.Harrison (Harmondsworth: Penguin, 1937), p.363.

8. Burwell, *Hemingway: The Postwar Years and the Posthumous Novels*, Notes, p.202.

9. Beongcheon Yu, 'The Still Center of Hemingway's World' in *Ernest Hemingway:Five Decades of Criticism* ed. Linda W. Wagner (Ann Arbor: Michigan State University Press, 1974), p.123.

0. Carlos Baker, *Ernest Hemingway: A Life Story* (New York:Scribner's,1969), p.522.

Exchange between Rivals : Faulkner's Influence on
The Old Man and the Sea

Peter L. Hays

Ernest Hemingway's antagonism to fellow writers, particularly to those who might be considered his equals, is well known, and William Faulkner was among his many targets for vituperation. Hemingway denounced him as "Corncob," "Old Corndrinking Mellifluous," and as the author of stories about "Octonawhoopoo" or "Anomatopoeio County."[1] Yet the situation was not simply one of unmixed antagonism. Hemingway told both James T. Farrell (in 1936) and Jean Paul Sartre (in 1944) that Faulkner was a better writer than himself.[2] And in *Death in the Afternoon* (1932) he praised Faulkner while mocking *Sanctuary*:

> My operatives tell me that through the fine work of
> Mr. William Faulkner publishers now will publish
> anything rather than to try to get you to delete the
> better portions of your works, and I look forward to
> writing of those days of my youth which were spent
> in the finest whorehouses in the land amid the most
> brilliant society there found.

Old lady: Has this Mr. Faulkner written well of these places?

> Splendidly, Madame. Mr. Faulkner writes admirably
> of them. He writes the best of them of any writer I
> have read for many years.
> *Old lady :* I must buy his works.
> Madame, you can't go wrong on Faulkner. He's prolific

too. By the time   you get them ordered there'll be
new ones out.
Old lady : If there are as you say there cannot be too
many Madame, you voice my own opinion.[3]

When Robert Coates, in his *New Yorker* review of *Death in
the Afternoon*, chided Hemingway for his "petulant jibes" at
Faulkner, Hemingway responded in a letter: "There weren't
any cracks against Faulkner...There was....a pretty damned
friendly mention....I have plenty of respect for Faulkner
and wish him all luck. I'm damned if I wrote any petulant
jibes against Faulkner and the hell with you telling citizens
that I did."[4] Hemingway wrote Malcolm Cowley (in 1945)
that Faulkner "has the most talent of anybody," then
qualified that praise by adding:

> He just needs a sort of conscience that isn't
> there....He will write absolutely perfectly straight and
> then go on and on and not be able to end it. I wish the·
> Christ I owned him like you'd own a horse and train
> him like a horse and race him like a horse – only in
> writing. How beautifully he can write and as simple
> and as complicated as autumn or as spring.[5]

Of Faulkner's work, Hemingway wrote Owen Wister (in
1932) that he liked *As I Lay Dying* but that *Sanctuary* was
"pretty phoney"; in another letter (1956), while calling
Faulkner a "no good son of a bitch," Hemingway praised
Sanctuary, Pylon, and "The Bear" but condemned *A Fable* as
night soil.[6] He did, however, include Faulkner's
"Turnabout," Faulkner's most Hemingwayesque tale, in his
wartime anthology *Men at War* (1942).

The major contretemps between them occurred in
1947 when Faulkner, questioned by students at the
University of Mississippi about his ranking of American
writers, put Thomas Wolfe, himself, and John Dos Passos –
in that order—ahead of Hemingway for their courage in
stylistic experimentation.[7] Hemingway chose to interpret
the published remarks as an insult to his physical courage.
He asked General Charles T. (Buck) Lanaham, with whom
he had served in the Second World War, to write to Faulkner,

which the general did, praising Hemingway's courage under fire. Faulkner replied, apologizing in separate letters to Lanaham and to Hemingway, inspiring this response from Hemingway:

> Awfully glad to hear from you and glad to have made contact.... Please throw all the other stuff away, the misunderstanding....
>
> You are a better writer than Fielding or any of those guys and you should just know it and keep on writing. You have things written that come back to me better than any of them......Have much regard for you. Would you like to keep on writing [letters].[8]

On the other side of the rivalry, Faulkner, as befitted his less bellicose nature, was consistently milder in his comments and more respectful of both Hemingway and his work. Most of his early correspondence deals with the man, not the books: e.g., he thanks Paul Romaine (1932) for a greeting passed on from Hemingway and remarks that he wished he had thought to initiate a friendship; he responds (1945) to Malcolm Cowley's letter about Hemingway's failed third marriage and loneliness, promising to write Hemingway (but not doing so for two years).[9] It is interesting that Cowley begins his correspondence with Faulkner in the spring of 1944 (he writes in February, Faulkner answers May 7), just after Cowley has finished compiling *The Portable Hemingway* and as Faulkner is finishing the screenplay of Hemingway's *To Have and Have Not*. Whereas Cowley mentions Hemingway frequently, Faulkner writes of him only twice: once in the letter of May 7 and once in another version of his much-repeated statement that Hemingway's fiction lacked experimentation.[10]

Elsewhere, however, Faulkner three times wrote high praise of Hemingway. In 1950, in a letter to *Time* magazine, seconding Evelyn Waugh's defense of *Across the River and into the Trees* Faulkner said, "the man who wrote some of the pieces in *Men Without Women* and *The Sun Also Rises* and some of the African stuff (some –most— of all the rest of it too for that matter) does not need defending."[11] When Harvey Breit asked Faulkner to review *The Old Man and the Sea* for the *New York Times Book Review*, Faulkner declined, but he sent Breit a letter praising Hemingway, repeating many of his *Time* magazine comments (but adding *A Farewell to Arms* and *For Whom the Bell Tolls* to his list of Hemingway's eminent achievements), concluding "that if even what remained [the other, unmentioned work] had not been as honest and true as he could make it, then he himself would have burned the manuscript before the publisher even saw it."[12] Faulkner finally did write a one-paragraph review of *The Old Man and the Sea* for *Shenandoah*, calling the book Hemingway's "best. Time may show it to be the best single piece of any of us, I mean his and my contemporaries."[13]

The two authors' works are also curiously intertwined. There is the coincidence of simultaneous publication by the New Orleans *Double Dealer* in June 22; there is the friendship of both with Sherwood Anderson, the lessons learned from him, and their coincidental mockery of their mentor, Hemingway savagely in *The Torrents of Spring*, Faulkner more gently in his introduction to *Sherwood Anderson and Other Creoles* (both published in 1926) and in his portrait of Anderson in *Mosquitoes* (written in 1926, published in 1927). Then there begin to be instances in their published works where one seems to have learned from, borrowed from, or be poking fun at the other (Hemingway's remarks in *Death in the Afternoon* are one example of the last). Malcolm Cowley makes the first attribution in 1945, saying that there is a suggestion of Hemingway in the way Faulkner presents a trout in a river (in the Quentin section of *The Sound and the Fury*?).[14] In 1952, French reviewers noted a similarity between *A Farewell to Arms* and *The Wild Palms;* similarities of theme aside, certain words make the connection obvious: Faulkner writes of "hemingwaves"; on the same page he picks up Hemingway's pun on "armor" (from Swift and Armour in "The Snows of Kilimanjaro") by making one of his own −"armorous"—and even writes of "aficianados"[sic].[15] The protagonist of *The Wild Palms* (1939) and *To Have and Have Not* (1937), just as the title of the contrapuntal novella within *The Wild Palms*, "Old Man,"

prefigures *The Old Man and the Sea*. As Thomas McHaney
notes, the last chapter of Faulkner's *The Unvanquished*
(1938), "An Odor of Verbena" (written in July of 1937),[16]
apparently owes its title to a phrase in Hemingway's "The
Short Happy Life of Francis Macomber" (published
September 1936), and references to Hemingway by name
occur in *Pylon* and *Requiem for a Nun*.[17] George Monteiro
suggests that Hemingway, in turn, borrowed from *The Wild
Palms* for the masturbation scene and the ending of *For
Whom the Bell Tolls*.[18] There also seems to be a passing
back and forth of the uses of bicycles grotesquely associated
with death probably based in Hemingway's own near-mortal
wound after cycling to the Italian front at Fossalta di Piave.
We see this conjunction first with Hemingway's *A Farewell
to Arms* (1929); then Faulkner picks it up for the Percy
Grimm section of *Light in August* (1932); then Hemingway
takes it back or "A Way You'll Never Be" (1933), "The Snows
of Kilimanjaro" (1936), and *To Have and Have Not* (1937).[19]
And John Howell sees the influence of *For Whom the Bell
Tolls* on "The Bear."[20] As Malcolm Cowley has written,
"Faulkner and Hemingway read each other's work with close
attention."[21]

Their lives, too, reveal curious likenesses.[22] Two
years separated their births, one year their deaths. Both
boys were taught a lifelong love of the outdoors, of hunting
and fishing, their fathers dominated by their wives. Both
boys played football in high school (Faulkner even repeated
the fall term of eleventh grade to play more football, in spite
of his slight size); and both unable to enlist with American
troops, found other means to join World War I forces. What
Carlos Baker wrote of Hemingway applies to Faulkner
equally well: "Because Hemingway was by nature and
inclination and profession a spinner of yarns, not all of the
stories relayed in his letters can be trusted as true. He
believed and often said that writers are liars and took
evident delight in living up to his own dictum in
conversation as in letters."[23] This love of invention, plus a
desire for some glorification, led to the reports of
Hemingway's serving as an infantryman with the Italian
army, printed on the back cover of many Scribner's

paperbacks; and to Faulkner's returning from Canada, not in the air cadet garb he should have been wearing, but in British officer's uniform, telling friends of his terrible crash and of the silver plate in his head.[24]

Though their writing styles are very different, both suggest a basic distrust of language. Hemingway avoids flowery rhetoric and highly connotative words; he purposefully omits certain details, trusting to a skillfully managed recording of fact and event to convey what he wants. Faulkner piles up synonyms as though no one word were adequate, insists as well, epistemologically, on the limits of human knowledge by never telling his readers enough for them to be sure of what has happened. Frederic Henry's comment "There were many words that you could not stand to hear and finally only the names of places have any dignity....Abstract words such as glory, honor, courage, or hallow were obscene beside the concrete names of villages" is very similar to Addie Bundren's "words are no good; that words don't ever fit even what they are trying to say at."[25] But the greatest similarity between the two men who hunted all their lives is the display in their fiction of their love of land: both show respect for wild creatures who inhabit wilderness, for the code of the hunter, and for anyone who acts with the dignity that they often ascribe to animals.

Faulkner praised *The Old Man and the Sea* as the work in which Hemingway discovered God and in which "he wrote about pity."[26] Pity has been present before in Hemingway's works, but God does not play a major role in *The Old Man and the Sea*;[27] in fact, the religion in Hemingway's novella, as in Faulkner's "The Bear," is more totemic or animistic than it is formally Christian.[28] If "Turnabout" is Faulkner's work most like Hemingway's, then *The Old Man and the Sea* is Hemingway's work most like Faulkner's – most specifically, it resembles "The Bear." Perhaps at least part of what appealed to Faulkner in this novella was what he had supplied himself. Some of the likenesses between "The Bear" and *The Old Man and the Sea* are obvious. Both stories involved the pursuit of a large anthropomorphized beast by an old man who has been responsible for the initiation of a boy into the craft of hunting or fishing and for instilling in the boy values, discipline, and a sense of respect. In both works, the authors are at great pains to establish a link between man and nature, a tight, interdependent community; beyond that, both works present social communities within the larger, natural one. And—unusual for both authors—women figure very slightly in *The Old Man and the Sea* and "The Bear," whereas women are the primary complicating figures in both the authors' longer works.

Both authors paid tribute to land or seascape repeatedly; such passages are too familiar to need repeating. Both authors hunted or fished all their lives and devoted much of their writing to the subject – Hemingway from "Big Two-hearted River" through *The Sun Also Rises, Green Hills of Africa*, to *The Old Man and the Sea;* Faulkner in *Big Woods* (which Edward Shenton illustrated, as he had *Green Hills of Africa*) and throughout *Go Down, Moses*. Even the pursuit of other men in their fiction is presented in terms of hunting; in Hemingway's Robert Jordan's discussion with Anselmo about killing men vs. killing bears,[29] or in Faulkner's "Red Leaves" or "Was". The animals pursued in "The Bear" and *The Old Man and the Sea* are clearly elevated and made human (or superhuman). Faulkner says that "the big old bear had earned for himself a name, a definite designation like a living man"; the bear is "widowed childless and absolved of morality – old Priam reft of his old wife and outlived all his sons." Faulkner describes Old Ben as Ike's instructor: "If Sam Fathers had been his mentor and the backyard rabbits and squirrels in his kindergarten, then the wilderness the old bear ran was his college and the old male bear itself....was his alma mater."[30] Hemingway emphasizes that Santiago loves and respects the fish as an equal. He has Santiago say of the marlin, "He is my brother. The fish is my friend too," and, "I have killed this fish which is my brother."[31] The identity Hemingway insists on between Santiago and the marlin common between hunter and hunted, can also be seen between Sam Fathers and Old Ben: both are aged for their kind, both unwifed and childless; both are Ike's tutors (and, like Isaac, were named from the Old Testament: Samuel the prophet and Benjamin, Isaac's youngest grandson, whose name means son of the South).[32] Both are doomed to die with the vanishing wilderness that both live in and represent. Although Hemingway does not deal with the ending of an era as explicitly as does Faulkner, the changing values of different generations are suggested in this passage:

> Some of the younger fishermen, those who used buoys as floats for their lines and had motorboats....spoke of [the sea] as *el mar* which is masculine. They speak of her as contestant or a place or even an enemy. But the old man always thought of her as feminine. (p.27)

More significantly, both authors make gods or demigods of the animals their protagonists hunt. Faulkner's bear is clearly an incarnation of Frazer's King of the Wood: Old Ben is the object of an attention approaching veneration "in the yearly pageant-rite of the old bear's furious immortality" (p.194). As many critics have noticed, Sam Fathers is the priest inducting Ike as "novitiate to the true wilderness" (p.195), but the bear is the symbol of that wilderness, its "apotheosis" (p. 193); it will die when he does (and Sam along with him). Isaac's approach to the bear – fasting one morning, and leaving behind his gun, watch, and compass – approximates the ceremony by which American Indian youth sought their personal totem, their *nigouimes*. Subsequently he confronts the bear "where it loomed and towered over him like a thunderclap....; this was the way he had used to dream about it" (p.211), another element of the *nigouimes* ceremony.[33] Thus Ike does not kill the bear, his personal totem, when the opportunity presents itself and he buries the bear's mutilated paw in the grave above Lion. Similarly, while Hemingway is content for the most part merely to link Santiago and the marlin in a chain of cruel kill-or-be-killed brotherhood, at one point he literally and symbolically elevates the marlin. For much of the

novella, Santiago has been identified with Christ: he bears
the name of a fisherman disciple, is scourged by the rope
line, earns stigmata (p.56), carries the mast falteringly,
stumbles various times, sleeps in a cruciform position, and
makes "a noise such as a man might make, involuntarily
feeling the nail go through his hands in the wood" (p.107).
At the death of the marlin, however, Santiago becomes the
centurion; and the fish, ICHTHYS, appropriately, assumes
the role of Jesus: Santiago drove the harpoon "into the fish's
side just behind the great chest fin that rose high in the
air to the altitude of a man's chest" (p.94). The subsequent
line, "showing all his great length and beauty"(p.66 "power
and glory," the only page where "Christ" is used as an
expletive), echoes "the Son of man coming in a cloud with
power and great glory" (Luke 21:27) or the more familiar
"For Thine is the kingdom and the power and the glory" of
the Lord's Prayer.[34]

   Also significant for comparison's sake is the
moment of death itself for both animals a moment
Hemingway describes as seeming like a dream, with "some
great strangeness" (p.98). Santiago's marlin "came alive
with his death in him and rose high out of the water.....He
seemed to hang in the air over the old man in the skiff.
Then he fell into the water with a crash"(p.98). Similarly,
Old Ben and his pursuers, also fixed in time for an instant
by Faulkner, "almost resembled a piece of statuary." Then,
as Boon probes and finds the bear's heart with his knife,
"the bear surged erect," and finally "crashed down....all of a
piece, as a tree falls"(p.241). Thus both authors attempt to
capture what Faulkner's favorite poem, "Ode on a Grecian
Urn," describes the fixing of a moment in time for all time,
the permanent presentation of the momentary and
ephemeral.

   Continuing with the totemic rites appropriate to both
beasts, one should note that both are killed not at a distance,
but by hand, with knives, as it appropriate for totemic
sacrifices. Both indictors-into-the-rites, Sam and Santiago,
initiate their hierophants into the mysteries of the hunt
with blood. When Ike killed his first buck, "Sam Fathers
had marked his face with the hot blood" (pp.209-10); and

when Santiago first took Manolin into his boat, the boy
was nearly killed when Santiago bought "the fish in too
green and he nearly tore the boat to pieces." Manolin
remembers 'feeling the whole boat shiver and the noise of
you clubbing him like chopping tree down and the sweet
blood smell all over me" (p.12).

The Old Man and the Sea is the only long work by
Hemingway published in his lifetime in which the
protagonist is not close to the author's own age; rather,
Hemingway makes Santiago as old as Sam Fathers so that
the fisherman can pass on a lifetime of values and
experience to the boy. "The old man had taught the boy to
fish and the boy loved him"(p.10), as is evident in the boy's
taking care of his tutor, feeding him, providing bait for him,
being willing to steal for him, and crying over his wounds
and his loss. So too in "The Bear." Sam teaches Ike safety
in shooting, woodlore, the craft of "hunting right,
upwind"(p.207); Ike "lay in wait for the buck at dawn and
killed it when it walked back to bed as Sam Fathers had
told him"(p.210). And when Sam wants to die, Ike stays
with Boon, to care for Sam, to help him to death and to an
Indian burial. And just as Santiago addresses the fish as
relative, brother, so Sam addresses a buck: "Oleh,
Chief....Grandfather"(p.184).

There are other, smaller similarities between the
works. Though "The Bear" is land bound, the surrey in
which Ike approaches the big woods is likened by Faulkner
to a "solitary small boat [that] hangs in the lonely
immobility, merely tossing up and down, in the infinite
waste of the ocean"(p.195), a sentence redolent of Conrad,
who influenced both authors. Santiago's hero, Joe DiMaggio,
is crippled with a bone spur on his foot and Ike's hero, Old
Ben, has lost toes on one foot. In both works also, the totemic
religion is celebrated with alcohol drunk in communion.
"The Bear" begins with "a bottle present, so that it would
seem to him that those fierce instants of heart and brain
and courage and wiliness and speed were concentrated and
distilled into the brown liquor which not women, not boys
and children, but only hunters drank, drinking not out of
the blood they spilled but some concentration of the wild

immortal spirit"(p. 198). This emphasis on the communion
between initiates into shared mysteries appears also in
The Old Man and the Sea:

> .....the boy said, "Can I offer you a beer?"
> "Why not?" the old man said. "Between fishermen.
> (p. 11)

Both books emphasize this sense of shared knowledge
denied outsiders. To underscore the contrasts, the authors
bring in awkward spectators: the tourists at the end of *The
Old Man and the Sea* who mistake the marlin's skeleton for
a shark's, and the uninitiated hunters in "The Bear": "In
camp that night—they had as guests five of the still
terrified strangers in new hunting coats and boots who had
been lost all day until Sam Fathers went out and got
them"(p. 225).[35]
      The presence of these onlookers is a reminder of the
social nature of the hunt in "The Bear"; indicative of the
many ties are the opening communal drink, the shared
social status of the land-and-slave-owning DeSpains,
Compsons, and McCaslins, and their shared values. The
social structure—Ike's coming to grips with his
grandfather's actions and determining a place for himself
in the South alongside his white and black cousins – is
central to "The Bear." Ike's relationship with Sam, Cass,
and even Old Ben are metaphors in the novel's study of
tangled human relationships and man's social
responsibilities. Hemingway has the reputation of being
primarily concerned with the individual, but as critics have
noted, he is much less so in his later works, especially *The
Old Man and the Sea.* Most obvious, of course, is Santiago's
close relationship with Manolin, which opens and closes
the novella, and which Santiago calls to mind throughout
his attempts to catch the fish when he needs strength and
inspiration. This small circle of two is concentrically
surrounded: Santiago is fed on credit by Martin (p. 29);
Pedrico saves newspapers for Santiago and cares for his
skiff and gear (pp. 17 and 125); Santiago knows that the
older fisherman will worry about his absence (p. 115); and
even the Coast Guard searches for him in boats and planes

(p.124). Then Hemingway surrounds this human community with a natural one in which Santiago feels kinship with green turtles, small birds, and the marlin.

Hemingway builds two other forms of social organization into his story: baseball and Santiago's dream lions. Although sport has long been a metaphor in Hemingway's work, usually it has been man against man – boxing—or man against beast—bullfighting, hunting, fishing. But in *The Old Man and the Sea* it is baseball, a team sport, and Santiago's code hero is Joe DiMaggio, the ultimate team player. Furthermore, lions are the only cats that are social, rather than solitary, a group of them being called a pride, an important virtue in both works.[36] (The natural habitat of lions is not the ocean beach. Perhaps these strong figures in *The Old Man and the Sea* were suggested to Hemingway by the strong dog named Lion in "The Bear.")

Finally, the basic likenesses of the two books lie in the similarity of themes discussed and virtues praised. Faulkner's ideal virtues are explicitly stated throughout "The Bear": "will and hardihood to endure and the humility and skill to survive"(p.191), "humble and enduring enough"(p.192), "the humility and the pride"(p.233), "pity and humility and sufferance and endurance"(p.257), "honor and pride and pity and justice and courage and love"(p.297). "Humility" and "pride" appear over and over, in paradoxical juxtaposition. Hemingway's ideal virtues have always been less explicit, usually left for the reader to infer from characters' actions. Endurance has always been present in Hemingway's work from "The Undefeated"(1924), through Jake's acceptance of his lot, through Hemingway's favorite motto –"*Il faut (d'abord) durer*" – to Santiago three days in his skiff; in Faulkner's work, however, it is a later addition. Endurance is not central or highly important in *Soldiers' Pay* (1926), *Mosquitoes* (1927), *Flags in the Dust* (1929), *The Sound and the Fury* (1929; the "They endured" of the "Appendix" dates from 1945, not 1929). It first becomes explicit in Addie's single monologue in *As I Lay Dying* (1930), is not major in *Sanctuary* (1931), or *Light in August* (1932). Endurance first becomes a major theme in *Absalom,*

Absalom! (1936). Often the demands Hemingway makes of
his characters' endurance is unrealistically superhuman,
from Romero's willing himself not to be knocked out by
Cohn, to Jack Brennan's sustaining Jimmy Walcott's foul,
all the way to Santiago's twenty-four-hour arm wrestling
match and his declaring that "pain does not matter to a
man"(p.84). Although these are exaggerations of probability,
they clearly underscore the values of endurance
throughout his work.

Pride, skill in one's ability, is also presented
throughout Hemingway's work, in his bullfighters, boxers,
fishermen, and writers. He always admired those "who were
pretty good in there." But there is not another work where
humility is praised as it is in *The Old Man and the Sea;* good
manners and decorum are virtues in Hemingway's works,
but not meekness and humility. Thus it comes as a
surprise, especially after the statement in *A Farewell to
Arms* that "abstract words.....were obscene," to read this
description by Hemingway of Santiago, not only mentioning
humility but (like Faulkner) coupling it with pride: "He was
too simple to wonder when he had attained humility. But
he knew he had attained it and he knew it was not
disgraceful and it carried no loss of true pride"(pp.13-14).
These many similarities are evidence that Hemingway's
long, close reading of Faulkner led him to include some
Faulkerian elements from "The Bear," that good hunting
story, into his own account of a man's attempt to subdue a
great beast. As he wrote Faulkner in 1945, "You have things
written that come back to me better than any of them."

There is another link between the two men at this
point in their career, a similarity that perhaps explains
why Faulkner began emphasizing endurance. *Go Down,
Moses,* of which "The Bear" is a part, is Faulkner's last
major work. He will follow it with *Intruder in the Dust, Requiem
for a Nun, A Fable, The Town, The Mansion,* and *The Reivers;*
but he will win the Nobel prize for what was written up to
and including *Go Down, Moses,* and he will never write with
such power and sustained authority again. For Hemingway,
The Old Man and the Sea would be the last book he would
publish in his lifetime. In 1952, when Faulkner read and

reviewed Hemingway's book, both felt themselves, in their own fifties, enduring, hanging on, wondering whether they could write well again. Responding to her questions about Faulkner's review, Hemingway wrote Lillian Ross: "You ask if I know what he means. What he means is that he is spooked to die."[37] In those years, as Carlos Baker records, so was Hemingway.

Of the two works, Faulkner's is the richer, the more complex, the more rewarding. Stylistically, there is the same demanding reader-involvement, epistemologically significant incomplete information, and moving rhythms of the hunt. Chapter 4 of "The Bear" also encapsulates most Western history, and the whole work presents many of the primary emotions: desire, fear, anger, ambition, disgust. It uses the Bible, both in the allusions of the book's title, *Go Down, Moses*, and in chapter 4 of "The Bear" and in the Genesis-like genealogy of that same chapter. It also uses ritual – the ancient patterns of the hunt and of initiation, and Frazer's more modern highlighting of them. Though these patterns are obvious, they are never so baldly asserted as Hemingway's use of Christ's Passion. Cass's role, however, is unclear: is he meant as a foil for Isaac – a wise and practical role model whom Isaac repudiates when he repudiates the land? Or is he (like Ike himself) another of Faulkner's failed heroes, in this case one who raises his cousin well but not well enough to preserve Ike's social responsibility? Certainly Faulkner succeeds admirably in presenting Ike's conflicting desires to prevent the continuing abuses of slavery and of the wilderness, to preserve his lot, his identity, his honor, and his marriage – those truths, as Faulkner has called them, of "the human heart in conflict with itself." It is with regard to internal conflict that *The Old Man and the Sea* is especially lacking. (Whether Hemingway's style in this book is a return to the famous earlier style or a parody of it seems impossible to resolve.)

Though *The Old Man and the Sea* is a moving tribute to the human spirit and to dignity, it describes no internal conflict. Santiago, in this touching parable, represents puny man against the might of nature. But Santiago never seriously questions his task, never doubts whether he should fish, never debates at length whether he should have allowed Manolin to accompany him. When he does question himself – over his right to kill the fish—the results are maudlin. Without this dimension of human conflict—of the heart in conflict with itself – Hemingway's novella remains a parable.

On the other hand, although Faulkner said in his Nobel Prize acceptance speech that man will prevail, this optimistic note is not evident in Faulkner's fiction. Hemingway, though he resents man as inevitably doomed, as fated for destruction, shows his protagonists fighting fate: even as they suffer they establish man's dignity and capacity for love. In the two works in question, Santiago and the Ike of "Delta Autumn" are much alike, but the similarities should not be overstated. Aged, father to none but uncle to many, both men are noble failures. Ike failed to reconcile his natural and social inheritances, failed to find an effective way to repudiate his grandfather's sin and to help his black cousins; as a carpenter, his emulation of Jesus adds to the spoliation of the wood he loves. Dignified in old age, still more in touch with nature than anyone else around him, he has failed through lack of nerve, lack of courage, lack of commitment. Tennie's Jim's granddaughter excoriates him for forgetting in practice what he has said love means – sharing. Santiago also fails, but not through want of nerve or effort. In Hemingway's cosmology, what the gods grant, they also take away. Santiago catches his fish and has the evidence to prove it, even though his victory is only symbolic – in the skeleton of the fish and in his example of man's courage. But he knows – as Uncle Ike does not – that love involves sharing, and he shares his knowledge and himself with the boy who loves him.[38]

NOTES AND REFERENCES

1. Carlos Baker, *Ernest Hemingway: A Life Story*. New York: Scribner's, 1969. pp. 661, 532, 495, 503.

2. Baker, *Life Story*, pp. 297, 439.

3. Ernest Hemingway, *Death in the Afternoon*. New York: Scribner's, 1932. p. 173. On a drive with Bumby to Piggott, Arkansas, subsequent to the publication of *Death in the Afternoon*, Hemingway found himself in a hotel in Oxford, Mississippi. Realizing that he was on Faulkner's turf and the disparaging nature of his remarks, he sat up all night beside Bumby, guarding the door with a shotgun. See Baker, *Life Story*, p.605, amplified in "Faulkner : An Orientation, 1940" *Faulkner Studies*, 1 (1980), 10.

4. *New Yorker*, 5 November 1932, pp.74-75; reprinted in *Ernest Hemingway: Selected Letters, 1917-1961*. Ed. Carlos Baker. New York: Scribner's, 1981. pp. 368-69.

5. Hemingway, *Selected Letters*, p.604.

6. Baker, *Life Story*, pp.227, 534.

7. *Lion In the Garden: Interviews with William Faulkner*. Eds James B. Meriwether & Michael Millgate. New York: Random House, 1968. p.58.

8. Hemingway, *Selected Letters*, pp. 623-25.

9. *Selected Letters of William Faulkner*, Ed. Joseph Blotner. New York: Random House, 1977. pp.61, 203. Cf. *The Faulkner-Cowley File* by Malcolm Cowley. New York: Viking, 1966. pp.29, 32.

10. Cowley, *The Faulkner-Cowley File*, p.104. Cowley also talked Robert Linscott of Random House into having Hemingway write an introduction to a new edition of *Sanctuary*. Faulkner told Linscott no. See Cowley, *The Faulkner-Cowley File*, p.87; Faulkner, *Selected Letters*, pp.229-30.

11. William Faulkner, *Essays, Speeches, and Public Letters*,. Ed.James B. Meriwether. New York: Random House, 1965.p.210. The letter was published in *Time* on November 13, 1950. Since Faulkner first learned of the Nobel Prize on November 10 of that year, this letter must have been written before he knew of the award.

12. Faulkner, *Selected Letters*. pp. 333-34. Breit passed the letter on to Hemingway, who once more misread Faulkner and believed himself again insulted. See Baker, *Life Story*, p. 503.

13. Faulkner, *Essays*, p. 193.

14. Malcolm Cowley, ed. *The Portable Faulkner*. New York: Viking, 1946, 1967. p. ix.

15. William Faulkner, *The Wild Palms*. New York: Random House, 1939. pp. 97 and 263. I am indebted to Thomas J. McHaney's close study of the two authors, *William Faulkner's "The Wild Palms."* Jackson: University of Mississippi Press, 1976. pp.12-20. The critic who first noticed Faulkner's pun on Armour from "Snows" was Melvin Backman, "Faulkner's *The Wild Palms* : Civilization against Nature," *University of Kansas City Review*, 29 (Spring 1962), 199-204.

16. Faulkner, *Selected Letters*, p. 100.

17. McHaney, *"Faulkner's "The Wild Palms,"* p. 21. William Faulkner, *Pylon*. New York: Random House, 1935, p. 50 ; William Faulkner, *Requiem for a Nun*. New York: Random House, 1950, 51. pp. 154, 158, 159-60.

18. George Monteiro, "Between Grief and Nothing: Hemingway and Faulkner," *Hemingway Notes* 1 (Spring 1971), 13-15.

19. Cf. Peter L. Hays, "Hemingway, Faulkner and a Bicycle Built for Death," *NMAL*, 5 (Fall 1981), Item 28. See also Fred D. Crawford and Bruce Morton, "Hemingway and Brooks: The Mystery of 'Henry's Bicycle,'" *Studies in American Fiction* 6 (1978): 106-9.

20. John M. Howell, "Hemingway, Faulkner and 'The Bear,'" *American Literature* 53 (1980): 115-26.

21. Malcolm Cowley, —*And I Worked at the Writer's Trade*. New York: Viking, 1978. p. 6.

22. Cf. Cowley, *The Faulkner-Cowley File*, pp.159-60.

23. Hemingway, *Selected Letters*. p. xii.

24. David Minter, *William Faulkner: His Life and Work*. Baltimore: Johns Hopkins Press, 1980. p. 32 Cf. Meta Carpenter Wilde & Orin Borsten, *A Loving Gentleman* . New York: Simon &

Schuster, 1976.p. 46 ; John Faulkner, *My Brother Bill.* New York: Trident, 1963. p.138. John'Faulkner also records the presence of a family friend who taught law at the University of Mississippi when Bill was enrolled there after the war – one Judge Hemingway (pp. 144-45).

25. Ernest Hemingway, *A Farewell to Arms.* New York: Scribner's, 1929.p. 185. William Faulkner, *As I Lay Dying.* New York: Random House, 193˙0, 1964. p. 163.

26. Faulkner, *Essays,* p. 193.

27. Hemingway didn't think so. When Lillian Ross sent him Faulkner's review, he responded to her: "The Old Man in the story was born a Catholic in the island of Langa Rota in the Canary Islands. But he certainly believed in something more than the church and I do not think Mr. Faulkner understands it   very well" (Hemingway, *Selected Letters,* p. 807).

28. Cf. Claire Rosenfield, "New World, Old Myths," *Twentieth Century Interpretations of "The Old Man and the Sea,"* ed. Katherine T. Jobes. Englewood Cliffs: Prentice Hall, 1968, pp. 42-44.

29. Ernest Hemingway, *For Whom the Bell Tolls.* New York: Scribner's, 1940. pp. 39-41.

30. William Faulkner, *Go Down, Moses.* New York: Random House, 1942. pp. 193-94, 210. All subsequent quotations from this work will refer to this edition and will be in parentheses in my text.

31. Ernest Hemingway, *The Old Man and the Sea.* New York: Scribner's, 1952. pp. 54, 59, 75, 95. All subsequent quotations from this work will refer to this edition and will be in parentheses in my text. See 'he discussion by Herbert Wilner, "Aspects of American Fiction: A Whale, a Bear, a Marlin," *Americana-Austriaca.* Ed. Klaus Lanzinger. Vienna: Wilhelm Braunmuller, 1966. p. 235.

32. *The Oxford Annotated Bible,* Ed. Herbert May and Bruce Metzger. New York: Oxford University Press, 1965. p. 45n.

33. Claude Levi-Strauss, *Totemism,* trans. Rodney Needham (Boston: Beacon, 1963) defines nigouimes on p.18. For initiation ceremonies, see The Encyclopedia of Religion and Ethics, ed. James Hastings. New York: Scribner's, 1961. vol.12, p. 405; and J.G. Frazer, Totemism and

Exogamy. London: Macmillan, 1910. vol.1.pp. 49-51. See also Francis Parkman, *The Jesuits in North America.* Boston: Little, Brown, 1895. pp. lxviii-lxxi.

34.   Cf. Arvin R. Wells, "A Ritual of Transformation: *The Old Man and the Sea*," originally printed in *University Review*, 30 (winter 1963): 95-101, reprinted in Jobes, *Twentieth-Century Interpretations*, pp. 56-63.

35.   This device of contrasts between initiates and outsiders is of course not new to *The Old Man and the Sea* and not dependent on Faulkner : Hemingway had used it in *The Sun Also Rises*, if not even earlier in "Indian Camp."

36.   Cf. Clinton S. Burhans, Jr., "*The Old Man and the Sea*: Hemingway's Tragic Vision of Man," *American Literature* 31 (1960): 451-52.

37.   Hemingway, *Selected Letters*, p.807.

38.   I am indebted to my colleague Karl Zender for many helpful suggestions regarding Faulkner.

The Old Man and the Sea and Riders to the Sea : An Inter-textual Encounter

Dipendu Chakrabarti

'A man can be destroyed but not defeated'

'No man at all can be living, for ever, and we must be satisfied.'

If Hemingway's novella *The Old Man and The Sea* and Synge's one-act play *Riders to the Sea* are juxtaposed one is at once struck for an inter-textual encounter that turns out to be mutually illuminating. The two texts challenge each other at so many levels, yet at the end they look like two supplementary angles for mapping the site of humankind's age-old struggle with nature. One critiques the other in so far as the contentions issues of gender, race, subjectivity and community are concerned. Neverthelesss, inspite of their mutually exclusive positions, they both gradually move towards a common perception of the primordial pattern of human vulnerbility vis-a-vis forces which are beyond human comprehension.

Such an encounter between two texts with thematic proximity may be conducted by the readers in terms of influence it there is any historical evidence to support it, as in the case of Flaubert's *Madame Bovary* and Tolstoy's *Anna Karenina*. But it would be difficult to prove that Hemingway in his novella tried consciously to appropriate Synge's text, as Bertolt Brecht did in his play *Senora Carrar's Rifles*; Brecht, of course, put upside down the story of a bereaved mother's acquiescence to fate. Such an inversion caused by an avowedly authorial intention makes the relation between two texts permanently antithetical. The

two texts I am dealing with—Hemingway's and Synge's—
cannot relate to each other either in terms of influence or
in terms of reaction.

Sometimes one text may act as a parodist in relation
to another, as we see *Waiting for Godot* parodying the theme
of waiting for God in *Murder in the Cathedral.* Hemingway's
The Old Man and The Sea neither negates nor neutralizes
the thematic concern of Synge's *Riders to the Sea* in a way
that suggests a parodic intention. As a matter of fact their
thematic affinity is just concidental, and because their
perspectives are different, they begin to interrogate each
other when placed side by side. How the sea affects the
people living in the coastal areas and how the sea functions
like fate when an individual interacts with the sea—both
the texts pursue this theme from two different
perspectives—male and female. *Riders to the Sea,* in spite
of its title is essentially concerned with a feminine
experience—a woman's response to the loss of her husband
and sons. 'The Old Woman and the Sea' would be a more
suitable title for the play.

Hemingway's novella not only adopts a male
perspective but also offers an exclusively male world. In
Synge's play female identity is, of course, represented as
passive and docile : women depend totally on men who risk
their lives to feed their families.The text does not raise
questions about this female identity as defined by
patriarchy, since the feminine experience at the heart of
the play does not lead to a feminist critique. Synge is simply
concerned with the kind of feminine response which is
inevitable in a community of peasants and fishermen in a
specific historical context. *The Old Man and The Sea* also
deals with the fisher folk who practice the classic division
of labour—men go out for fishing while women work at
home. But Hemingway does not represent men and women
working in their respective spheres and claiming equally
authorial attention. Exclusion, not passivity, of women is
what shapes the world of *The Old Man and the Sea.*

If *Riders to The Sea* were written from the point of
view of the riders, that is, the menfolk, it would have ended
with the message that man may be destroyed but he cannot

be defeated. For Bartley, disregarding his mother's protests, takes the hazardous journey to the sea that is not basically different from Santiago's plan to catch another big fish after his defeat. Had *The Old Man and the Sea* been written from the point of view of Santiago's wife, we would have got the reverse side of the story of a lonely man who defines his identity only in terms of personal success or failure. It is just an accident that Santiago has lost his wife, and it is just a matter of luck that he comes back alive from his solitary fishing expedition at sea. Let as reverse the course of events and we shall see Santiago's wife, like Maurya, lamenting the death of her husband. The novella, then, would have been called *The Old Women and the Sea.* This is not just idle speculation encouraged by irresponsible playing with the two texts. This is rather like an exchange of arguments between two interlocutors, each trying to expose what the other is lacking by offering an alternative perspective. Hemingway's text when placed against Synge's challenges the exclusion of a male point of view : as a result the experience of menfolk struggling with the malevolent sea has been left out in *Riders to the Sea.* What we have instead is the agonised waiting of the three women— Cathleen, Nora and Maurya—for the disaster that would strike them. Synge's text similarly challenges Hemingway's privileging of the male discourse which puts under erasure the female voice.

Santiago even at his age displays a physical stamina befitting the heroic image of the male. The graphic description of how he fights with his injured hands only confirms this idealised construct. He recalls time and time again great DiMaggio's physical strength and wishes to emulate him. If DiMaggio can do all things perfectly with the pain of the bone spur in his heel, Santiago, too can win the game at sea with his injured hands and say 'But I with show him what a man can do and what a man endures'. Even his dreams throw up images of male power represented by the African lions. It should be noted that when Santiago is in his shack, that is, on the land, he is usually seen lying down like a typical weak old man, ready to be looked after by a boy. Essentially a creature of the sea, on land he behaves like a fish out of water, but when he goes out into the sea on a fishing boat he acquires superhuman energy. To him life of land means doing nothing—an unbearable passivity ; but the sea rouses the male in him and the sea is imagined to be a woman. The sea is also a stage for an exhibition match between a man and a beast. Santiago knows quite well that 'man is not much beside the great birds and beasts' ; still he must accept the challenge thrown by 'the beast down there in the darkness of the sea'. Like the bullfight, a favourite game and a metaphor in Hemingway's fictive world, Santiago's fight with the fish and then with the sharks valorizes a concept of heroism that is not applicable to all men, let alone women. He is exceptional even in his own community—a man without a family, a man who is perpetually out of luck, a man who is old but more ambtious and more adventurous than a young man. What is a practical question of livelihood for his fellow fishermen becomes the pursuit of a heroic model for Santiago, and this would be passed on to Manolin the boy whom Santiago has trained, ensuring a continuity of the male heroic traditon. The menfolk in *Riders to the Sea* die for the sake of their family yet their sacrifice is not presented as heroic ; it is the women who show a power of endurance in times of disaster that turus out to be heroic. Maurya, the protagonist, is not an exceptional case of infinite capacity for suffering and endurance. There are women in her community who have met with similar fate and there will be other women, who 'will be keening'. Maurya, thus, represents a community, but Santiago remains a unique individual. Because he has no family to look after, he can desperately pursue his ambition. He has removed the photo of his dead wife from the wall because he feels too lonely to look at it. This deliberate effacement of the memory of a woman is like a preconditon for the exclusivity of the male world Santiago inhabits. He thinks of DiMaggio and his only companion is a boy. Even the fish he kills is a male and calls him 'brother': 'He took the bait like a male and he pulls like a male and his fight has no panic in it.' It is Hemingway's familiar world of men without women in which Santiago feels at home, and for this reason he cannot be a representative of his community. The only glimpse of a woman permitted at the end of the novella is a tourist who does not belong to his folk and fails to tell a fish from a shark. It is only symbolically that the female is allowed to enter the text : the sea is conceived as a woman: 'The moon affects her as it does a woman, he thought'. The sea like a woman shows a streak of whimsicality in giving or withholding great favours.

The sea in Synge's play can also be seen as a woman, since she enjoy torturing the women on land by snatching away the male members of their family. When Maurya cries out, 'They're all gone now, and there is not anything more the sea can do to me...' her sense of personal rivalry seems to underscore this feminization of the sea. Like the sea in the Hemingway-text, the sea here has by implication a dual role—a source of sustenance and a force of destruction. That is why people in Aron islands cannot think of migrating to a safer place far away from the sea.

In the Hemingway-text the sea is not just a background but the centre of action—a battlefield where killing is a biological necessity. 'Everything kills everything else in some way,'— the principle of mutual violence which is a law of nature is thus presented in terms of food chain. But Santiago is a man and as a man he has a consciousness that raises him above this level of biological compulsion. Which is why he becomes sympathetic to the fish he is going to kill. In fact, Santiago while fishing at sea speaks sometimes as Everyman when he meditates on man and the beasts. He is, then, no longer a unique individual, 'a strange old man', an outsider in his own community ; he becomes a spokesman for mankind, as he says, 'And pain does not matter to a man?' or 'A man is never lost at sea!'

Maurya is universalised as a mother figure. Santiago is also a father figure to Manolin, but this particular role has no scope in the text for further development. Maurya and Santiago share the infirmities of old age; but as an old woman she is not taken seriously by her daughters and son. Santiago has seen spared this sense of isolation in

the family, since he has no family. He has been more lucky
than Maurya in more than one way. His surrogate son
Manolin has proved more dutiful than he expected. Besides,
he lives in that part of Cuba that is technologically more
advanced than Aron islands. 'The glow of Havana', the rich
fishermen having 'radios to talk to then in their boats', an
aeroplane passing overhead 'on its course to Miami'—all
this makes an appropriate background for Santiago's
determination to be in command in the aquatic world.
Cultural differences determined by historical and
geographical forces account for the different responses of
the protagonists of the two texts. But at a deeper level they
share a common perception of the mediation of
supernatural forces. Inhabitants of the Aran islands
inherited a whole set of beliefs in the supernatural. The
ghost of Michael riding a grey pony behind Bartley, as seen
by Maurya, suggest a predetermined scheme of things that
human willpower cannot change. Santiago, more rational
and knowlegeable, has no such superstitious obsession.
He is not religious, but cannot help praying to Mother of
God and even promises to make a pilgrimage to the Virgin
de Cobre 'if I catch him'. But his prayer gives him more
confidence and strength. His acknowledgement of the
supernatural intervention is borne out by the frequent use
of the words 'luck' and 'lucky' :

'We were born lucky'

'It is better to be lucky'

'No, I am not lucky. I am not lucky any more!
Santiago starts as 'salao' and maybe said to end up as 'salao'
in spite of his heroic success in catching a big fish. His
success as a fisherman, however is nullified by the sharks
who seem to function as agents to fate in the same way as
the horses do in *Riders to the Sea.*

Santiago's final plan to go out fishing with Manolin
is usually seen as a gesture of his invincible spirit. But its
inferent ambiguity is often overlooked. It is Manolin who
first suggests this joint venture to go out to the sea to catch
a bigger fish, and Santiago's consent may be seen as
nothing but an attempt to please the boy who has done so
much for him. *The Old Man and the Sea* ends, not with a

dream of a more adventurous fishing expedition, but with a dream of the African lions. Since the lions are not aquatic animals the question we face is : Does Santiago turn his back on the sea and wish for a display of his prowess on land? The dream can symbolically prove that Santiago is destroyed, but not defeated. At the same time we cannot deny that a dream may not translate into reality. Next time Santiago would be older and weaker, and there is no guarantee that the sharks would not spoil his chances of the glory he aspires to. In his sleep he can transcend reality, but before he drifts off to sleep he has to accept his failure: 'I am not lucky any more'. This admission of continuous failure designed by fate brings Santiago closer to Maurya. The only satisfaction he can have now is that he has done his best to achieve his objective and this is what maintains his dignity. Maurya, too, after a prolonged period of keening becomes calm and silent and achieves a new sense of dignity by accepting what is inevitable. *Riders to the Sea* is more often than not compared with Greek tragedies; *The Old Man and the Sea*, I think, is closer to the Greek model in its portrayal of the conflict between mau and his fate. But the invocation of the Greek concept of tragedy is irrelevant in both the cases. Given her social background and cultural parameters, Maurya can only be a passive sufferer, which is the lot of the poor people in all the ages. Santiago is locked in a combat with his fate like a bullfighter fighting with a bull. The conflict between man and fate is thus given the shape of an athletic match, which the Greeks would not have appreciated. Maurya's passivity and Santiago's activism are best understood in relation to their race, gender and historical context which force the two texts interrogate each other from two different perspectives. Such a mutual interrogation, however, leads the two texts beyond the domain of familiar binaries (man/ woman, Irish/Cuban, backward/advanced) to a shared awareness of humankind's need for dignity in a losing battle with the forces which neither women nor men can comprehend fully.

Note : All quotations are from *The Old Man and the Sea*. (Harper Collins Publishers, India) and from *Riders to the Sea* (O.U.P.)

The Old Man and the Sea in the Light of Rasa Theory: An Indian Reading of Hemingway

Priyadarshi Patnaik

The Theoretical Background

In this paper, I wish to read *The Old Man and the Sea* in the light of the *Rasa* theory – a very significant reading tradition in ancient Indian aesthetics. The theory, expounded for the first time in the *Natya Sastra* of Bharata (1st to 4th century) emphasises the fact that "without rasa there can be no drama" (*Natya Sastra*, Book IV, verse 31). This statement is to be taken in the light of the fact that the *Natya Sastra* discusses elaborately other significant issues of literary language like *alamkaras* (figures of speech), *dosas* (faults) and *gunas* (good qualities). What is implicit in the statement is the fact that for all these above mentioned components, a literary work does not achieve completion or merit unless it contains the elements of *rasa* and results in the *rasa* experience.

Rasa, which can be roughly translated as aesthetic emotion or rapture, was dominated by the other schools of aesthetics like that of *alamkarikas*, *vakroktivadins* (dealing with indirections of language), *achutavadins* (dealing with appropriateness), etc., till the 10th-11th century. Then, the advent of two significant Kashmir aestheticians, Anandavardhana and Abhinavagupta, changed things. Anandavardhana, from a linguistic stand point, showed that literary language signifies at three levels – at the level of denotation (*abhidha*), indication (*lakshna*) and suggestion (*vyanjana* or *dhvanim*). To his mind, a literary work that made use of suggestion was of the greatest literary merit. Abhinavagupta, who commented on both Bharata and

Anandavardhana, applied the concept of suggestive meaning (*dhvani*) to the *Rasa* theory of Bharata, where he fit it in brilliantly. Since then the *Rasa* theory has become the most popular and accepted theory of Indian aesthetics.

But what is *Rasa* theory? According to Bharata, it is from a combination of *bhavas* (in the work) that *rasa* arises. *Bhavas* can be roughly translated as psycho-physiological states in a person and are of three kinds – *sthayibhava, vyabhichari* or *sancharibhava*, and *sattvikabhavas*. *Sthayibhavas* can broadly be said to be stable or permanent states that persist through or dominate a work. In other words they set the mood(s) of the work – angry, sad, terrifying, etc. The various transitory or fleeting states are generated along with them – *sancharibhavas*. In fact, the audience, on observing these indications infers the *bhava*. It is thus that suggestion (*dhvani*) becomes significant in *rasa* realisation. The *sancharibhavas* can be manifest as panic, fear, trembling, anger, paralysis, stuttering, etc. Within the work, there must be a cause that generates such emotions. These causes are the *bibhavas*. For instance, a tiger in a forest would generate fear. The tiger is the *bibhava* (cause) of fear (*sthayibhava*) which is accompanied by trembling, stuttering, tremor, etc (*sancharibhavas*). According to tradition, the *rasas* are nine in number, dealing with nine broad emotions[1]: *srngara* (love), *hasya* (comic), *karuna* (sorrow), *raudra* (fury), *vira* (heroic), *bhayanaka* (terrifying), *bibhatsa* (disgusting), *adbhuta* (wonderous) and *santa* (peaceful).

A literary or dramatic work might contain one or many of these, but finally, only one of these must dominate the work and lead to a point of culmination that is experienced by the audience or reader as a *rasa* experience. The theory is significant, thus, from the modern context since it takes into cognisance the various factors that constitute a text starting from the writer and his genius (*pratibha*) to the reader and his reading experience that might finally culminate in *ananda* (bliss). Besides, the successful generation of emotion in and by the work – which bring in the notion of subjectivity and reading conventions – is also highlighted.

In this paper, I wish to highlight a reader's response to a work (here, *The Old Man and the Sea*) from within a theory that takes into account the reader's personality, his tradition as well as his training. Thus, this culture and context-specific theory, when used in a traditional way to a modern Western work results in a typically Indian and even spiritual reading of *The Old Man and the Sea*.

According to Abhinavagupta, be it poetry or play, the experience of the reader must be such that one feels that things are happening "before our very eyes" (*Aesthetic Rapture*, Vol.II, p.71). This points to the degree of involvement that is expected from the reader or audience. But the reader or audience is not to be taken as an unknown or untrained quantity. Reading traditions, in ancient India, were traditions controlled, regulated and sustained by conventions and practices. Only then could one hope to have consistent meanings and consistent readings. In philosophical discourse of ancient India, subjectivity was generally not encouraged. Besides, for the clarity and orderliness of a literary theory, innumerable interpretations (or misinterpretations) could not be encouraged. But most important, in ordinary communication, where the writer/speaker wants to communicate a specific thing to the reader/hearer all interpretations save one, all understanding expect what is intended cease to be meaningful in that framework. It is here that the ideal reader comes in – the one who is trained in convention, the one who is the best person to understand what is intended.

Convention, here, plays an important role because it is only through conventions that communication, however incomplete, is possible. A convention assumes that certain things are to be understood in certain ways. "The acting out of the various *bhavas*" - *bibhavas* and *anubhavas* - refer to the manifestation or suggestion of emotion through words, expressions and gestures (described) which are culturally accepted. For a reader, to translate these various gestures and expressions into meaning, training in the convention of language is necessary.

Bharata, in *Natya Sastra* uses the expression *sumana*

to talk of such a reader or audience. *Sumana* is a conjunction of *suddha* (pure) *mana* (mind). Though literally it simply means, "healthy minded," Abhinavagupta seems to have interpreted it in the first sense. Here, we become aware of the reader as a subjective entity. *Sumana* assumes a stage when the mind is not unhealthy and polluted. By what? — emotions. About this Abhinavagupta writes:

> With a mind that is completely free from any kind of obstruction from any sense organ (i.e., completely controlled) because they are completely absorbed in the thrill of imaginative experience. . . . (*Aesthetic Rapture*, Vol.I, p.47.)

In other words, nothing must come between the text and the reader - neither external disturbances nor the personal memories and experiences of the reader. Abhinavagupta later explains this further in the concept of the ideal reader - *sahrdaya* (the sympathetic perceiver) in *Abhinavabharati*:

> . . . these people who are capable of identifying with the subject-matter, since the mirror of their hearts have been polished through constant recitation and study of poetry, and who sympathetically respond in their own hearts are known as sympathetic readers. (*Aesthetic Rapture* Vol.I, p.6.)

"Identification" with the text involves an Eliotian "escape from one's personality." The personality must not come in the way. As in *Yoga*, here the five senses distract actively through outside influence and latently through memory. In a reading experience, these must be brought under control through practice, as is done in *Yoga*. And this is possible only through training and practice.

In this practice of reading or interpreting, two significant concepts are used by the *rasavadins*. The first one is known as *samskara* – the socio-cultural convention. This has already been discussed. The other one is *vasana* -- latent emotions, tendencies of past life, unconscious memory. The first component takes care of the socio-cultural dimension of reading. But it is the second component, vasana, that answers questions about individual differences in not only understanding, but also in enjoyment. According to the *Rasavadin* interpretative tradition, in spite of individual differences, the ideal readers who get involved in the work savour similar tastes or experiences. And all successful readings finally lead to a transcendence of ordinary emotions to *ananda*.

Thus, in *Rasa* theory it is this emotional content that emerges into its own. *Rasa*, relish, enjoyment, pleasure, delight suddenly question the all importance of the text. The text loses its rigid boundaries, enters into the space in the mind of man, interacts in and with his living, and suddenly the reader is seen in a different light. He is no more a secondary neglectible component who can be forgotten. In the reader the text and its author attain culmination. What emerges is not a reader, not a text but the sheer pleasure of an experience - *ananda*. It is for this reason that *Rasa* theory has not only to talk about the reader, it has also to talk about an ideal reader; subjectivity here is assumed as is objectivity in most other theories.

Bharata says (*Natya Sastra*, VI, 31):

> As gourmets (*sumanas*) are able to savour the flavour of food prepared with many spices, and attain pleasure . . . so sensitive spectators (*sumanas*) savour the primary emotions (*bhavas*) suggested by the acting out of the various *bhavas* and modulation of voices, movement of body and display of involuntary reactions, and attain pleasure . . . . (*Aesthetic Rapture*, Vol.I, pp.44-47)

Both food and text involve an interpretation; whether the product is enjoyable or not and the reasons for such a feeling. The moment we talk about *sumana* (gourmet/ideal reader) we accept the possibility of a taster of food or literature who is not the ideal. In other words, we see scope for many interpretations only one of which can be declared (according to tradition and trying to keep the writer's intention in mind) to be the ideal. Reading and misreading, both, are thus acknowledged.

But beyond all that, what is implicitly acknowledged in the concept of *ananda* is that all reading or viewing experiences aim at a transcendence – of one's own identity, one's world, one's differences. Analysis must be transcended in favour of experience, an experience that can be shared. This is beautifully brought out where Abhinavagupta says that all *rasas* finally culminate in *santa rasa* and all *rasa* becomes one indescribable *ananda* or aesthetic ecstasy – almost like a momentary *brahman* realization (*Santa Rasa*, p.142).

An Indian Reading of *The Old Man and the Sea*

The Old Man and the Sea, according to the *Rasa* theory would be centrally about the emotions related to courage and wonder generated by such courage. Thus, here we will look at *The Old Man and the Sea* from the point of view of vira *rasa* (the heroic *rasa*), its accompanying emotion of *utsaha* (energy), and its culmination in *adbhuta rasa* (wonder). But as we have discussed, each rasa, when extended to its limit culminates in the *santa rasa* (peace). *The Old Man and the Sea* justifies this claim comprehensively.

The novella often considered Ernest Hemingway's best and most lyrical work, has an almost universal appeal largely due to its apparently simple style and theme. In the Western context both religious and epic aspects of the text are highlighted to emphasise its popularity.   But according to the *Rasa* theory, the success of the text can be ascribed to the successful realisation of *Vira rasa* and the transcendence of that emotion to the attainment of *Santa rasa*.

According to *Natya Sastra*, prior to the state of *rasa* being achieved, an intermediary state is to be seen - the *sthayibhava* (permanent/stable state) which pervades the work. The features listed under *vira rasa* are very interesting (at least from a Western point of view) since they indicate qualities such as valour, humility, courage, patience, endurance etc., all together. It is thus, in an

Indian context, that heroism can not only be related to physical conquests and courage, but to spiritual as well. In the Indian tradition, *vira* has always been an important *rasa*. In both the epics, where we see a lot of war and heroic action, it is to be found. Besides, in many of the plays of the Sanskrit dramatist, Bhasa (A.D.,fourth century), they prevail. *Vira* as endurance, in Indian literature, can be epitomised in two supreme examples, first, in the episode of Karnasena's endurance of pain in *The Mahabharata* and secondly, in the story of Raja Hariscandra[2].

In *The Mahabharata* when Karna (the sixth and the identitiless Pandava) goes to learn war skills from the great Brahmin master Parsurama, one day Parsurama, after a tiring day lays his head on Karna's lap and takes rest. At that time an insect starts biting Karna's leg. Although in agony, Karna does not even budge, afraid that his Guru's rest might get disturbed. It is only when the blood from his wound flows up to Parsurama's head that Parsurama wakes up[3].

In case of Raja Hariscandra, it is the test of the endurance of suffering - at a psychological, moral and metaphysical plane. Considered a great giver (he gives away whatever one asks for) one day Hariscandra is tested by the gods. Indra sends the sage, Viswamitra who asks for his kingdom, his wealth, and even, finally for his removal from his own kingdom. When the sage asks for *danadakshina* Hariscandra has nothing else to give. So he sells his wife and son, and with that money gives the *danadakshina*. In another country, in the end Hariscandra lives as a *chandala* (one who burns the dead). When his son dies of snakebite and his wife brings the body to the crematorium, Hariscandra unable to recognise them asks his wife for money for the burial. And then he realises who it is. At that moment his total world collapses. But still he never complains. Once this supreme test is over, the gods restore everything back to him.

In both these examples, what comes out most prominent is endurance. But what is it that makes one endure? - conviction, steadfastness, a sense of purpose. In *The Old Man and the Sea* we see all these qualities. In fact, as we read it, we are reminded again and again of the passage in the *Natya Sastra* describing *vira rasa*:

> *Virarasa* is a dynamic energy (*utsaha*) which arises from various causal factors (*arthavsesa*) such as decisiveness, not giving way to depression, not being surprised or confused. (*Aesthetic Rapture*, Vol. I, p.54).

"Decisiveness," "not being surprised" and "not giving way to depression" briefly sum up the attitude of the old man all though the novel. Santiago, an old fisherman, is a veteran fighter and is prepared for anything. All his life he has caught big fish and in all his lonely battles out in the deep see with the big fish, he has won. In that he is like an undefeated warrior. But then comes a long period of no luck when he catches nothing. But he never gives up hope.

> He was an old man who fished alone in a skiff in the Gulf Stream and he had gone eighty-four days now without taking a fish. In the first forty days a boy had been with him. But after forty days without fish the boy's parents had told him that the old man was definitely and finally *salao*, which is the worst form of unlucky . . . . It made the boy sad to see the old man come in each day with his skiff empty . . . . (*The Old Man and the Sea*, p.5)

When the old man endures two long days of battle with the marlin, it is sheer physical endurance. But when the old man loses his fish to the sharks, what he endures in not merely physical. When the old man is taking his big fish home, the sharks are waiting. Knowing that there is a battle to come the old man says:

> "Don't think, old man," . . . . "Sail on this course and take it when it comes." (*The Old Man and the Sea*, 103)

And a little later when the suffering comes in the form of sharks that tear his fish apart:

> "*Ay*," he said aloud. There is no translation for this word and perhaps it is just a noise such as a man might make, involuntarily, feeling the nail go through his hands and into the wood. (*The Old Man and the Sea*, 107)

The implication of suffering here at a more than physical or emotional plane is intensified by the crucifixion imagery present in the description. For that matter, moral and physical endurances cannot be separated. They stem from the same root. But we can speak of moral or physical endurance in terms of degrees.

In the *Natya Sastra* it is said (VI.97):

> *Virarasa* is properly acted out by firmness, patience, heroism, pride, dynamic energy (*utsaha*),bravery, might, and profound emotions. (*Aesthetic Rapture*, Vol.I, 54)

These are the qualities that a character manifests in *vira rasa*. "Heroism" and "pride" are related. In fact, pride can often manifest itself as "arrogance" and in that case would not be "heroism" anymore. The "pride" indicated here is the pride at one's skill, a pride that is necessary for self-esteem. The pride of the old man is such - it is born of faith in oneself and paradoxically is integrated with humility:

> He was too simple to wonder when he had attained humility. But he knew he had attained it and he knew it was not disgraceful and it carried no loss of true pride. (*The Old Man and the Sea*, 10)

But the key words here are "firmness" and "patience." It is these that are usually not recognized as of primary importance in any heroic act. But they are so, for without them one will act rashly. "Firmness" indicates a steadiness of purpose and a "conviction" that one's action is right. And "patience" later can lead to humility. Both these aspects are amply evinced in the old man. His ceaseless struggle with the fish, his strong determination to catch it indicate his firmness. And from his patience, he learns much more than mere skill. He learns humility.

The Natya Sastra (VI.66) says:

> Now (the *rasa*) called *vira* has (only) noble people for its characters and consists in dynamic energy (*utsaha*). (*Aesthetic Rapture*, Vol.I, 54)

But the "nobility" of the character need not necessarily be determined by birth. What determines nobility is the action. In *The Mahabharata*, Karna, for all purposes is the son of a charioteer. Ekalabya, the only disciple of Dronacharya who could equal Arjun, is a tribal boy. Thus, the fact that Santiago is a common fisherman does not diminish his nobility in any way. It is his action that determines what he is.

Utsaha or dynamic energy is the *sthayibhava* or the primary state of *vira rasa*. In other words, without the enthusiasm or the "dynamic energy" - however prudent or insightful or calm one is - one cannot act. Thus, this positive state of excitement is at the root of any action, or even "patience" that causes a courageous act (or waiting). It is this frame of mind that is indicated at the beginning of the novella when the author says that the old man had gone eighty-four days without catching a fish. Yet, at the worst phase of his lucklessness he is in a positive frame:

> Everything about him was old except his eyes and they were the same colour as the sea and were cheerful and undefeated. (*The Old Man and the Sea*, 6)

Of the relation of *rasas*, the *Natya Sastra* (VI.39) says:

> The awesome (*adbhuta rasa*) comes from the heroic (*vira rasa*). . . . (*Aesthetic Rapture*, Vol.I, 48)

In *vira* the response is that of *adbhuta* or wonder. In the audience or reader, there can be the dual response of courage and wonder. If the heroic acts are unachievable they lead to a response of wonder. This is a response, where distancing is involves. But if it is the heroism of a common man (someone with whom we can identify) then both sympathy and identity will operate. Thus, here is the possibility of inspired courage. In this instance, the boy, Manoloine, is the subject that is affected with wonder at the old man's skills and achievements.

Coming back to the problem of "patience," one might ask, how can patience (which involves no action but a stasis) lead to *vira*? For one thing, as here, patience is what determines the right moment to strike. Thus, valour without prudence will lead only to disaster. But even otherwise, the very act of patience, of waiting, against all despairs, is an act of courage. An illustration is the way the old man waits patiently for eighty-four days without a fish.

The causes or the *vibhavas* of *vira* are the following (*Natya Sastra*, VI.66):

Correct perception, decisiveness (*adhyavasaya*), political wisdom (*naya*), courtesy (*vinaya*). an army (*bala*), eminence (*pratibha*), etc. (*Aesthetic Rapture*, Vol.I, 54)

"Correct perception" is at the root of any positive act. If it is not there, even in the face of challenge, one might act rashly. In other words, it is "correct perception" only that can lead to any decisive (and positive) action. *Naya* has been translated as "political wisdom." The word also implies goodness and a sense of justice. Thus, when one is good and just, it leads to "correct perception" and thus to right action. This is important from our point of view since "correct perception" also holds the key to any spiritual seeking. In *The Old Man and the Sea*, fishing is the old man's livelihood. It is his *dharma*, his life. The old man kills not for pride, but for making a living. Thus, it is the right way to act for him - a fisherman must fish. Yet he loves the fish, calls it his brother. And when the sharks attack he thinks:

> I am sorry I killed the fish . . . (*The Old Man and the Sea*, 103)

"Bravery in battle," "courage," etc., are inner qualities that lead to or cause heroic action. But "courtesy" or *vinaya* is a little problematic. *Vinaya* also means humility. We can understand it as an accompanying state of *vira rasa*. In fact, in *The Old Man and the Sea*, in the end the old man learns humility of a higher order. In that transcendence, Santiago becomes the true warrior. For in the end when he admits he was beaten:

> "They beat me, Manolin," he said. "They truly beat me." (*The Old Man and the Sea*, 124)

There is no sense of defeat or despair in it – just a statement of act. And when Manolin points out that the fish never beat him, it was the sharks, his acknowledgement of this fact also has no pride in it:

> "*He* didn't beat you. Not the fish"
> "No, Truly. It was afterwards." (*The Old Man and the Sea*, 125)

Bala can mean both "an army" and also "power." *Sakti* similarly can mean both "skill in battle" as well as "strength." These give one confidence in oneself and thus can lead to heroic action in the face of necessity. These qualities are amply evidenced in the novella and need no discussion.

The *Natya Sastra* (VI.66) tells us that *vira*:

> . . . should be acted out by such *anubhavas* as firmness, patience, heroism, generosity and shrewdness (*vaisaradya*). (*Aesthetic Rapture*, Vol.I, 54)

The manifestations or effects of *vira rasa* should depict such qualities as mentioned above. We have already discussed "firmness" and "patience." "Heroism" is a rather vague categorization that includes valour, courage, correct perception etc.

Though the element of sadness (*karuna*) is innate here, what we notice is the old man's stubborn "patience." This is one element that we have been trying to highlight right from the beginning. For it is usually something that is not associated with heroism. Or if at all it is mentioned, it never is given the kind of priority it finds in the *Natya Sastra*. In *The Old Man and the Sea*, interestingly, it is this aspect which comes out most sharply. Even when the boy is gone and he is alone, he still continues with his efforts. When the narrative begins, he is going out for the eighty-fifth time, without a fish. This single-minded and dogged determination becomes more clear as the narrative proceeds:

The old man is battle-scarred and there are marks of sea-battles (with fishes) upon him

. . . his hands had deep-creased scars from handling heavy fish on the cords. But none of these scars were fresh. They were as old as erosions in a fishless desert.
Everything about him was old except his eyes . . . .
(*The Old Man and the Sea*, 5-6)

Thus, we have the picture of a warrior who has nerves of steel. The *sthayibhava* or the primary state of dynamic energy is always present. Even after eighty-four days out of luck, his eyes are still undefeated. It is perhaps his long experience that has made him overcome anger. Thus, in his action there is always control, and never anger, not even when he is ridiculed:

They sat on the Terrace and many of the fishermen made fun of the old man and he was not angry. (*The Old Man and the Sea*, 7)

Thus he has learnt the essence of heroism: "humility" and

"forgiveness":

> . . . he knew he had attained it and he knew it was
> not disgraceful and it carried no loss of true pride.
> (*The Old Man and the Sea*, 9-10)

Yet, even this is to be tested at the end, when the ordeal is over. The old man's conviction, that he can never be beaten, is "defeated". But this does not "destroy" the old man. He accepts the fact that he is beaten as courageously; and it is here that the "humility" of a true warrior sees him through. At the end he is absolutely unaffected. He is not truly beaten for he can still go on dreaming about the lions (*The Old Man and the Sea*, 127).

A very important element that is the response to *vira* - the response of *adbhuta* - is to be found in the reaction of the boy (Manolin) who considers Santiago the best fisherman in the world:

> "There are many good fishermen and some great
> ones. But there is only you."
> "Thank you. You make me happy. I hope no fish will
> come along so great that he will prove us wrong. (*The
> Old Man and the Sea*, 19-20)

But actually such a big marlin does come along and challenges the old man. On the eighty-fifth day, the old man goes deep into the sear and there a fish takes the bait on one of his lines - a huge marlin, as the old man comes to know in good time. From now on it is a battle of courage, intelligence and patience. What the fish tries to do then is to run the old man out of courage and patience. It does not come out until almost the very end, and hence the old man has no way of knowing how big he really is. Thus, the battle turns slowly into a test of patience and endurance, a war of attrition:

> He held the line against his back and watched its
> slant in the water and the skiff moved steadily to the
> north-west.

> This will kill him, the old man thought. He can't do this for ever. But four hours later the fish was still swimming steadily out to sea . . . (*The Old Man and the Sea*, 43)

In this battle an entire day and a night pass and now it becomes a battle of sheer will and endurance: for neither is ready to give up:

> "Fish," he said softly, aloud, "I'll stay with you until I am dead." (*The Old Man and the Sea*, 50)

In this there is an absolute steadfastness of purpose. There is no question of turning back. An interesting point to be noted is that the old man is very sensitive about weaknesses. When his left hand cramps he says:

> "What kind of a hand is that," . . . . . "Cramp then if you want. Make yourself into a claw. It will do you no good." (*The Old Man and the Sea*, 56)

Thus any kind of weakness, indecisiveness etc., is inimical to *vira* or the heroic emotion. As the day progresses, finally the fish comes out and the old man kills him, but that is not the end of his ordeal. On his way back the sharks attack his fish which is tied to the side of his skiff. They come large numbers and he fights them with his harpoon, and when it is gone, with a knife and then with the tiller. But in the night they eat away most of his great fish. Despair attacks him:

> It was too good to last, he thought. I wish it had been a dream now and that I had never hooked the fish and was alone in the bed on the newspapers.(*The Old Man and the Sea*, 103)

But immediately he says:

> "But man is not made for defeat," . . . . "A man can be destroyed but not defeated." I am sorry that I killed the fish though . . . . (*The Old Man and the Sea*, 103)

What emerges above everything else is that "energy" that always latches on to a hope. This, the *sthayibhava* of *vira*, is ever present.

In the *Natya Sastra* (VI.66), the *vyabhicharibhavas* or the accompanying states of *vira rasa* have been listed as follows:

> . . . happiness, attentiveness, pride, panic, violence, resentment, remembrance, and horripilation. (*Aesthetic Rapture*, Vol.I, 54)

"Happiness" and "pride" follow from the sense of achievement. When the old man finally kills the marlin, he achieves his goal and so is happy. Thus, the possibility of reaching a goal and happiness (and thus the possibility of *santa*) is to be seen here. "Resentment" can lead to action. It might also result from an encounter, on the part of the victim of the heroic action. "Panic" and "horripilation" thus apply mostly to the object on which the heroic act is being enacted. But even in the reader, there is the possibility of fear (or awe) at the enactment of a great heroic deed. Thus, there is the possibility of both *bhayanaka* and *adbhuta*. In fact, in *The Mahabharata*, after the war, what is to be seen is only death and devastation. Thus, *vira rasa* can also lead (apart from *karuna*) to a sense of fear and pity at the waste. This holds the possibility of a "worldly weary" feeling and so of leading to *santa rasa*.

But coming to the question of "happiness," in the end, when the old man goes off to sleep and dream of lions, does that state of mind have anything to do with his achievement or failure? It is here that the aspect of "humility" stands out prominent. When the old man admits that he is beaten (at the end) he transcends his ego, his little self. At the end we find him completely without any self-awareness. When the boy asks:

> How much did you suffer?
> "Plenty," the old man said. (*The Old Man and the Sea*, 126)

But he is not aware of his suffering, or of his victory, or of
his defeat. He has transcended beyond. In an Indian context
he can be said to have transcended into a state of bliss, of
ananda.

It is thus that *vira rasa* can lead beyond itself to *santa rasa,*
which is the goal of every other *rasa.* In that, beyond
Christian "humility" and "suffering," beyond epic "strength"
and "courage" the old man can be said to have achieved
santa where the heroic and the religious merge and are
transmuted. Abhinavagupta comments on the
transformation of *vira* to *santa* as follows:

> . . . if he resorts to extraordinary energy dominated
> by the absence of delusions (in order to overcome
> worldly temptations). (*Santa Rasa,* 129)

it can lead to *santa.* Now, *vira* and *santa* have certain
similarities. The *vibhava* or cause of *vira* is "correct
perception." The cause of *santa* is "knowledge of Truth."
Both have "steadfastness," determination, patience, etc.,
among their *vyabhicharibhavas* or accompanying states. But
the basic difference between the two is that while in *vira*
"pride" plays an important role and thus there is the
affirmation of ego, in *santa* ego gets diluted in the
realization of the bigger Self (*Santa Rasa,* 93)

But in order for one to achieve Self-realization, a lot
of hardship, temptations etc., have to be overcome and this
needs courage - a basic ingredient of *vira.* On the other
hand, in a life of courage, one learns "humility." The old
fisherman's lonely and brave struggle against a big and
fighting fish teaches him humility:

> He was too simple to wonder when he had attained
> humility. But he knew he had attained it and he
> knew it was not disgraceful and it carried no loss of
> true pride. (*The Old Man and the Sea,* 9-10)

Once "pride" is transmitted, there is the effacement of the
ego, and one is one the road towards self-realization. Thus,
in the end, even if the old man is tired, and dead tired, he

has nothing to be sad about. In his sleep, in the last page, we find him dreaming of Africa and of lions.

Where steadfastness and perseverance are (at one point of time) detached from egotism, *vira* gets transformed into *santa*. According to Abhinavagupta, the culmination of all great works of art must be in *santa*. As mentioned earlier in the context of ananda, the experience of santa by the perceiver holds the possibility of transcendence of the self and the realisation of moksha or enlightenment where all emotions and their causes dissolve. *Santa*, to Abhinavagupta, is like a white thread that holds coloured jewels together (the other eight rasas). It is neutral and can absorb the colours of the jewels, yet hold them together in a thread of continuity and is capable of leading to a state where the soul (*atman*) shines through.

A reading of *The Old Man and the Sea*, with *Rasa* theory makes one realise that the old man transcends ordinary emotions at the end. For the reader, also, the smooth and continuos development culminates at a point, where, if (s)he identifies with the central character, (s)he holds the possibility of an aesthetic experience that is tranquil and gives a sense of peace.

NOTES & REFERENCES

Ghosh, Manmohan, (tr). *The Natya Sastra*, Calcutta: The Royal Asiatic Society, 1950.

Hemingway, Ernest, *The Old Man and The Sea*, Delhi: Surjeet Publishers (reprint), 1970.

Masson, J. L. and M. L. Patwardhan, *Aesthetic Rapture*, 2 Vols., Poona: Deccan College, 1970.

Masson, J. L. and M. L. Patwardhan, *Santarasa and Abhinava Gupta's Philosophy of Aesthetics.*, Poona: Bhandarkar Oriental Series, 1969.

1.   Controversy rages whether there are eight or nine rasas. It is usually felt that *santa*, the ninth *rasa*, is a later addition. However, for Abhinavagupta it is a very important rasa, in fact the driving force behind the *rasa* theory.

2.   The episode of Raja Hariscandra is to be found in the 12th canto of *The Mahabharata* and later, in a more detailed way, in *The Markandeya Purana*.

3.   In the 8th canto of *The Mahabharata*.

Santiago : A Sinless 'El Campeon'

Pralhad A. Kulkarni

A boat with sail "patched with flour sacks and, furled"[1] sets sail in the Gulf Stream, far away from the land, with the old man with sun-burnt skin, wrinkles in the back of his neck, and deep blue "cheerful and undefeated"(5) eyes for fishing. Whenever he went fishing, the sun had hurt his eyes, so he prefers to go to the sea quite early in the morning. He knows that the glare on the water disturbs him. Santiago is a Cuban fisherman. His first love is the sea. He wants to show his skill and ability in fishing. In fact, "thousand times he had proved it meant nothing"(114). He dreams of a big fish for eighty-four days continuously. But it seems that luck has turned its face from him. He is with his boy friend Manolin there. Manolin adores him as a hero but later his parents prevent him from accompanying Santiago because he was an unlucky man. When Santiago returns with empty hands, he becomes the focal point of fun. Like a sage, he remains calm and quiet and never pays any attention to such things.

On the eighty-fifth day, luck favors him with a big fish "two feet longer than the skiff"(52). His eyes sparkle with joy. He perhaps feels for a while that his struggle has come to an end. He feels that he "was born for"(32) the sea and hence, prefers to go to the unexplored part of the deep sea and he wants to find the fish "beyond all people. Beyond all people in the world"(41). Slowly he begins to realize that all the evil forces have come to him in the form of a fish.

Now the fish begins to shake the boat, first northwards and then eastwards. For some time he feels that the declining age and diminishing strength may not give him power to meet the challenge posed by the marlin.

But his long experiences have taught him about "many tricks" and "resolution" (emphasis mine; 17). He prepares himself to face the challenge. The water-surrounding loneliness and the complete isolation helps Santiago to peep into his past. It reveals to him his successful encounter with the strong Negro "a fine man and a great athlete"(59) from Cinefugos; his uncanny interest in baseball; his unfaltered faith in Di Maggio, the best player of the Yankees. Naturally even the thought of defeat upsets him. He believes that "a man can be destroyed but not defeated"(89) . He remembers Manolin's words: "There are many good fishermen and some great ones. But there is only you."(17) Somewhere at the core of his heart he is elevated.

Santiago believes in Christianity. He follows his religion of humanity scrupulously. He speaks with the fish, "I love you and respect you very much. But I will kill you dead before this day ends"(45). He pities the fish and says that, "If I were him I would put in everything now and go until something broke."(53) In his fight with the fish, Santiago receives both: the crown and the grave. He observes that fish disturbs him. Perhaps the fish does not like any invasion in their territory, and, hence, become more fierce and aggressive in their defence. The marlin becomes more violent and it hurts the ego of Santiago. He decides to show it "what a man can do and what a man endures"(55). But his efforts could not save the marlin nor could save himself too! It is as if a battle lost but war won.

The blackhole creates fear in Santiago's mind and naturally he turns his mind towards God. Probably he seems to be in search of a peace of mind. He believes that God is kind and his prayers are full of faith. The beauty of the fish tempts him and he begins to feel for the marlin. Slowly he begins to search for the self. Perhaps he knows the meaning of oneness in the universe, and hence, does not feel any difference in "who kills who."(79). He contemplates over the killing of the fish. He does not think that killing is a sin. His concept of sin has a wider domain. He feels that "Perhaps it was a sin to kill the fish – even though I did it to keep me alive and feed many people. But then everything is a sin." (90). He thinks that killing of the fish is a natural religion of a fisherman. Further he stretches at length his assumption and thinks that he is not a sinner. He says that "everything kills everything else in some way. Fishing kills me exactly as it keeps me alive."(91)

Douglas Hewitt says that, "It is very difficult to be wholly joyous or wholly sad on this earth."[2] Santiago, though strong and courageous, is unable to be happy all the time. Fear of loneliness haunts him and he begins to speak with the fish. His monologues become more articulate. The loneliness symbolizes Inferno – a self-torturing process. He thinks that man cannot be alone at sea; the deep waters, fish, and the sky above form the nucleus of his friendship. Further, he assumes that physically man may suffer from the isolation but spiritually he remains in chains.

Now he begins to return to his shack. He looks back and finds the skeleton- "the great tail of the fish standing up well behind the skiff's stern"(104). It reminds him of his great loss – physical as well as spiritual. His loss o faith, loss of hope, loss of courage – all these mark the end of everything. We are reminded of man's predicament as defined by Joseph Conrad – a lonely being in the universe. He is unique and lonely in the hostile and insurmountable universe and is constrained to live within this hostility. But the champion proves himself to be superior to his mediocre colleagues. As an unarmed warrior he fights the fish successfully. Even in killing the fish he is aware of his humanistic sensibilities. Perhaps Hemingway treats fishing as a sport and Santiago plays with the fish. He makes it dance to his tunes. He remembers DiMaggio, who symbolizes strength. But Santiago does not like to be defeated and with the same sense he plays with the Negro in the hand-game and defeats him. The champion is further rewarded with both the things – the crown and the grave.

The champion wants to restore the faith of man again. His going too far into the deep waters has resulted in destruction and total annihilation. It has ruined him and the marlin. He realizes that his skiff is too small in the sea. Now he seems to be tired of the sea but he still dreams of the marlin. He probably dreams of a new world – a world of faith, courage, love, compassion and, humanity. He knows that he can do it better. The fish has become more violent and it started to upset Santiago and he felt as if all the evil forces had united together to fight with him. He strongly endures the attacks and at last kills the fish.

Ernest Hemingway is not a religious writer but he talks about sin, salvation and suffering. In his undaunted courage and his experiences, Santiago resembles Christ. He calls the fish a brother, loves the birds on the sea, and pities the sharks, and ultimately faces crucifixion. Perhaps in the destruction of Santiago and the marlin, Hemingway seems to have anticipated the Apocalypse. Further, he expects a new world to emerge – a world of hopes, certainty, happiness; a world without hostility, enmity and war. Santiago fights for the right of a life worthy of humanity and becomes a flickering hope for it. Thus he becomes a sinless 'El Campeon'- the Champion.

NOTES & REFERENCES

1. Ernest Hemingway, *The Old Man and the Sea*. London: Triad Panther Books, 1985, p.5. Further quotes from the text will be marked in parenthesis.

2. Douglas Hewitt, *Joseph Conrad: A Reassessment*. London: Bowes and Bowes, 1952.

A Look At The Manuscript of *The Garden of Eden*

P. G. Rama Rao

Though Hemingway wrote it in 1946, The *Garden of Eden* appeared in 1986 and at once created a sensation and became a Book of the Month Club main selection in the same year. People began to talk about androgyny and Mark Spilka presented a paper on "Hemingway's Quarrel with Androgyny" at the 1988 International Hemingway Conference at Schruns in Austria. Kenneth Lynn wrote at length about it in his biography in which he gives an account of how Hemingway's mother used to dress him when he was a little boy and his sister Marcelline alike to look like twins and how it had a lasting impact on his mind.

In the novel, David Bourne, the writer, and his wife, Catherine, honeymoon in a lovely little coastal town in France. David is writing about their life together, obviously, at the insistence of his wife and they conduct strange experiments in lovemaking, again at the insistence of the wife; their experiments include transsexual role-reversal. Put in simple terms, Catherine wants him to pretend that he is Catherine and she call herself Peter and they make love in the woman above position. Then one day she goes to a haircutting salon and has her hair cut short like a boy's and then she makes David also have his hair cut short, exactly as short as hers, and then they have their hair bleached exactly alike so that they might look like twin brothers. Then she says that both of them are boys and brothers too and wants to make love as such. David does not like it, resists, but acquiesces in because of his infatuation for her. Then she wants to become dark and both of them tan themselves lying naked in a hidden beach. Then one day, another girl called Marita comes along. They become friends and Catherine asks her to stay with them and be her girl and David's girl also, and have a *menage' a trios* situation. Told in a nutshell, the story hinges first on role-reversal, then cutting hair, then having sex, both as boys, and a perversion compounded with incest, as brothers, and then a third person entering the scene and becoming the mistress of the husband and the lesbian partner of the wife.

But the protagonist is a writer and has alredy written a successful novel and is now writing a narrative about their present life. Catherine who is wealthy and crazy, as we find her from her obsessions, funds their honeymoon and makes it possible for him to write in freedom of a sort. She wants him to write only about their life and sexperiments together, but when he interrupts it to write an elephant-hunt story set in Africa, in which his father hunts the elephant and he accompanies his father, she does not like it. The story is coming up very well and Marita likes it and encourages David while Catherine feels jealous, not of Marita, but of the African story, and one day burns the only copy of the story together with the reviews on his first novel. Meanwhile Marita falls in love with David and drifts away from Catherine, thus bringing normalcy into David's life. Catherine, who has become a confirmed lesbian now, makes an exit from their life. David rewrites the story destroyed by his ex-wife and leads a normal life with Marita. This is the story of the printed text.

Hemingway's publisher, Charles Scribner, Jr. says in his preface to the paperback edition of the book, that one day Mary Hemingway brought a large shopping bag full of photocopies of unpublished material to his office and this contained the manuscripts of *The Garden of Eden*. They found that the manuscript could be published with some pruning. Mr. Tom Jenks was asked to give it a shape, which he did.

I have gone through the first draft of this novel, 1189 pages long, in the John F. Kennedy Library, Boston, and have found some interesting passages that are vital to the structure of the novel, and need not have been omitted. I strongly feel that all that pruning by the publishers was not necessary, or could have been minimal. In fact, the novel need not have been published, as Hemingway probably never intended to publish it.

An important opinion is the reference to the Rodin statue of two lesbians making love. As they are making love, Catherine reminds David of the statue that they saw together when they visited the Rodin museum, and asks him to change like in the sculpture:

> "Will you change and be my girl and let me take you? Will you be like you were in the statue? Will you change?"

Later she thanks him and says, "Please know I never made love to a girl before."[1] But David is worried. He wonders what will become of them if things go this wildly, this dangerously, and this fast.

Catherine wants to look as though she belonged to a different race with a different pigmentation e.g. like a Somali woman (there were several pages on the Somalis) whom Hemingway seemed to like and admire.[2] She wants to look different, not as God made her. She wants to look like and play the role of man in sex. If it is confined to the physical part, there is no problem. The woman above position is one of the many variations accepted in lovemaking, described in erotica from Ovid's *The Art of Love* and Vatsayana's *Kamasutra* to the present day. But what matters is the mind. Jesus says that sin pertains to the mind in his Sermon on the Mount. Here Catherine's mind is affected by perversion and she is conscious that it is wrong. David is actually aware of it. They have a sense of sin repeatedly voiced by both in the manuscript. Catherine calls what they are doing "the devil things." David jokingly calls her "devil."

Having been affected by the Rodin statue, Catherine meets another couple, Nick Sheldon, the painter, and his wife, Barbara, friends of David who have already conducted the experiments Catherine is obsessed with viz., androgyny, lesbianism, and unisex. Both have their hair cut the same length. This makes her "feel strangely" in her words. Nick and Berbara seem to be the immediate cause of Catherine's decision to go ahead with the experiments. She has seen the Rodin sculpture. She had read Proust's *Sodome et Gomorrhe* which is revealed during a conversation between David, Andy (Andrew Murray, a writer) and Catherine, which is also omitted in the printed text. Nick and Barbara and Andy do not figure in the printed text at all.[3] The reference to *Sodome et Gomorrhe* is also omitted. According to the Biblical story, God promises Abraham not to destroy Sodom if there are ten good people there.

Proust's *Sodome et Gomorrhe* is the 4th section of his classic *A la Recherche du temps perdu [Remembrances of Things Past]* published in 1946, while Hemingway was working on *The Garden of Eden* with the enmity and incomprehension between the sexes. God will withhold His wrath from Sodom and Gomorrha if even one couple can be found there who are happy in the normal union of man with woman. Hopes center on the couple Lia and Jean, but they are dashed. The end of the world itself cannot still the dissension between these two. The reference to this book should not have been omitted in the printed text.[4] Her mind already powerfully affected by the sculpture and the book, Catherine meets Nick and Barbara. It is like King Lear, who, already ranting and raving after being betrayed by his daughters, meets Edgar disguised as Tom of Bedlam.

David's perspective is different from Catherine's. He takes it as a passing fancy of his wife's but when she persists, he gets worried. She is actually going through a state of transformation. She longs at first to be both boy and girl, i.e. sometimes a boy and sometimes a girl. Later on in the novel, she is no longer a woman in mind. She becomes a complete lesbian and wants, not a man, but a woman. When she walks out of the *menage a trios,* she hopes to have an affair with Barbara (in the manuscript) who is made "another woman" in the printed text, as Nick and Barbara are totally dropped in the printed text without any justification. If it is just a variation of position without the sexual identity being affected, it is all right; but when either the man or the woman thinks and believes that they belong to the same sex, The Garden of Eden turns into Sodome and Gomorrah for it is the mind that matters.

Later, when Catherine expresses her desire to go to Marita's room and do the lesbian act, David repeatedly warns her not to. When she reminds him that he had changed into a girl for her, he answers, "But it was for us and it was in the dark." But she disregards David's words and goes to Marita. She tells Marita that she is committing a sin and David is her partner. All this is once again, omitted in the printed text. The first draft presents Marita as a good, normal girl, a virgin, but with an initial inclination for lesbianism which stopped with kisses only. She tells David that she never did really bad things. This slight inclination vanishes and she is completely cured of it and restored to normal sex life like Maria in *For Whom the Bell Tolls* after her contact with Robert Jordan.

Apart from his autobiographical reflections, Hemingway in this novel, seems to think of Catherine, the very romantic heroine of *A Farewell to Arms* who has long hair and who loves Fredric Henry with all her mind, with all her heart, and with all her soul so that she completely identifies herself with him, "I want what you want. There is no me anymore" and of Maria of *For Whom the Bell Tolls* with her close-cropped hair like a rabbit's fur, who becomes Marita here and grows her hair. The Catherine of *The Garden of Eden* has her hair cut like Maria of *For Whom the Bell Tolls*, the victim of Fascist cruelty.

Some very good dialogues and interior monologues of David and Marita which could have made contributions to meaning of the novel are omitted in the printed text. Again, another episode where Marita and David drive to Cannes is dropped in the text. Here Marita tells David that she will grow her hair long and wear it down over her shoulders, and David says, "You'll be beautiful."[5] The elephant story runs parallel with the David and Catherine story. David is in both of them. He is sorry for the elephant whose whereabouts he unwittingly passed on to his father, the hunter, and thus became an accomplice in the killing of the elephant, which he regrets. The elephant story belongs to the past -his boyhood -and he is now reminiscing it in a story. "In the story he had tried to make the elephant alive again.... .Maybe I can make Catherine whole again," he says hoping against hope (omitted in the printed text).[6]

There is a very interesting passage of two long pages in which David looks at himself in the mirror while shaving and reflects on his predicament. "How crazy could you have been to let her do that to you?..1 love her and I loved everything we ever did together.... .except that I had remorse and nothing could be right for me to do that gave that remorse. But she had no remorse.... .I'm not doing so good now, he told the mirror. But things are not going so good in the story either."[7] The mirror image is a recurring image. They want a mirror in the bar which takes a long time to come. Finally, when it comes and reveals his soul to David in the manuscript, Tom Jenks, the Scribner's editor removes it from the printed text.

In the manuscript, Catherine takes a reluctant David a second time to the haircutting saloon. David repeatedly says as he submits to the barber, "The hell with it." Later she says, as Eve must have said to Adam after they had both eaten the forbidden fruit, "You were so good to be damned with me." Then he says like Adam had after eating the forbidden fruit, "I'm really spooked this time.... We really shouldn't have done it." David repeats again and again, "I am spooked." "David looked at her eyes.... .and he began to realize what a completely stupid thing he had permitted."[8]

Marita tells David in another censored portion that she read the narrative he wrote about himself and Catherine. When David asks her what she thought of the sexperiments part, she says, "it was the bad part" and adds, "I knew all about that because I am just the way you are." David says, "You mean that you're a remorse girl?" David and Marita are remorseful unlike Catherine who is stubborn, unrepentant and crazy.[9] Therefore she cuts her hair and cuts herself adrift from David and the Garden of Eden while Marita wants to grow her hair and grow into David's heart and grows another Garden of Eden with David.

Hemingway was a devout Catholic. He went to churches and prayed. He read the *Old Testament* narratives when a schoolboy, as part of his course, and the Bible was a powerful influence on his thinking and writing. His works are positive affirmations of "The earth abideth forever" and pay homage to the everlasting things. "The palm fronds of our victories, the worn light-bulbs of our discoveries and the empty condoms of our great loves float insignificantly on the one single lasting thing—the stream," he says about the Gulf Stream in *The Green Hills of Africa*. The title, *The Sun Also Rises*, as well as one of the two epigraphs is from *The Ecclesiastes;* the Catholic priest in *A Farewell to Arms* is central to the novel as he defines true love for Frederic Henry: "When you love you wish to do things for, you wish to sacrifice for, you wish to serve." *For Whom the Bell Tolls* is inspired by one of John Donne's devotions: "No man is an island... .and therefore never send to know for whom the bell tolls, it tolls for thee." Santiago is Saint James. "In our time" is part of a prayer. Hemingway presented his Nobel prize medal to the shrine of *Neustra de la caridad del cobre* or *Virgin del cobre* near Santiago in Cuba in 1956, two years after receiving it. Not everybody could part with such a prestigious medal.

　　Questions therefore can be logically raised as to why did such a religious man write this novel, or to put it better, how could he write such a novel as this? Why did he never mail it to the publisher even though he revised, it again and again? I guess he wrote it for himself and he wrote it as a private, confessional novel. Having started it in 1946, he interrupted the writing as he wrote other novels and stories even as David interrupted his narrative about the sexperiments and wrote other stories, which Catherine could not tolerate. But Hemingway never neglected his Garden. He went back to it from time to time till his death adding a passage here and removing a passage there or rewriting an episode. For example, he rewrote the elephant episode in 1958. He himself wrote in the margin giving the date on which he rewrote it (22 November, 1958). But he never mailed the manuscript to the publisher. For one thing it dealt with what happened in his own marital life or lives (Hadley and Pauline) and later Martha. Secondly, it might have been an exorcism of whatever nocturnal forces troubled his soul, his consciousness of guilt and sin, against which he wrestled in private. I personally am inclined to think that this novel was a fourteen-or-fifteen-year long and a 1200 page confession of a devout Catholic in the church of his heart. Maybe it was Hemingway's attempt at psychotherapy. When asked, "Who is your psychiatrist?" he had once answered, "My Smith-Corona typewriter." Confession is a sort of psychotherapy and whatever his biographers say about his Catholicism, the fact remains that Hemingway was a Catholic and a believer and therefore the manuscript is filled with words like sin, devil, wicked and remorse.

According to Carlos Baker, Hemingway confessed to Buck Lanaham that he wrote the novel at enormous speed. Starting in January, he wrote 400 pages by mid- February, 700 pages by the end of April, and 1000 pages in mid-July. He could never stick to a preconceived pattern but invent as he went from minute to minute without knowing what was going to happen next. Besides, he was spurred to the effort by a big impending sense that would die within a year. If he had foreseen that Charles Scribner and Jenks would give it a shape of their choice, he himself might have hurriedly given it a shape or destroyed it. He could not have destroyed it since he preserved every piece of paper including train tickets and lots of junk for editors and researchers to ferret out his secret confessions.

NOTES & REFERENCES

Places in the printed text (cited as PT) where the omitted passages in the manuscript should have figured (Courtesy: Hemingway Room, J.F.Kennedy Library, Boston: Box no. 422).

1. Reference to Rodin's sculpture PT p.17; (Ms. P.20 of 422-1-3) and the birth of Catherine's lesbian desire.

2. Reference to Somalis (422-1-17. Chapter 23 of Ms.) omitted in PT pp.134-5.

3. Reference to Andrew Murray (Andy) and Nick Sheldon, the painter and Barbara (422-1-5 of Ms.) Totally dropped in PT.

4. Reference to Marcel Proust's *Sodome et Gomorrhe* in conversation between Andrew and Catherine (422-1-6, Ch.9 p.1 of Ms) totally dropped in PT.

5. Trip to Cannes (422-1-22. Ch. 28 of Ms) omitted in PT.

6. Elephant hunt episode rewritten (422-1-23. Marginal note Chapter 29 Rewritten 22/11/58 by Hemingway) reflection on the parallel Catherine story.

7. David shaving and looking at his face in the mirror and reflecting (422-1-23 pp.18-20) omitted in PT. Pp.167-68.

8. Second visit to the haircutting salon (422-1-25 omitted in PT. p. 177-78)

9. David and Marita having remorse (422-1-27) omitted PT.p.185.

Biblical Resonances in Hemingway's Short Fiction : Moving Testaments to His Art

Ajanta Paul

Though individual works by Hemingway, such as *The Old Man And The Sea* and the short story 'Big Two-Hearted River', have been examined for their affinities with Biblical myth and imagery, his short fiction as a whole, I believe, has never been approached for the same. Attempting to remedy the oversight, in the circumstances, would be a step not only towards canonical restitution, but also a reorientation of the balance of the stories around a fresh fulcrum of meaning. Interesting though the exercise promises to be, a detailed execution of the same, for all practical purposes, is beyond the scope of a short exegesis. Hence, I propose to limit my investigation to a few stories especially evocative of such influence.

That Hemingway was influenced by the Bible in matters of craft is clear from his use of simple narrative, repetition and poetry. While the 'simple narrative' is only too evident in Hemingway's minimalist plots and stark evocation of scenes, the famous repetitive manner, frequently parodied and commonly summed up as an element of 'anti -style', may actually be seen as a throwback to the Biblical mode, an incantatory technique that is resonant in its reach and effect. The poetics of purity, evident everywhere in Hemingway's work, develops in the best of his short stories into certain fine, bare effects, which recall in mood as well as tonality, the austere modulations of the Old Testament.While it is true that certain general Biblical beneficences of style did accrue to Hemingway, influencing the narrative and rhythmic cast of his stories in a significant way, it is his exploitation of Christian echoes, allusions, texts and prayers, for ironic as well as harmonistic purposes, which really calls for inquiry. From the outset, the phraseology of prayer informs Hemingway's stories.

'In Our Time', the title of one of his first collections of stories, is a breakaway splinter of the supplicatory line: "Give peace, O Lord, in our time". 'Now I lay me', the title of one of his short stories, is a fragment of the popular prayer "Now I lay me down to sleep". 'The Light of the World', the title of another story by Hemingway, refracts the rays of several Biblical texts at once. While it seems to catch the glow of Jesus' declaration in the Sermon on the Mount, "Ye are the light of the world", it is also iridescent with the promised brilliance of his exhortation in the Gospel of St. John, "He that followeth me shall not walk in darkness but shall have the light of life." While in the first instance cited, the actual petition: "Give peace, O Lord, in our time" eludes Hemingway, and we catch only the receding whimper of the line in the phrasal echo "In our time", in the second instance, 'Now I Lay Me Down to Sleep' the childhood prayer ostensibly evoked in the title is not the real concern of the protagonist. Rather, he is concerned about his inability to complete the Lord's prayer, unable as he is, to go beyond the first few lines. Vestiges of prayer and prophecy, thus reduced to a residue, articulate in their broken cadences the disruption and dismemberment of a post-war society even as they reflect a curious peripheralization of integrals, in that the prime dilemma of the author or protagonist frequently appears as a sort of a deflected discourse.

As in title, so in text, the scriptural element fosters the aesthetics of ambiguity, inviting comparisons and guiding intuition to the allegorical and parabolic plangencies of the prose. In the story 'A Clean Well-Lighted Place' the "shadow" in which the old man sits, recalls both in its pastoral ambience and in its sense of present suffering, the shadow-haunted valley of death evoked in the Twenty Third Psalm. Certain images, because of their closeness to the Bible, resonate with a particular intensity. The notion of shelter so ritualistically adumbrated in *Isaiah* 4:6, "And there shall be a tabernacle for a shadow in the daytime for heat, and a place for refuge, and a covert from storm and rain", prefigures in an almost uncanny manner the tent imagery in 'Big Two-Hearted River'. It is no idle speculation, therefore, to suggest, that the tent pitched by Nick Adams in 'Big Two-Hearted River', and regarded by him as "the good place", expands into the allegorical contours of the Biblical tabernacle. The tabernacle as described in *The Old Testament* was not only the portable sanctuary in which the Jews carried the Ark of the Covenant, it also denoted a temporary dwelling, of the kind used by the Jews during the Exodus. The notion of a sanctuary combines with that of a shelter to suggest a habitation that is not very different from the physical and psychological properties of Nick's tent in the riverine wilderness. If the tent in 'Big Two-Hearted River' operates as a powerful scriptural symbol multiplying Biblical resonances, the river itself becomes identified with the primordial; baptismal waters in which Nick Adams experiences a spiritual renewal. In this connection, the comparison of the two-hearted river with the iconic and mythicized Jordan becomes one of the imperatives of the argument. Though critics have consistently located in the celebrated two-heartedness of Hemingway's river the conventional binaries of birth and death and those of progress and primitivism, there has been little or no attempt to trace in the polarities and dualities of the Biblical river the literary antecedents of the fictional one.

In ancient times, the river Jordan used to link the northern and the southern parts of Herod's kingdom, thereby connecting what were essentially two centers within the same geopolitical dominion, or two hearts beating the rhythm of the same Jewish life. In modern times, the upper course of the Jordan remains distinct from its lower course in that plots of farmland flank the former while the latter is threatened by the wilderness. The cultivable and the wild aspects of the Jordan translate immediately into the confluent currents and the swampy

stretches of the northern Michigan river evoked in
Hemingway's story. Moreover, the fact that the swirling
waters of the Jordan derive their emotional momentum
from the miracles performed by the prophets Elijah and
Elisha, further push back the boundaries of association to
accommodate the notion of a dual source of animation.

Images of fluidity lead one inevitably to that of the
overflowing cup evoked so memorably in the story 'A Clean,
Well-Lighted Place'. When one of the waiters poured brandy
into the old patron's glass, some of it spilled over. The act
of pouring the brandy, as described in the story, recalls the
inspired metaphysics of Isaiah who had likened the Creator
to the "Spirit that is poured upon us from high". Hemingway
literalizes in the image of the overflowing cup one of the
most familiar metaphors of the Twenty Third Psalm — "my
cup runneth over". The cup of brandy, as a correlative for
the chalice of spiritual bliss, ironically underscores the
emptiness of the old patron's life and, through it, the
pervasive hollowness of modern existence. It is this
pervasive hollowness which returns to haunt Hemingway's
stories as the "nada" seen to most striking effect in the
story 'A Clean Well-Lighted Place' where it wreaks havoc
on two archetypal addresses — the Lord's Prayer and the
Hail Mary. It induces in one a sense of awe at the syllabic
subversion wrought in and the grammatical genocide
inflicted on the form of the prayers through the
indiscriminate replacement of substantives and transitives
with the ubiquitous "nada". The Lord's Prayer and the Hail
Mary, which are bound up with the roots and rituals of daily
Christian life at the individual, familial and congregational
levels, have been parodied by the so-called older waiter in
the story as "Our nada who art in nada, nada be thy name".
What has been long regarded as a subversion of stereotypes
turn out to be an exercise in self-satire, for established
above and beyond the parody of forms and utterances, are
the power of the prayers and the insecurity of the denouncer
before them. This is borne out in the fact that the prayers
may not be cancelled at one stroke by a simple negative,
but must be repeatedly hammered upon and ritualistically
demolished through an almost manic deployment of the

word "*nada*".

Well from *nada* or nothingness to the Creation and Adam is but a mandatory movement and it is no coincidence that Nick Adams, at first glance, comes across as Adam the original man partaking of an Edenic repast. This is especially evident in those stories dealing with Nick's boyhood. The innocence of the boy Nick, his empathy with nature, along with the luminous quality of some of the settings and images, has strong suggestions of a prelapsarian world. At the same time, one realizes that all is not tranquil, for knowledge lurks close by, ever seeking to disturb the tranquility of Adam's garden. While the shadow of death falls across the morning mist in the story 'Indian Camp', the stories 'The End of Something' and 'The Three Day Blow' introduce the note of separation, signifying not only the end of the relationship between Nick and Marjorie, but also the end of Nick's companionship with his father. In sharp contrast to such poignant awakenings arrives the specter of violent death in the story 'The Killers' where the adult Nick is traumatically initiated into the potency of evil. The process of initiation, theologically explained as recognition of evil, is powerfully present in Nick's experience in 'The Killers' though, of course, explained from an entirely secular perspective.

If in these stories Nick is Adam the original man, in 'Big Two-Hearted River' he is also Lazarus returned from the dead, working out the practicalities of a fresh lease on life. Leaving behind the burnt townscape of Seney, as also his smoldering memories, Nick camps by the Northern Michigan river, attempting to negotiate a journey to mental and emotional balance and spiritual health. From the image of Lazarus and a remembrance of Christ's mission and ministry as described in the Gospels, one moves down in time to recognize, in Nick's journey in the same story, the quest of the medieval knight for the Grail as has been pointed out by Leo Gurko in his penetrating analysis of Hemingway's pursuit of heroism. From blasted terrain to steep hill, Nick's is a compelling odyssey and his figure, climbing a hill with a heavy burden on his back, is not only rife with intimations of Cavalry but is distinctly reminiscent of Bunyan's pilgrim. The centuries thus converge in the character of Nick Adams, giving rise to a protean persona that is resistant to temporal categorization and is identifiable with more than one Christian archetype. The old mythos generated by the ancient Hebrew narratives with their historical projection of Adam is prevailed upon and tempered by the newer, messianic mythos heralded by Christ. For it can be scarcely denied that, in addition to the Adamic myth, Hemingway uses the motif of Christ's life in both novel and interesting ways. In the story 'The Light of the World', for instance, Hemingway creates the legend of a contemporary Christ figure in the character of the dead boxer Steve Ketchel who is effectively mythologized in the words of one of his admirers as "the greatest, finest, whitest, most beautiful man that ever lived".[1]

From surpassing eulogy to Eucharistic apprehension of character, the Christ motif serves a variety of uses in the Hemingway short story. In the story 'The Undefeated', for instance, the ageing bullfighter, Manuel, develops into a Christ-like figure who must be sacrificed over and over again in celebration of the Mass. Just as Christ, in the form of the consecrated host, is distributed among worshippers, and is reconstituted in the spiritual wholeness of the partakers of the sacrament, Manuel Garcia comes apart in his ritual defeat and death only to emerge spiritually stronger and, in a sense, more complete in the cumulative insights of his colleagues and readers. In his striving, not for the corruptible but the incorruptible crown, and in his adherence to the Pauline admonition "Let all things be done decently and in order." Manuel exemplifies a Christ-like commitment to truth. It is equally interesting to observe how a Biblical terminology pervades Hemingway's philosophy and aesthetics. Commenting on his notion of the actual Hemingway describes it as being made up of, among other things, "knowledge, experience, wine, bread, oil, salt, vinegar"[2]. The words "wine, bread, oil, salt, vinegar" exceed their mundane, naturalistic brief to discharge certain Biblical exclusivities of meaning, which come, inevitably with their powerful emotional accretions. Such exclusivities, when encountered in

Hemingway's aesthetic formulations, are found to assume ecumenical proportions, as for example, when Hemingway clarifies in his interviews and writings, that a writer's job is to "tell the truth". Ecumenical euphonies, such as truth, grace and honor, richly fraught as they are with moral and religious overtones, are nevertheless subsumed into Hemingway's short fiction as verities of temperament and situation, not to be compromised at any cost. Thus it is seen that from its use of Christian motifs in the development of character, and the forging of consonances with Scriptural situation and mood, to its appropriation of images directly or indirectly related to both the Testaments, and its frequent adoption of the rhythms of the King James Bible, the Hemingway short story demonstrates a closeness with the Authorized Version that virtually begs investigation. The Biblical echoes in Hemingway's short fiction, though not overwhelming in their consistency, may yet be recognized as mythic multivalencies of character and style which yield resonances far in excess of their materials, even as they generate ironies and resolve ambiguities in the manner of most provocative fictions.

NOTES AND REFERENCES

1.   Hemingway, Ernest. *The Short Stories of Ernest Hemingway*, New York: Charles Scribner's Sons, 1966: 388.

2.   Hemingway's Introduction to Elio Vittorini's novel *In Sicily*, New York: 1949.

True at First Light : Our Centennial Gift

Somdatta Mandal

"There are always mystical countries that are part of one's childhood. Those we remember and visit sometimes when we are asleep and dreaming. They are as lovely at night as they were when we were children. If you ever go back to see them they are not there. But they are as fine in the night as they ever were if you have the luck to dream of them....In Africa when we lived on the small plain in the shade of the big thorn trees near the river at the edge of the swamp at the foot of the great mountain we had such countries. We were no longer, technically children although in many ways I am quite sure that we were."

— *True at First Light*

"The bull-fight has become formalized. My interest is now in Africa, and all I am here for is to make enough money to return to East Africa."

– *Ernest Hemingway*

After completing *Winner Take Nothing*, Ernest Hemingway fulfilled his ambition expressed in *The Sun Also Rises* of "going to British East Africa to shoot." Having received $25,000 for a safari paid by Uncle Gus, Hemingway and his second wife Pauline traveled to Africa for big game hunting in the winter of 1933. Africa had always fascinated Hemingway. His son Patrick opines that probably the impression that Teddy Roosevelt's writing about Africa made on his father as a young fellow drew him to his first safari. According to his biographer, Jeffrey Meyers, (261-262) the Hemingways set sail from Marseilles and arrived at Mombasa on December 8th. From there they traveled inland to Nairobi, spent a few days hunting near Philip Percival's farm at Machakos (twenty miles from Nairobi), and on December 20 started south to the Serengeti plain in Tanganyika. The campsite was in eastern Tanganyika, off the road to Handeni. It was near the cone-shaped, snow-covered Mount Kilimanjaro, a very nice place to camp, and filled with thousands of wild animals. They were also accompanied by Hemingway's Key West friend, Charles Thompson and their trips had a way of turning into contests. The safari was interrupted in mid-January 1934 when Hemingway suffered a serious attack of amoebic dysentery, which he had contracted on the voyage to Africa. Before he was flown back to Nairobi in a private plane, Hemingway shot three lions, a buffalo and twenty-seven other beasts until hunting stopped, after seventy-two days in Africa, when the rains came. In mid-February, they returned to the coast at Malindi, north of Mombasa, and after a week sailed back to France.

The events of this real life safari were quite obviously detailed in *Green Hills of Africa* once Hemingway returned to Key West. He had read extensively about big game hunting, but the book tried to capture the initial enthusiasm rather than synthesize his expertise on the subject. In the Foreword he somewhat defensively states: " The writer has attempted to write an absolutely true book to see whether the shape of a country and the pattern of a month's action can, if truly presented, compete with a work of the imagination." (Meyers, 264) It is interesting to note that Hemingway's first African safari would have almost as great an impact on his life and writing as the discovery of Spain and bullfighting had ten years earlier. As in *Death in the Afternoon*, the focus is on Hemingway's literary persona, autobiographical reflections and incidental opinions as well as on the ostensible subject matter. Hemingway was interested in the African landscape and animals, but not in the customs and people; his account of hunting in Africa conveys the excitement of getting close to wild beasts in their natural element, but lacks the artistic and cultural context of bullfighting in Spain. The whole African adventure lasted not more than ten weeks, but Hemingway's consciousness was so stimulated by his enthusiasm and curiosity that every event seemed to have been indelibly etched in his memory. The wealth of their detail created the impression of a much longer time in Africa that the writer actually spent. Thus, although factual and autobiographical, *Green Hills of Africa* was designed to have the same psychological effect on his readers as a work of the imagination. Hemingway rearranged the sequence of the events accordingly, constructing the scenes of each part with that purpose in mind.

But Hemingway saved the best of his African experience for his fiction. He had a psychological need to write well and truly, and maintained his artistic integrity. When he wrote directly about himself in *Green Hills of Africa* he pretended to - though he did not - confront the writer's problem of drink, women, ambition for money and fame. He had composed "an absolutely true book" in the first person immediately after the safari, but failed to capture and recreate the essence of his African experience. By 1936, however, he had achieved the necessary objectivity, irony and self-scrutiny, and transmuted his hunting expedition into two undisputed masterpieces: " The Short Happy Life of Francis Macomber" and "The Snows of Kilimanjaro". Both these stories successfully blend historical and literary material with personal experience to produce fictional characters that are much more subtle and substantial than the complacent, one-dimensional self-portrait of *Green Hills of Africa*. Also, Hemingway had written a short story entitled "An African Story" about an elephant hunt in Africa. This story was later interpolated in various chapters as 'a story within a story' in his novel, *The Garden Of Eden*. The protagonist, David Bourne is a writer who is writing a "story about Africa back before the 1914 War. In the time of the Maji-Maji War. The native rebellion of 1905 in Tanganayika" and Hemingway includes the earlier story verbatim. His love of the place is also revealed in a very short and humorous story entitled "The Good Lion" where a good "pasta and scampi" eating lion, "being a lion of culture", is confronted by bad lions who "especially liked to

eat Hindu traders", flees to Venice to complain to his father
how savage Africa was and ends up drinking at Harry's Bar.

Hemingway's best essay on Africa, "The Christmas
Gift," published in *Look* (April-May 1954) was written in
Nairobi while he was recovering from extensive injuries.
All these years, Hemingway *aficionados* were upset that
the second safari produced no literary work comparable to
the two great African stories of 1936. Hemingway published
a minor article, "Safari," to accompany Theisen's
photographs and fulfill his obligations to *Look*. Ten years
after his death, when Mary published what Hemingway had
written in 1954-56 and chosen to keep back, a quarter of
his 200,000-word "African Journal" appeared in *Sports
Illustrated* (December 1971-January 1972). It must be
mentioned here that in an online interview, Charles
Scribner III is of the opinion that scholars have wrongly
referred to Hemingway's manuscript by the title given it
by *Sports Illustrated*, "The African Journal". Hemingway
never called it that and to call it a journal would be to
misrepresent the nature of the manuscript. Patrick, who
had been all along on the safari and knew full well that it
was not a journal pointed out very emphatically that the
title was totally misleading and would confuse people. This
lifeless boy's adventure story is an unintentional parody of
the worst aspects of *Green Hills of Africa*. Hemingway and
Percival, portly and puffing, are twenty years older; Mary
instead of Pauline now stalks a lion. Despite the Mau Mau,
the Africans - including N'Gui, nephew of the original
M'Cola - are as faithful as ever. Nicknames and Swahili
words provide *verismo* - there is plenty of whiskey to soften
the rough life. The flat narrative - "The day that Miss Mary
shot her lion was a beautiful day. That was about all that
was beautiful about it" (*Sports Illustrated* 36,January 3,
1972.p.36) is accompanied by hideous drawings but the
articles are also interspersed with nostalgic and
sentimental memories - positive on Ezra Pound and
negative on Ford Maddox Ford.

In the last decade of his life, Hemingway attempted
to recapture the past by returning to Spain and Africa, and
by writing again (though not nearly as well) about the places

that had inspired him in the 1920s and 1930s. He also returned to his work as a journalist and arranged for *Look* to subsidize the trip with lavish fees. They paid $15,000 for a picture story of the safari, to be photographed by Earl Theisen and another $10,000 for a 3,500-word article that appeared in the magazine on January 26, 1954. (Meyers 497) Hemingway's son Patrick was then living in East Africa and in a letter written from Texas on April 10, 1950 to Adriana Ivancich he proudly declared that "Patrick loves Africa as though Africa were a girl." (quoted in Mary Hemingway, 389) On August 6, 1953 the Hemingways set sail from Marseilles to Mombasa, and met his friend Mayito Menocal and Earl Theisen in Nairobi. The government of Kenya had persuaded Philip Percival to come out of retirement in the hope of reviving tourism during the Mau Mau emergency - the fierce independent movement led by Jomo Kenyatta. Though this was, as Hemingway said, "an actual state of war," the danger was primarily in the Kikuyu district north of Nairobi; there was no trouble where he hunted, south of the capital. Accompanied by another white hunter, Roy Home, they first hunted near Percival's farm at Machakos and were then granted permission to hunt during September in the game reserves at Kajiado and Magadi, which were under the supervision of the game warden, Denis Zaphiro. Kenya was the center of safari business at that time but why Hemingway went particularly to Kimana was that it was a wonderful place made available to him on a special basis by the Kenyan government. Moreover it was a very nice place indeed to camp and offered a wonderful view of Mount Kilimanjaro.

In October, Hemingway visited Patrick in Tanganyika. Perhaps to escape from the strain of the hunting trip or his failure to embody the ideal image of the photo-magazine , Hemingway did something very unusual. Though going native was especially frowned upon during the Mau Mau period, after killing a leopard on his own, he began celebrating by shaving his head, hunting with a spear, dyeing his clothes the rusty Masai color and while Mary was off Christmas shopping at Nairobi, by having an elaborate courtship of his African "fiancee," Debba, a native of the Wakamba tribe. The group of local women who caroused and cavorted with him in his tent were sent home when one of the men cautioned him that things were becoming unseemly. In a letter written at the time, Hemingway extols the virtues of "African girls" - their impudence, cheerfulness, beauty, and ability to give him "a hardon." He boastfully refers to his African "finacee" and suggests a sexual liaison that Mary knows about and condones. Zaphiro described her as "an evil-smelling bit of camp trash"; but Hemingway, using considerable imagination, connected Debba to his youthful infatuation with an Indian girl and later told Archibald MacLeish (letter dated March 29, 1954) that she was a cross between Prudy Boulton and an impudent, dark, short-haired version of Marilyn Monroe. Mary, who understood enough about his mental state to remain aloof, tolerated his absurd behavior : "she just stays the hell away from it and is understanding and wonderful." (*Letters*, p.826) The letters are jocular, though not absolutely tongue in cheek, and so the door is open for gossip (Jenks 54). Before Hemingway died, he boasted to Charles Scribner Jr., his publisher, that he had several unpublished manuscripts in a safe that would someday earn good royalties for his heirs if he didn't live to complete them. With the posthumous publication of *True At First Light : A Fictional Memoir* edited by Patrick Hemingway and released with a lot of fanfare on the 21st of July 1999 to coincide with the hundredth year of the writer's birth, the author's forecast is true and the story of the African sojourn is probably complete.

II

Though edited from the abandoned 800-page manuscript, in *True at First Light* the close parallels with real life events are easily discerned. The title was chosen from the text itself: "In Africa a thing is true at first light and a lie by noon and you have no more respect for it than for the lovely, perfect weed-fringed lake you see across the sun-baked plain." This title is admittedly unfortunate because the events in the book do not take place at Hemingway's first light. They lie more or less in the dusk of his life and career. Patrick's arch choice of the subtitle, "A Fictional Memoir," also involves the reader unnecessarily in questions of what is true and what is made up in the text. It is a warning that *True at First Light* is not a novel, but rather a collection of material out of which a novel might have been constructed. The line between what is fiction and what is memoir is never clear, and neither does it seem particularly significant. It shows that he has no idea what an author actually does in building a virtual reality out of words. It is also possible that the author no longer cared to distinguish. When the story begins, the glory days of the "great white hunters" are over and the Mau Mau rebellion is violently dislodging European farmers from Kenya's arable lands. But to the African gun bearers, drivers and game scouts who run his safari in the shadow of Mount Kilimanjaro, Hemingway remains a lordly figure - almost a god. Two parallel quests propel the narrative: Mary, Hemingway's fourth and last wife, (though called Miss Mary throughout) doggedly stalks an enormous black-maned lion that she is determined to kill by Christmas, the "Birthday of the Baby Jesus", while Hemingway becomes increasingly obsessed with the nubile African woman Debba. What makes the novel especially strange and compelling is that Mary knows all about Debba and accepts her as a "supplementary wife," even as she loses no opportunity to rake her husband over the coals for his drinking, lack of discipline in the camp, and condescending protectiveness. When the weather and tracking conditions are deemed correct by Hemingway and the Game Warden, Mary gets the first shot at the "wonderful and long and dark and beautiful" lion, but the killing blow is administered by none other than Hemingway. It is an anti-climax for Mary, who wanted desperately to shine. The pursuit had given meaning to their existence for over three months, so the killing was met with mixed emotions of relief that no one had been injured, and sorrow for the death of so formidable a creature. Despite the Ngoma (dance) held in her honor, Mary feels cheated. When not busy looking after her, Papa has plenty of time to play Bwana. He's the local arbiter of disputes, a medicine man, and a quasi-military leader charged with defending the area in case of a Mau Mau attack. These roles afford the old man plenty of opportunities to swagger but yield trivial dramas, barely integrated to the story of Miss Mary, Papa and his African "fiancee". The seduction between Papa and Debba occurs in vague, mutely couched passages of Papa's self-serving reflections. Their attraction leads to a scene in which they tryst on a riverbank while waiting for a troop of marauding baboons Papa must kill. Debba and Papa caress and Papa declares his love in the typical simple style that is Hemingway's hallmark:

> I told her in Spanish that I loved her very much and that I loved everything about her from her feet to her head and we counted all the things that were loved and she was truly and very happy and I was happy too and I did not think I lied about any one of them nor about all of them.

Later, when tribal customs force him to give up the girl, Papa reports: "This was the beginning of the end of the day in my life which offered the most chances of happiness."

Whether we're intended to take his assertion seriously or as an exaggerated expression of his disappointment is unclear, but from that point onwards, *True at First Light* pursues a drawn-out conclusion in which Papa and Mary go on, as if contentedly, with their marriage. As usual with Hemingway, atmosphere and attitude are far more important than plot. Mary at one point berates her husband as a "conscience-ridden murderer," but this is precisely the moral stance that gives the hunting scenes their tension and beauty. For instance, "I was happy that before he died he had lain on the high yellow rounded mound with his tail down," Hemingway writes of "Mary's lion," "and his great paws comfortable before him and looked off across his country to the blue forest and the high white snows of the big Mountain." Also, in the course of the ninety-six days it takes them to stalk the marauding male lion, the novel wends its way through philosophical digressions on the nature of love, friendship, the soul and the meaning of cultural differences. Hemingway combines his intimate knowledge of nature with his well-honed instincts about people, as he narrates in a loose, diary-like form the trials and tribulations of an encampment with a single purpose. Patrick was even impressed by his father's total recall of the backdrop of the story, but the amazing thing is that Hemingway was writing the manuscript at all, given that the safari ended in two plane crashes.

Even before the actual release of the book, the news about this forthcoming publication (including an excerpt from Chapter One online and another one in the May 24th 1999 edition of *The New Yorker*) swept the literary arena like wildfire. Charles Scribner III, the New York publisher, is one who offers a positively valid argument for his publishing venture:

> After Hemingway's death, my father oversaw the publication of several posthumous works, beginning with *A Moveable Feast* and including *Islands in the Stream, The Dangerous Summer,* and *The Garden of Eden.* At his retirement I "inherited" this one final manuscript, which I first read with great excitement over a decade ago and then kept under wraps until the perfect editor could be engaged - the author's son Patrick, who accompanied his father and Mary Hemingway on their final safari and who alone could appreciate its status as a work of fiction, "a fictional memoir."

The "perfect editor" Patrick, who had been along on the safari and knew inside-and-out the subject matter of the book as well as the author and his voice believes that the book is

> ...I think, a very good picture of, among other things, safari life. Hunting safaris were a very characteristic type of travel experience. It was sort of ike an ocean voyage. You took off with a crew and you were isolated for weeks at a time without communication really with anybody. And the crew was made up of certain jobs. There were the people who did the tracking of

the animals, the people who prepared the meat and the skins, the cooks, the drivers. And *True at First Light* very much describes this life and the different people's jobs and how they thought and what they did in the course of the work.

III

Reactions to *True at First Light* have ranged from positive affirmation to total negation. For some critics the book is a Hemingway lover's dream come true - an unexpected centennial gift. Previewed in Prepub Alert, *Library Journal* 3/1/99 Michael Rogers seems to have been swept off his feet as he writes in the same journal on May 1:

> Like Zeus descended from Olympus, Hemingway returns with one last bolt of lightning in his hand......
> Plot-wise, the book is fairly subdued, simply following the daily activities of the African hunting camp. The book's contribution to the author's canon is first-person narrator "Papa", essentially EH himself, who refreshingly is far older and less spry than the usual Hemingway supermen.....here it is wife Mary who is the aggressor, hell bent on killing a lion, while Papa acts as a game ranger and medic for local natives........Hemingway's unequaled power to describe a locale is in full vigor, and readers will feel the sun hot on their necks, the weight of the rifle in their hands, and the taste of the gin after the hunt.
> ....Twentieth century American literature could not end on a brighter note than the publication of this book. (p.79)

Malcolm Bradbury is equally forthcoming in his assessment. The book according to him is an attempt to cast a heroic glow over a disturbing episode in Hemingway's life. It offers a mythicized version of the safari, transposed into a tale of African imperial adventure in the manner of Rider Haggard. Moreover he feels that tucked into the book is a weirdly disturbing sexual fantasy about male and female possession.

> There is good, engaged writing here, when Hemingway forgets his vanities and pretensions, stops searching for humour, turns to dealing directly with nature or matters of precise observation. There are marvellous passages on African birds, others of solemn meditation. Hemingway has not lost his talent, but he has certainly not found his bearings. No editor could give this material dramatic tension or strong narrative structure.
> .....*True At First Light* (incidentally a seriously good Hemingway title) will not engage the reader as a great lost novel. Rather it's a lesser, disturbing work, by one of the century's truly great writers, showing what is good and bad about him. It will not enhance his reputation, but it will help illuminate it.

We are all aware that pruning was a part of Ernest Hemingway's art. He once remarked that he a writer could omit anything if he knew what he omitted, and the omitted part would make the story stronger. But the question naturally arises, can we trust another with that judgment? Patrick Hemingway, the author's son and literary executor, who prepared the manuscript for publication condensing it to half its length, has a logical explanation to the barrage of questions targeted at him: "The only trouble is (Ernest Hemingway) did leave the material. He didn't destroy it. Perhaps he didn't intend to have it published, but when people are dead it's hard to know what they want. Somebody, some day, was going to publish these works, and I had particular insights about this particular work." When questioned by the online interviewer about what criteria he chose for editing the manuscript, Patrick categorically stated that though condensing the book inevitably reshaped it, he had not intentionally changed any of his father's words:

> It was essentially to keep as strong a story line as

the original manuscript would allow. I had identified what I felt were the principal story lines. There are two main story lines: One is a lion hunt, the second is a leopard hunt. And then there is a more complex story line that involves sexual politics and the triangle between a husband and wife and another woman. I wanted to make them as strong as possible and as integrated as possible. My tool was cutting, not making up material or inventing transitional passages. Just cutting. We ended up taking about a quarter to a third of the manuscript.

Asked whether he was able to sense where his father was headed, Patrick replied in the affirmative:

I think I could see where my father was headed, I think he was planning to incorporate his actual plane crashes in it. He did have two plane crashes in Uganda. There is a certain amount of forewarning: that he's very reluctant to leave this place, that he doesn't see why then they should go to central Africa. I think his description of the crashes would have been horrific. He was building up some tension there that would have been very explosive.
But given what we had to work with, we simply couldn't indulge ourselves in that.

Perhaps the most matter-of-fact logic for the publication of the book is offered by Michael Reynolds, the recent and most prolific Hemingway biographer. Leaving the critics to decide whether the book was good or bad, he emphasized one point about unpublished manuscripts:

He left five books unpublished. They've all been published. They were not left unpublished because he hid not want them published. In the 1950s his income-tax situation was horrific. At one point he was paying 85 cents out of every dollar he made to the IRS. Rather than publish books and pay the money to the IRS, he left all the five of those books to his

heirs tax-free. (Today, we have more favorable codes.)
But Hemingway intended eventually to publish those
manuscripts. Some of them, as far as he was
concerned, were ready to publish. *True at Firs Light*
was perhaps the least revised before he died, but he
spent a year writing it, and he always revised as he
wrote. So the people who say that none of these should
have been published because Hemingway didn't want
them published don't understand the situation.

Unlike Michael Reynolds, Patrick Hemingway's mention
of "cutting" is what troubles people like novelist Joan
Didion. She wrote in *The New Yorker* last November that
condensation inevitably works to alter what the author may
have intended. Hemingway, she claimed, "was a writer who
had in time made the English language new, changed the
rhythms of the way both his own and the next few
generations would speak and wrote and think .... This was
a man to whom words mattered. He worked at them, he
understood them, he got inside them. His wish to be
survived by only the words he determined fit for publication
would have seemed clear enough." Didion noted that from
excerpts published already, it was manifest that the
manuscript of *True at First Light* was "something not yet
made, notes, scenes in the process of being set down, words
set down but not yet written." She even went on to describe
the book as "the systematic creation of a marketable
product, a discrete body of work different in kind from, and
in fact tending to obscure, the body of work published by
Hemingway in his time." Didion even quotes from
Hemingway's own letter written in 1952 to Charles A.
Fenton to support her point of view:

> Mr. Fenton I feel very strongly about this. I have
> written you so before and I write you now again.
> Writing that I do not wish to publish, you have no
> right to publish. I would no more do a thing like that
> to you than I would cheat a man at cards or rifle his
> desk or wastebasket or read his personal letters.

Fans of Hemingway who find the book a disappointment
also have their own logic for such an attitude. They accuse
that there is no dramatic structure or plot. What suspense
there is – Will the marauding Mau-Maus attack the camp?
Will Miss Mary kill her lion? – is disposed of before the
book is half over. The dicta on writing are no longer fresh
and the other observations tend to be of the throwaway
variety. David Gates in the *Newsweek* states that "much of
it reads like B-plus Hemingway - with some of the passages
he ever wrote" , Rose Marie Burwell, a professor who
specializes in his unfinished late work ... sees it as a
daring, if ultimately thwarted, expedition into postmodern
narrative and the strange country of [Hemingway's]
obsessions. Adam Fein feels that the book's failure is not
in its fascination with sex, drinking and hunting, but in
its inability to explain this preoccupation.

> While *The Sun Also Rises* made the drifting, amoral
> lifestyle of its characters a fulcrum of its commentary
> in his novel, Hemingway and his wife live with a belief
> system that has neither meaning, nor interest in
> explaining itself. Although the novel focuses on the
> interplay of human relationships, age and
> enlightenment, spirituality, and even the power of
> Africa itself, in the end it simply has no meritable
> substance.

Another critic, Tom Jenks, is of the opinion that
Hemingway, in his last book, writes his own sad epitaph.
According to him, "As an icon of mid-century American
masculinity, Hemingway lives on everywhere, reinforcing
the perception of his vitality and success..."(53). Yet,
"certain to be an international best seller, *True at First
Light* in no way resembles anything like Hemingway's best
work. In fact, it can't be viewed as a book in the usual
sense but only as a published rough draft whose claim to
our attention lies not in its characters or story per se but
in an author whose failing effort at writing the book presents
an unfortunate self-portrait of the deterioration behind of
the surface of his heroic image. (54). Jenks concludes his

argument with a strong sense of disgust:

> *True at First Light* candidly shows Papa at his worst:
> self-conscious, self-pitying, self -indulgent, self
> aggrandizing. The book is so unformed, fragmentary,
> digressive, and anecdotal that no one can say what
> Hemingway's intention might eventually have been.
> There are numerous themes he seems to have
> wanted to explore; however it seems clear that the
> existence of the book owes more to a determined
> habit of writing than to any clarity of purpose. I think
> it is reasonable to say that in drafting the manuscript,
> Hemingway was more or less, just writing. There's
> little tension in the book except the knowledge that
> it is Hemingway doing the writing, aimlessly for the
> most part, yet with hope - his occasional successes
> must have tantalized him, as they do the reader, but
> he's clearly very tired. Too much of the dialogue
> between characters reads like the author talking to
> himself. (60)

In another review of the book, James Brady's tone is equally
outrageous:

> Has anyone been given less opportunity to "rest in
> peace" than Papa sincehe said adios? Has any great
> writer   been   so   relentlessly   milked,
> marketed,manipulated and exploited in death as poor
> Hemingway? .....Since the 1961 suicide in Idaho,
> they've gotten four full books out of a dead man....
> There is some wonderful stuff in these books plus
> much literary dreck. The Hemingway who once told
> George Plimpton that he re-wrote the final paragraph
> of *A Farewell to Arms* 39 times, "to get it right," would
> probably not have recognized any of these works in
> their posthumously published form.

"I hope I won't offend with heresy when I say that
Hemingway never had both feet down on Africa, never really
was in Africa," Nadine Gordimer, the Nobel-prize winning

author, said. "For a country is its *people*, Africa is its people,"
and Hemingway "chose Africa as one of those panoramic
three-dimensional postcards where at first light animals
seem to leap out of the thorn bush." She finally added, It's
an insult indeed to his lifelong integrity to his art to regard
his work in this shabby, prurient way."(Goldberg, 4) Charles
Scribner Jr. likes to call Hemingway " a Scribner author,"
and writing about the association that Hemingway
maintained with their firm for the rest of his life, he said
way back in 1993: "I sincerely hope that if Ernest is keeping
a watch on the fate of his writings from someplace beyond
the grave he will be pleased by what we have done and
what we are doing, If he is not pleased I am sure to hear
about it should we meet in the hereafter." (35) Earlier, he
had justified his claim for publishing a selection of
Hemingway's letter in 1981 by stating: "Hemingway left
strict instructions that his letters should not be published.
But with Mary's approval, I published them and I think I
did the right thing.....I considered that I was justified. It is
well known that Virgil left instructions for the *Aeneid* to be
burned after his death. Fortunately not all literary executors
obey such requests." In a way, this assertion seems true
because though a lot of ire has been vented out against
the publication, Charles Scribner's Sons must be happy
with the rising sales records. A letter from the present
executor of the firm, Charles Scribner III even eulogizes
the book openly:

> The last of the Hemingway books, *True at First Light*
> combines in a memorable way the hallmarks of
> Hemingway's talent: action fused with reflection,
> psychological insight, and humor - *Green Hills of Africa*
> meets *A Moveable Feast* as it were. The first appraisal
> of this unpublished work was written by my father
> twenty-five years ago, and I can think of no better
> one to share with you now. As a result of its
> informality it provides a delightful self-portrait of
> Hemingway, if not in his slippers, at least with his
> mosquito boots on, in front of the campfire with a
> scotch and soda. The narrative is zestful, self-

disparaging, humorous, and at times outrageous. It also contains exquisitely sketched memories of the past.

Herb Greer, who called this a "piece of virtual reality", feels that the virtues are several levels above those of the pompous and expensive flash that passes for literature today. According to him,

> This book, clearly neither a novel nor a memoir, is best described by the ambiguous French term *Ácrit* , which the dictionaries say means tale or narrative butproperly connotes something more subtle, in which questions of detail like "is it really true?" or "did it literally happen like that?" are irrelevant. The virtual reality of the tale has its own integrity, and if that satisfies the reader, it should be enough for anyone except, as I say, the professional or amateur critic who is determined to cavil and carp. If the narrative in general feels stretched out here and there, that is not Hemingway's fault but Patrick's. The point is that no one will read this book unless he is interested in Hemingway. That interest, plus the very real virtues, which are all his, ought to satisfy the honest (as opposed to vulpine) reader.

IV

Discussions regarding the sharply divided opinion of the publication and reception of *True at First Light* can go on endlessly but it would be missing one vital point. If we can accept the posthumously published *A Moveable Feast, Islands in the Stream, The Dangerous Summer* and *The Garden of Eden* to be integral texts in the Hemingway canon, one should not have any qualms of conscience in accepting *True at First Light* as Hemingway's work too. Though Edmund Wilson had edited the notes and unfinished drafts of F. Scott Fitzgerald's *The Last Tycoon*, the published version definitely helps one to understand better the author's final years of stay at Hollywood. So also, Hemingway's

posthumously published last novel can offer us insights,
however fleetingly, into his *oeuvre*. The book begins with
the observation that Africa has changed. Hemingway must
have soon come to see that the cultural gulf between him
and the Africans was far too wide for any close relationship,
and that in any case the tribal system was rotting, almost
ready to make way for the tribally corrupt caricature of
Western European government that came to rule Kenya.
The theme of war, a favorite of the novelist, is relegated to
the sidelines too. Though the war hovers in the early
chapters – wary preparations for a possible attack that never
materializes – it quickly fades into the middle distance
and Kenyatta and his Kikuyu tribe are not featured. The
dedication with which his hero in *For Whom the Bell Tolls*
had joined the Spanish Republicans is absent here and
the narrator speaks much about his closeness to the
Wakamba tribe, not very involved in Mau Mau.

Stylistically, it is unfortunate that there are too few
passages that have the unique technique for which
Hemingway received the Pulitzer Prize and the Nobel Prize
for literature. There are sections of stiff dialogue and
condescension to his wife and the Africans that make the
reader cringe. Nevertheless, more humorous than most of
his other novels, the narrative also contains enough
hunting scenes for Hemingway and others to show the
requisite grace under pressure. As the reviewer of
Publisher's Weekly states, the book is more a curiosity than
a major contribution to Hemingway's *oeuvre*. Yet the old
Hemingway magic flashes sporadically, like lightning, but
not often enough. There are a series of sentences intoning
"I wished..." reminiscent of his earlier linguistic triumphs,
and some dialogue, crisp and to the point, like the
stichomythia of Greek tragedy. Lines like "So I carried her
in and she weighed just what a woman that you love should
weigh when you lift her in your arms..." still resonate. The
incident where Hemingway recalls a poignant moment in
which years earlier in Montana, he had shot Old Kite, his
aged, favorite horse and left the carcass as bait to catch
bears can be probably called Hemingway at his best. He
describes the horse's reaction "when he saw the gun come

up. I thought I could keep him from seeing it but he saw it and his eyes knew what it was and he stood very still trembling." The voice of Hemingway that American writers and readers have grown up on is heard as the writer explains how a man of honor can have the heart of a child. We hear it again in the single paragraph in which he watches an airplane land at a campsite, and later as he talks about what it is like to lie in your bed listening to a lion roaring in the night. His memories of growing up in Michigan are also fine and exquisite.

Sometimes his technique is almost invisible. In one episode, for instance, we meet his gun bearer and native guide Nguili, who "loved to pour beer and see that the foam rose just at the very last and topped the beer without spilling." Hemingway then goes on to describe the young man, his background, and his talents in depth, including that unimportant detail that he was "almost as good looking as a girl without being at all effeminate." But the careful reader watches how the writer segues out of this description and effortlessly back into the narrative by repeating that, for Nguili, "one of his great pleasures, since he was not yet allowed by tribal law to drink, was to pour beer for those who were allowed to drink it."

Apart from his style, what really surprises us in *True at First Light* is the similarity of certain situations, certain concurrent themes within the Hemingway canon, which occurred in his earlier *Green Hills of Africa* and the African short stories. While reading the book it is difficult to know when Hemingway is telling the truth, and when he has fictionalized his story. By altering details and creating new stories, is he proving that writers have the power to blur the line between what is real and what is imaginary - and sometimes even rewrite history? Though based on big-game hunting, all these works contain detailed description of the actual setting and location in Africa - the green plains covered with grey mist, zebra and gazelle traversing the horizon, cool dark nights broken by the sound of the hyena's cry - but they also digress into other issues relating to a writer's creative talent, his craft etc. For instance, the incident of the hunting of the big kudu in *Green Hills of*

Africa or the charging buffalo in "Francis Macomber", is
replicated by Miss Mary's lion; the talk about "what is it
that happens to American writers" (*GHOA*, 27) , the idea of
the dying Harry in "The Snows of Kilimanjaro" that he
"would never write the things that he had saved to write
until he knew enough to write them well", is once again
reiterated by Papa when he talks about the writer's craft.
In *Green Hills of Africa*, apart from the now oft-repeated
statement of Hemingway that "All modern American
literature comes from one book by Mark Twain called
Huckleberry Finn" (26), Hemingway tells us about "the kind
of writing that can be done. How far prose can be carried if
anyone is serious enough and has luck. There is a fourth
and fifth dimension that can be gotten."(29) He even
classifies various categories of American writers:

> At a certain age the men writers change into Old
> Mother Hubbard. The women writers become Joan of
> Arc without the fighting. They become leaders.....The
> others try to save their souls with what they write.
> That is an easy way out. Others are ruined by first
> money, the first praise, thefirst attack, the first time
> they find they cannot write, or the first time they
> cannot do anything else, or else they g frightened
> and join organizations that do their thinking for the.
> Or they do not know what they want. Henry James
> wanted to make money. He never did, of course.(27)

Though most critics find Hemingway's practice of attacking
writers and critics sloppy and egotistic - the attack on
Julian/F.Scott Fitzgerald in "The Snows of Kilimanjaro" is
too familiar an instance - nevertheless, when Hemingway
does discourse on writing and writers he does so
insightfully, stating: "Our writers when they have made
some money increase their standard of living and they are
caught. They have to write to keep up the establishments,
their wives, and so on, and they write slop.... Or else they
read the critics... At present we have two good writers who
cannot write because they have lost confidence through
reading critics." He was speaking of Fitzgerald who was

having trouble finishing *Tender is the Night*, and Sherwood Anderson who was never the same after *Winesburg, Ohio.*

In *True at First Light*, Hemingway reminisces about encounters with other writers and his days in Paris and Spain and satirizes, among other things, the role of organized religion in Africa. He also muses on the act of writing itself and the author's role in determining the truth. What is fact and what is fiction? This is a question that was posed by Hemingway's readers throughout his career and is one of the principal subjects here. He dismisses his critics at one sweep:

> Lately I had read with distaste various books written about myself by people who knew all about my inner life, aims and motives. Readingthem was like reading an account of a battle where you had foughtwritten by someone who had not only been present but, in some cases,had not even been born when the battle had taken place. All thesepeople who wrote of my life both inner and outer wrote with anabsolute assurance that I had never felt.

Nothing has changed about the complex connection between lying that is truer than the truth and daily journalism's onslaught of facts that are accurate but total lies. These are more dangerous than the inaccuracies, because the inaccuracies can be corrected, but there is nothing to remedy a factual, untrue lie except art. Figuring out what that means, acquiring an intuitive understanding of all that, lies at the heart of the slow, painful, wonderful process that is the fiction writer's apprenticeship. Hemingway knew this better than anybody and said this better than almost anybody and demonstrated this in a body of work as good as anybody's. So we find him stating in his "fictional memoir":

> ...[A]ll a writer of fiction is really is a congenital liar who invents from his own knowledge or that of other men. I am a writer of fiction and so I am a liar too

and invent from what I know and what I've heard.....
My excuseis that I make the truth as I invent it truer
than it would be. That is what makes good writers or
bad. If I write in the first person, stating it isfiction,
critics now will still try to prove these things never
happened tome. It is silly as trying to prove Defoe
was not Robinson Crusoe so therefore it is a bad book.

The issue of a writer's craft also figures within the
conversation of the story as well.

We are [crazy]," I said. "But you musn't tell outsiders".
"But you don't really mean all writers are crazy?"
"Only the good ones."
"But you got angry when that man wrote a book about
how you were crazy."
 "Yes, because he did not know about it not how it
worked. Just as he knew nothing about writing."
"It's awfully complicated," Miss Mary said.
"I won't try to explain it. I'll try to write something to
show you how it works."

From such examples it is clear that the true book, *True at
First Light*, is less in its events than in the unmonitored
voice of its author. However unrevised, unpolished it might
be, Hemingway's talk here offers a compendium of his
familiar old symbols, themes, moods, feelings, details. We
cannot but agree with the reviewer of *Kirkus* when he states
that the book is "uneven, imperfect, irritating, amusing,
moving, and of treasurable importance to an understanding
of this massive, however flawed genius of our literature."
For people who love Hemingway and even for those who
hate him, *True At First Light* is a great book that will teach
us more about him. Michael Reynolds says that what he
has tried to do all along in his writing is to explain
Hemingway the writer and so his focus has always been
on his writing, trying to encourage his readers to go back
to his text, because ultimately this is the moat important
aspect of Hemingway. Had he never written, we would not
be celebrating his centennial. It was not the public man

who made history, it was Hemingway the writer.

NOTES & REFERENCES

Baker, Carlos.   *Ernest Hemingway: A Life Story*. New York: Scribner's, 1969.

Bradbury, Malcolm.   "It Really Is a Very Important Centenary" True at First Light by Ernest Hemingway. *Literary Review*.

Brady, James.   "Tome from the tomb: Another work by Hem comes to light".

Advertising Age, September 7, 1998. p.21.

Didion, Joan.   "Last Words: Those Hemingway wrote, and those he didn't". *The New Yorker*, November 9, 1998.pp.74-80.

Fein, Adam.   Review in *The Yale Herald* via U-WIRE, 1999.

Goldberg, Carey.   "Hemingway Gets a Kick In a Kickoff." *The New York Times*. April 14, 1999.

Greer, Herb.   "True at Dusk". *World and I*, November 1999.

Hemingway, Ernest   *Green Hills of Africa*. Penguin, 1966.

————.   "The Good Lion". *The Complete Short Stories of Ernest Hemingway*. The Finca Vigia Edition. New York: Scribner's, 1987. pp.482-484.

————.   "An African Story" op.cit. pp. 545-554.

————.   *True At First Light: A Fictional Memoir*. Edited with an Intro. by Patrick Hemingway. New York: Scribner's, 1999.

Hemingway, Mary   *How It Was*. New York: Ballantine, 1976.

Hemingway, Patrick   Online interview copyrighted by Charles Scribner,III, 1999

Jenks, Tom.   "The Old Man and the Manuscript" *Harper's Magazine*, May 1999.pp.53-60.

Macintyre, Ben   "The Importance of being Ernest". *The Statesman*, April 14, 1999. p.9. (Reprinted from *The Times*, London).

Meyers, Jeffrey	*Hemingway : A Biography.* New York: Harper & Row, 1985.
Reynolds, Michael	Online interview dated 21.7.99 discussing the final part of his biography, *Hemingway, The Final Years.* http:// barnenandnoble.com
Rogers, Michael	"An Earnest Celebration". *Library Journal.* May 1, 1999.p.79.
Scribner, Charles J	"The Secret of Being Ernest (and the Secret of Keeping Ernest)". *In the Web of Ideas: The Education of a Publisher.* New York: Scribner's, 1993. Pp. 35-62.
Scribner, Charles III.	"Hemingway: A Publisher's Assessment"; "Hemingway. Remembered"; "A Letter from Charles Scribner III", an Online interview. (Available through several Hemingway websites).

Picasso, Hemingway, And The Bull

Indrani Haldar

That Hemingway possessed, as an inventory reveals, no less than seven books on Picasso[1]—albums, critical surveys, and Sabertes' *Intimate Portrait*—does not seem to be a mere accident when one recollects his association with the members of Gertrude Stein's charmed circle in Paris (Miss Stein herself possessed 30 Picasso paintings), and the letter he wrote to Charles A. Fenton in 1952 asserting that Picasso, Braque, Masson and Miro were friends of his. In an interview, he confessed, "I respected a lot of painters, some of my own age, others older—Gris, Picasso, Braque, Monet—", later adding almost as an explanatory footnote, that he had learned "as much from painters about how to write as from writers,"[2] an admission not unexpected in the context of his frequent forays into the Luxembourg Museum and the Prado.[3]

With Picasso, Hemingway shared, in particular, an enthusiasm, amounting almost to an obsession, for the drama of the *corrida*, which is reflected in the importance of the bullring and in the centrality of the bull-symbol in the work of the two contemporaries. For both artists, the bullfight is of complex and ambiguous significance equally as visual experience and metaphor. Both depict the actual drama in all its crude reality but infuse it with patterns of symbolic meaning.

Familiar with the bullring from his childhood, Picasso had so intimate a knowledge of bull-fighting that in the Spring of 1936, he was able to engrave, within a few hours, twenty-six aquatints illustrating the different stages of the drama for the classic bullfighting manual of Pepe Illo, a contemporary of Goya.[4] His earliest recorded drawing, at

the age of ten, had been of a bullfight, the subject recurring
in a number of early paintings, made before his visit to
Paris in 1900 and on his return to Barcelona in 1901, in
which the traumatic coexistence of life and death in the
bullring had been conveyed by the two halves of the arena,
one brilliantly-lit and the other in deep shade. Towards the
end of the First World War, the bullring reappeared in
Picasso's art to acquire increasing importance in the early
thirties when, in a series of haunting paintings and
sketches, the artist portrayed the savage drama of
slaughter so forcefully that during the Picasso Exhibition
at Barcelona, Ramon Gomez de Serna, who recited some of
the artist's poems, would call him "the toreador of painting."[5]
The torrid thirties also saw the evolution of the Minotaur
figure in the artist's work, first in May 1932, clasping a
dagger, on the cover of the journal *Minotaure* designed by
Picasso, and latter ininnumerable paintings and sketches,
namely the four remarkable etchings included in the
Vollard Suite under the title *The Blinded Minotaur* (1934)
and the paradoxical *Minotaurmachy* (1935). At the same
time, the bull remained the focus of attention in the series
of engravings entitled *The Dream and Lie of Franco* (1937),
a satiric commentary on the dictator's rule, and most
bafflingly, in *Guernica* (1937). In the still-lifes of the forties,
especially the famous *Bull's Head* of 1943, a bronze cast
from a bicycle saddle and handlebars, the bull becomes
almost an emblem for the artist reminiscent of the
Minotaur. The late fifties saw Picasso executing bullfighting
sketches of high artistic quality while, in the last paintings
of 1961 and 1962, the bullfighter hero emerges as a symbol
of inviolable devotion to art.

"To me heaven would be a big bullring with me holding
to seats,"[6] wrote Hemingway to F. Scott Fitzgerald from
Spain in July, 1925. And to Paul Romaine, in 1932, he
confessed, "About bulls—forteen years or so—bull-fighting
was my recreation and amusement as whatever might be
yours if you have any need to think about anything but
your work."[7] Bullfighting meant, in fact, more than
recreation and amusement to Hemingway for all those
years since his introduction to the sport on a trip to Spain

in 1923. Of Nick Adams he was to say in the posthumously published piece, "On Writing": "His whole inner life had been bull-fights all one year."[8] For Hemingway, the disturbingly violent drama of the bullring, which he yet witnessed compulsively as an *aficionado*, demanded to be metamorphosed into a coherent artistic experience embracing a meaningful way of looking at life. On one plane of experience, the prismatic range of vivid visual impressions afforded by the bullfight could not but stimulate a writer as painterly in his perception of the sensate world as Hemingway was. On another plane, imaginatively transformed, the bullring could become an arena for the enactment of a drama of deep, spiritual significance enabling the writer to test out, in its conflicts and confrontations, a positive and humanistic philosophy of life.

In a despatch to the *Toronto Star Weekly* in October 1923, "Bullfighting a Tragedy," Hemingway had explained the sport to an American readership emphasizing however, that bullfighting was not a sport but "a very great tragedy."[9] A second dispatch, "Pamplona in July," had testified to the artistry and dedication of the two matadors Maera and Algabeno, thus establishing bullfighting as a test of skill and courage. More remarkable were the six brief bullfighting vignettes of 1924 in *in our tune.* Dramatic and visual on the level of pure description ("Villalta standing straight and the red hilt of the sword sticking out dully between the bull's shoulders,"[10] they yet betray an ironic and distanced stance. Occasionally the spectator's point of view overlaps with that of the protagonist, man or bull (as for instance, in the account of Maera's death[11]), opening up possibilities of a triple identification for the reader.

While bullfighting is both the central event and the central symbol in Hemingway's first novel, *The Sun Also Rises* (1926), the spiritual distance separating the actor, the heroic individual from the spectator, is almost as distinctly emphasized as in Picasso's *corrida* paintings. Jake Barnes is the spectator *par excellence*, consoling himself with a *barrera* seat and the ironical epithet *aficionado*, and deriving vicarious pleasure from Pedro Romero's exploits, but denied the matador's privilege to kill or create in love or hate. In its devastating commentary on the spiritual torpor prevalent in modern life, the novel expresses anguish equal to that of Picasso's tormented bullfights of the thirties.

For a more didactic treatment of bullfighting and its significance to the artist, the Hemingway-enthusiast usually plods his way through *Death in the Afternoon*, published in 1932 and anticipated in an article entitled "Bullfighting, Sport and Industry," written for *Fortune* magazine in 1929. Predictably, in this work, which also constitutes his most protracted analysis of his own craft, Hemingway traces analogies between the arts of bullfighting and writing. That superb story of the late twenties, "The Undefeated," however, presents the matador-artist equation in more imaginative terms, combining visual experience with psychological drama, and introspection with an objective approach. The undefeated hero of the story, Manuel Garcia, may not be as great a bullfighter as Maera or Juan Belemonte, matadors Hemingway apotheosizes in *Death in the Afternoon*, or even Sidney Franklin, the American bullfighter Hemingway formed a friendship with, but in his dedication to his art and his intuitive understanding of the moment of truth in the bullring, he furnishes an aesthetically satisfying version of Hemingway's concept of the artist.

To his father, Hemingway wrote in 1925, explaining his artistic aims, "You see I'm trying in all my stories to get the feeling of the actual life across—not to just depict life—or criticize it—but to actually make it alive. So that when you have read something by me you actually experience the thing."[12] Not to narrate, or explain, the reporter's goal, but to convey direct experience was obviously what the painter, and especially the inheritor of Impressionism, the modern painter, aimed at. Picasso, in fact, did not mince words when he remarked, "In the case of a painting people have to understand—people who try to explain pictures are usually barking up the wrong tree.."[13] Hemingway's tours of the Musee de Luxembourg, the Chicago Art Institute, and the Prado had unquestionably prepared him to share the painter's method and objective. At the same time, in the direct, violent and swift action of the bull-ring, and the strong elemental feelings it unleashed, did Hemingway, like Picasso, or Goya to whose bullfighting engravings both the twentieth-century artists were indebted, find an experience that could be conveyed with immediate dramatic vividity and yet reverberate with a meaning beyond the raw physical data, the "fourth and fifth dimension," perhaps, that Hemingway mentioned in *Green Hills of Africa.*

Interestingly, both Hemingway and Picasso were averse to intellectual interpretations of their work and unswervingly resisted attempts to clamp rigidly limited symbolic meaning to it. To Kahnweiler, Picasso asserted in a discussion on *Guernica,* "it isn't up to the painter to create the symbols; otherwise, it would be better if he wrote them out in so many words instead of painting them. The public who look at the picture must see in the horse and the bulls symbols which they interpret as they understand them."[14] Hemingway's anti-cerebral bias is too well-known to be reiterated at this point but it is obvious even from the casual remarks he throws out in *Death in the Afternoon* that he considered intellectually imposed symbols to be too restricted to be aesthetically acceptable. In the intensely-lived sequence of moments in the *corrida,* however, both painter and writer discovered a drama that would yield rich symbolic nuances with the actors assuming different and often interchangeable roles from time to time.

For both Picasso and Hemingway, the slaughter of the bull is essential, a ritualistic act, as in a Dionysian vegetation rite, through which a renewal of life and manhood is achieved. The paradoxical juxtaposition of death and life in the bullring, an affirmation of life being reached through the act of death-dealing, thus convincingly conveys the duality of the universe. As the arena on which this strange but timeless drama is played out, the bullring is sacrosanct in Spanish tradition, and realized as such by Picasso and Hemingway. Indifferent to the sympathy or apathy of the spectators outside the halo-shaped *barrera,* the matador confronts the sacrificial bull alone. His isolation is emphasized by Picasso who spatially separates the two worlds of spectator and actor, contrasting the public with the private, and the known with the magical. Hemingway's bullfighter, too, is isolated by being inarticulate, uncommunicative like Manuel Garcia in "The Undefeated," or completely immersed in his art to the exclusion of all else like Pedro Romero in *The Sun Also Rises*. This *noli me tangere* envelops him even when, like Maera in *in our time*, he bleeds to death in the bullring.

The toreador, then, has a crucial role to play in what Hemingway considers a three-act tragedy.[15] In Picasso's paintings, this role is never stressed but left implicit. Like his *saltimbangue*, Picasso's bullfighter lives precariously on the edge of life, asserting both his humanity and his manhood in each solitary confrontation with death. Yet, he always remains an ambiguous figure, somewhat withdrawn, harlequin-like in significance, for the bond that unites him with the bull he must kill is also one of love, even of love for a part of himself. The central protagonist in Picasso's work, always in the foreground, and assuming fresh significance in each new painting, is the *toro* rather than the *torero*. In most of Hemingway's fiction, on the other hand, the matador, in a sense, creates the bull, bending the animal to his will, his virtuoso performance raising him to the status of a creator.

Savage and brutal in the paintings of the thirties, Picasso's bull seems maddened by the ugliness and torpor of the world he seeks to destroy. It is also a world in which manhood has gone to seed, like the dilapidated, mangy horses ridden by the picadors only to be disemboweled by the bull. In a terrifying bullfight painting of this decade, the bull even devours the entails of a horse in its rage. Hemingway, at his toughest, wrote that the degutted horses of the bullring contributed a comic element to what he else deemed a tragedy but the ironic conversation of the picadors in "The Undefeated" serves to show that he considered the wretched animals to represent the cupidity of men rather than masculine virility. It is the bull, on the other hand, who in Picasso's work, seems to acquire a double connotation, symbolizing both creative energy and man's deep, unconscious ties with the physical, instinctual world. In destroying him, the matador sacrifices the raw, physical instincts so that a new imaginative reality may emerge and man's immortality assured. At the same time, it is the creative energy released by the blind demoniacal world the bull represents which ultimately enables the act to be performed. To Hemingway, indeed, the supreme matador is he who kills *recibiendo*, using the bull's own impetus to drive in the sword at the crucial moment in an act that unites the victim and the slayer.

Both Hemingway and Picasso, thus present, Hemingway directly and Picasso in an oblique and implicit manner, the enigmatic bond between man and bull, a hermetically sealed relationship that excludes even the privileged spectator. All Hemingway's matadors love and admire the bulls they kill. In *Death in the Afternoon*, the writer sees the killing as an act of exchange and substitution since matador and bull are linked both in life and death, each enabling the other to display consummate courage and an artistry surmounting death while, for each, death is equally real. For all Hemingway admiration of the skill his matadors display, there is never any attempt to gloss over to the stark reality of death in his bullfighting stories. Of the matador he writes in *Death in the Afternoon*, "He is performing a work of art and he is playing with death, bringing it closer, closer, closer to himself, a death that you know is in horns—"[16] Similarly, Picasso's still-life paintings with bull skulls, for instance, the *Still Life with Red Bull's Head* and the *Still Life with Black Bull's Head*, both painted in 1938, suggest the co-existence of creativity and morality even while the bull's head becomes almost as emblem for the artist.

In his book on *Guernica*, Anthony Blunt writes, "Picasso's symbols are never static, they can never be exactly pigeon-holed but develop as his ideas develop."[17] As a complex symbol of the man-bull relationship, Picasso evoked the Minotaur figure, which he invested with a dual personality like the Harlequin. In a series of paintings in the thirties, the Minotaur appears as alternately violent and tender, menacing and yet suffering, tragically blinded and yet searching for light and beauty. In the aquatint, Blind Minotaur Led Through the Night by Girl with Fluttering Dove (1935), the Minotaur strains toward the starry sky and is helped forward by a girl who seems to represent man's spiritual self and his lost innocence. In *Minotaurmachy* (1935), he advances threateningly but is stopped by an unfearing girl who holds out a candle, interpreted either as imagination or as the light of reason, to light his way through the darkness. This ambivalence of the protean creature reflects the ambivalence of human nature in which the instinctual vies with the intellectual, the physical with the spiritual, and the lust for destruction with the yearning for a renewal of life. At the same time, the Minotaur becomes a conscious means of self-identification for the artist as destroyer and creator in one. "If all the ways I have been along were marked on a map and joined up with a line," Picasso once wrote, "it might represent a Minotaur."[18]

Picasso's later bulls are all, in a sense, Minotaurs, half-human, keepers of virility, and identifiable with the artist himself. The only heroic figure in *The Dream and Lie of Franco* is the noble, humanized bull who boldly confronts the polyp-like excrescence riding on a degutted horse. Amidst the devastation of *Guernica*, the taurian presence diversely symbolizes courage, fortitude, and an indomitable life-force. Strangely observant and quizzical in aspect, he may also represent the artist as both spectator and actor, looking forward through the confusion and turmoil of an agonized age to a timeless moral destiny.

In 1951, Hemingway wrote a fable entitled "The Faithful Bull" about a "great bull" that "fought wonderfully" but was killed "because he was faithful."[19] Underneath the irony, it is possible to detect in the story, almost a Picassoesque desire to identify with the bull in his serious dedication to his art. As a model of integrity in an irrational world, the bull seems to represent Hemingway's concept of the artist and may thus offer a positive approach to life in a problematic world. While the earlier writing had tended to identify the artist with the matador or, as in the case of

Jake Barnes, even with the spectator, this last taurian fable suggests that like Picasso, Hemingway was aware that the metamorphic possibilities of the *corrida* also included a final merging of the god-like creator with the sacrificial victim to emphasize the inescapable connection between suffering and creation.

For both Hemingway and Picasso then, the bull, bullfighter, and bullring seemed to crystallize the human experience of living in a world chaotic, destructive, and indifferent by turns, and yet, simultaneously suggest the means of a redemptive transcendence. Equally aware of the tragic destiny of the individual, which they saw reflected in the violence and bloodshed of the bullfight, both artists created images of death and horror. Yet, in the courage and beauty born of this terrible drama, they were able to envisage an affirmation of life and an assurance of the immortality towards which man eternally aspires. The role the artist must play in achieving this rebirth, always a major concern with Picasso and Hemingway, could also be examined and invested with dramatic significance through the triple masks of bull, matador, and spectator.

Whether this remarkably similar response of writer and painter to a primarily visual experience was consciously striven after or accidental is a question which will continue to intrigue sensitive readers. Visual images do indeed cut across the different arts to convey their messages. And, if the writer, in making a Daedalus-like voyage into unknown arts, had seen a trail-blazer in one who was possibly the greatest artist of our age, that recognition need not in any way detract from the merit of his own creative work. Rather, the discovery of correspondences should not only facilitate an understanding of his aims and philosophy, but also lead to the realization, necessary to validate a comparative approach, that while in this century, the arts are ceaselessly expanding their parameters, an overlapping of territories also becomes unavoidable.

NOTES AND REFERENCES

1. "Ernest Hemingway and the Arts: A Necessary Addendum,"
    Fitzgerald; Hemingway Annual, 1974. Michigan: Gale Press,
    pp.145-54.

2. George Plimpton, "An Interview with Ernest Hemingway,"
    in *Hemingway and His Critics: An International Anthology,*
    ed. Carlos Baker. New York: Hill & Wang, 1961. pp.26- 7.

3. See letters to Bernard Berenson in *Ernest Hemingway :
    Selected Letters:1917-1961.* New York: Scriber's, 1981. p.
    790, pp. 823-24. Ernest Hemingway, *A Moveable Feast.* New
    York: Scribner's 1964. p.13, 69; and Lillian Ross, *Portrait
    of Hemingway. New* York : Simon & Schuster, 1961. p. 57.

4. Jean Leymarie, *Picasso, The Artist of the Century.* London:
    Macmillan, 1972.p.152.

5. *Ibid.* p. 158.

6. *Letters,* p.165.

7. *Ibid.* p.366.

8. Ernest Hemingway, *The Nick Adams Stories.* New York:
    Scribner's, 1972. p. 236.

9. Ernest Hemingway, *By-Line: Selected Articles and Dispatches
    of Four Decades.* Harmondsworth: Penguin, 1970. p. 102.

10. Ernest Hemingway, *in our time.* Paris: Three Mountain
    Press, 1924, facsimile edition, 1970. p. 24.

11. *Ibid.* p.27.

12. *Letters,* p.153.

13. Dore Ashton, ed. *Picasso on Art: A Selection of Views.*
    London: Thames and Hudson, 1972. p.23.

14. *Ibid., p.155.*

15. *By-Line,* p.102.

16. Ernest Hemingway, *Death in the Afternoon.* New York:
    Scribner's, 1960. p.213.

17. Anthony Blunt, *Picasso's 'Guernica'.* London: Oxford
    University Press, 1969. p.14.

18. *Picasso on Art,* p. 159.

19. Ernest Hemingway, "The Faithful Bull," *Holiday,* 9 March
    1951. p. 51.

The Real, The Imaginary and the Hyperreal Text: Hemingway's Fiction and Hollywood's Visual Fiction

Sanjukta Dasgupta

Hemingway was invariably sceptical about Hollywood and its methods of adapting fiction into film. One main reason for this dissatisfaction on the part of one of America's most flamboyant of writers was that the author's hegemonic control of the text had to be surrendered to the filmmaker who directed the film through systematic approximation, appropriation and abrogation. For the author of the fictional text this was sacrilegious and expectedly the film version invited the wrath of the author. But the mass appeal conscious commercial cinema industry of Hollywood had to primarily concern itself with the entertainment value of a film. Anticipation of viewer reception forms an important part of filmmaking as this is directly related to the commercial viability of cinema. The financial input in making a movie is most often so formidable that the maker of a commercial movie generally treads a beaten track adapting erstwhile success formulas of celebrated box office hits. This practice often mars the fiction irremediably but the cash registers sing out in adulation. Very recently while interviewing in New York one of America's most powerful contemporary writer E. L. Doctorow I happened to mention to him that I had watched the Hollywood adaptation of his dynamic historiographic text *Ragtime* and he immediately dismissed the movie version as a failure and devastatingly stated "it has about ten good minutes in it".

So Hemingway's reaction was not extraordinary. Time and again writers have expressed their dissatisfaction with Hollywood for steamrolling the original text or sometimes apart from the title or the names of characters everything else in the film from locale to story underwent a metamorphosis often at the behest of producers who would not like to screen anything that might dissatisfy the establishment or be politically incorrect or inflammatory. The fictional narrative is technically accredited to be the closest compounding of a sign system that represents the real. The imaginary is directly interlinked with the real in its representation of history. Jean Baudrillard categorically accuses the cinema for destroying the real and the imaginary, history and fiction through its projections of cinematic myth as real and thereby producing the hyperreal:

> Concurrently with this effort toward an absolute correspondence with the real, cinema also approaches an absolute correspondence with itself-and this is not contradictory.
> : it is the very definition of the hyperreal. Hypotyposis and specularity. Cinema plagiarizes itself, recopies itself, remakes its classics, retroactivates its original myths, remakes the silent film more perfectly than the original, etc all of this is logical, *the cinema is fascinated by itself as a lost object as much as it (and we) are fascinated by the real as a lost referent.*[1]

So how do we distinguish between what is real and what is hyperreal? Baudrillard writes,

> It is a question of substituting the signs of the real for the real, that is to say of an operation of deterring every real process via its operational double, a programmatic, metastable perfectly descriptive machine that offers all the signs of the real and short-circuits all the vicissitudes. Never again will the real have the chance to produce itself-such is the vital function of the model in a system of death, or rather of anticipated resurrection that no longer even gives the event of death a chance. A hyperreal henceforth sheltered from the imaginary, and from any

distinction between the real and the imaginary, leaving room only for the orbital recurrence of models and for the simulated generation of differences.[2]

Referring to the distinction between historical myth and the myth created by the cinema Baudrillard asserts that the mediation of history into cinema and vice versa has resulted in a double destruction:

> Because cinema itself contributed to the disappearance of history, and to the advent of the archive. Photography and cinema contributed in large part to the secularization of history to fixing it in its visible "objective" form at the expense of the myths that once traversed it...Today cinema can place all its talent, all its technology in the service of reanimating what it itself contributed to liquidating. It only liquidates ghosts, and in itself is lost therein.[3]

A truly morbid world of simulation. But what were Hemingway's own reservations about this extremely powerful medium that has enthusiastically and repeatedly translated his fictional texts into visual fiction? Though he advocated that "take the money and run" would be the appropriate manner in which a writer should negotiate with Hollywood yet we find most of his major texts were translated into the visual fiction mode while he was living, implying that a tacit agreement existed between the producer, director and the author—primarily the trinity that is responsible for constructing visual fiction. Unlike Faulkner who was such an enthusiastic screenplay writer Hemingway however mostly turned down requests for writing scripts and screen plays based on his fiction and whenever screenplays had been forwarded to him for approval he is known to have often re-inserted all the passages from his original text that the scriptwriter had rejected. Hemingway could never reconcile himself to the transcreation of the narrative image into a visual image that appeared to be recognizably different. It is a fact however that the distinction between narrative and spectacle, the text on the page and the on-screen text often creates a gulf between the author's intended image and the image on celluloid. ·

In 1929 Hemingway's immensely popular novel *A Farewell To Arms* was published. The novel was a unique aesthetic achievement and established Hemingway's reputation as heralding a new era in the craft of writing. Narrative acquired a kinetic force for the novelist's sparse use of signifiers aroused the reader, coaxed him out of ennui and ensured participation. Description, introspective ruminations, monologues, dialogues, all these attributes of narrative art gained dimensions hitherto quite unprecedented. Many regarded the inimitable Hemingway style with its chiselled expresssions and terseness to be overwhelmingly cinematic. However, during the construction of the screenplay and in transferring the dialogue as real-life exchanges between characters the difficulties of the textual transference from the printed page to the celluloid screen became only too apparent. But not only the linguistic signifiers, even the non-verbal and aural signifiers posed problems and the Hemingway text needed to be filled out with relevant padding that understandably met with the writer's disapproval. The priorities were clear. Marketability of the film was far more important than the fidelity to the author's text. The semiotic effects of the printed text and that of the cinematographic text were sometimes quite distinct and instances of the kinetic power of Hemingway's prose seemed far more formidable than cinematic impact.

The very first chapter of *A Farewell to Arms* illustrates quite unequivocally the limitations of cinematic art despite the sophisticated technology. Though the camera panning the surroundings can recreate the Hemingway text that begins with the following sentence- " In the late summer of that year we lived in a house in a village that looked across the river and the plain to the mountains". The spectacle can be sensitively refigured in the cinematic image. But what can be a possible substitute image for the concluding sentence of the first chapter that makes the reader sit up with a sense of shock and outrage confronted with historical fact and statistics?

> At the start of the winter came the permanent rain
> and with the rain came the cholera. But it was
> checked and in the end only seven thousand died of
> it in the army.[4]

Nevertheless, A Farewell to Arms, released in 1932 fared
well at the box office grossing the highest sales figures for
that year, was nominated for best picture and won Oscars
for cinematography and sound recording. This first screen
adaptation of the novel had two endings, one maintaining
the fidelity to Hemingway's text ending with the tragic
death of the heroine Catherine and the other ending happily
for the lovers as Catherine regains consciousness.
Hollywood was always squeamish about intense love stories
ending in separation as it apprehended adverse viewer
response. This first screen adaptation of Hemingway's
fiction was made by the noted film maker Frank Borzage,
the screenwriters were Benjamin Glazer and Oliver
H.P.Garrett. The cast included Gary Cooper as Frederic
Henry and Helen Hayes as Catherine Barkley.

However, even the ending that bears fidelity to the
Hemingway text and ends in tragedy could not transfer the
nuances of the original text into the visual fiction. The
dead Catherine is seen in the arms of Frederic who
murmurs "Peace, peace" which is highly melodramatic if
not outright ironic along with the strains of Wagner's
"Liebstode" from Tristran and Isolde and the tolling of church
bells. This impression is further intensified if we compare
the film version with the compact tension of the fictional
ending:

> But after I had got them out and shut the door and
> turned off the light it wasn't any good. It was like
> saying goodbye to a statue. After a while I went out
> and left the hospital and walked back to the hotel in
> the rain.[5]

The alternative happy ending that deviated from

Hemingway's text and infuriated him had Frederic carrying
Catherine to the hospital window. Catherine who was
unconscious revives and Frederic whispers "Armistice" and
she answers smilingly "Peace" as the church steeple and
fluttering doves are seen on screen and church bells are
heard. Such a scene amply bears out the veracity of
Baudrillard's apprehensions about the destructive impact
of cinematic re-creations.

But Hollywood's visual fiction of 1932 which was such
a blockbuster was a passionate love story whereas
Hemingway's text had juxtaposed the two planes of reality,
the subjective or perceptional and the objective or
experiential. The horrors of the First World War which are
foregrounded in the fiction receive peripheral significance
in the film thereby abrogating the very purpose of the
original text. As a result the entire text that unfolds from
the point of view of Frederic Henry and his initiation into
the war environment loses its purpose. Frederic Henry's
cynicism, detachment and disenchantment that are so
powerfully expressed in the following introspective passages
do not in anyway become an integral part of the visual
fiction:

> I was always embarrassed by the words sacred,
> glorious and sacrifice and the expression in vain. We
> had heard them, sometimes standing in the rain
> almost out of ear-shot, so that only the shouted words
> came through and had read them, on proclamations
> that were slapped up by billposters over other
> proclamations, now for a long time, and I had seen
> nothing sacred and the things that were glorious had
> no glory and the sacrifices were like the stock yards'
> at Chicago if nothing was done with the meat except
> to bury it.[6]

Frederic concludes his dismissal of values by stating
without hesitation.

> Abstract words such as glory, honor, courage or
> hallow(sic) were obscene beside the concrete names

of villages, the numbers of roads, the names of rivers, the numbers of regiments and the dates.[7]

Interestingly, in 1957 *A Farewell To Arms* was re-made. This time the producer was the celebrated David O. Selznick of *Gone with the Wind* fame. The director was the intrepid Charles Vidor. Rock Hudson, Jennifer Jones and Vittoria de Sica were cast in the roles of Frederic Henry, Catherine Barkley and Rinaldi respectively. The re-make was of 152 minutes duration whereas Frank Borzage's screen adaptation was of 78 minutes. Selznick planned to craft it into a super spectacle. The war scenes and the ignominious retreat of the Italian army received serious attention in the re-make. But reviews of the film indicated that these scenes were more in the nature of documentaries and did not satisfy viewer expectation. The viewer was eager about Frederic's plight and experiences and was not interested in a general survey of the retreat of Caporetto. Apart from other drawbacks such as mis-castings, Rock Hudson seeming too boyish in comparison to the elderly Jennifer Jones. The Legion of Decency designated the movie as "morally objectionable in part for all audiences" because of its persistent emphasis on illicit love. Ironically however, Gene D. Phillips observes that:

> The picture is also marred, ironically enough, by too liberal a use of Hemingway's dialogue which...reads well on the printed page as highly wrought literary language but can for that very reason sound somewhat stilted when verbalized on the screen. Carefully crafted by Hemingway to illuminate Frederic's subjective psychological states, the novel's interior monologues appear rather mannered when articulated by Rock Hudson on the screen. Thus Frederic's ruminations about death and defeat in the final hospital scene seems to be a genuine cry of anguish in the book, but appear self-conscious and overwrought in the movie.[8]

The visual text once again fails to capture the nuanced

impact of the printed text.

But what about the Hemingway films made in-between 1932 and 1957,that is a period of twenty-five years? In these two and a half decades the visual fiction based on Hemingway's novels and stories that were released included *For Whom the Bell Tolls* (1943) and *To Have and Have Not* (1944) starring Humphrey Bogart as Harry Morgan and Lauren Bacall as Marie Browning and directed and produced by Howard Hawks. This film was re-made twice with different titles- *The Breaking Point* in 1950 directed by Michael Curtiz and *The Gun Runners* in 1958 directed by Don Seigel. Incidentally this novel considered the least satisfactory of Hemingway's creative output curiously had three movie versions each time dismissing the original as definitely not "Holy Writ" and shifting locale and re-constructing characters and situations as the screenwriter demanded. Inevitably, the original Hemingway text was lost. Also, in 1957 *The Sun Also* Rises was released directed by Henry King and the roles of Jake Barnes and Brett Ashley were played by Tyrone Power and Ava Gardner. Though Hemingway was consulted before the script was finalized Hemingway criticized the film and walked out of the screening after about thirty minutes.

The film adaptations of Hemingway's stories included *The Killers* (1946) based on the story with the same name starring Burt Lancaster as Swede and Ava Gardner as Kitty Collins. The director was Robert Siodmak. Siodmak tried to retain the flavor of the fictional text as much as possible in the visual fiction. Hemingway was known to have been satisfied with the production. However, in 1964 the movie was re-remade which Hemingway did not live to see. The director of the re-make was Don Siegel and Lee Marvin and Angie Dickinson acted in the lead roles. While the 1946 version was in black and white Siegel's film was in color. It departed considerably from Hemingway's story and was intended for the small screen.

In 1947, *The Macomber Affair* was released. The original story was titled, " The Short Happy Life of Francis Macomber". This film is generally regarded as one that is

closest to Hemingway's text in details and spirit despite
the superimposed love story. In 1950 Twentieth Century
Fox released *Under my Skin* based on " My Old Man" and in
1952, *The Snows of Kilimanjaro* starring Gregory Peck as
Harry and Ava Gardner as Cynthia created quite a
sensation. The advertisements for each of these films
included a focus on Hemingway's own alternative lifestyle
choices, for the American writer had become a cult figure.
While one advertisement boasted of a macho and a sadist-
masochist Hemingway- "a mixture of cruelty and yearning"
and "love like a lash of a whip Hemingway style"[9] another
stated, "only Ernest Hemingway, author of *For Whom the
Bell Tolls* and *The Killers* could have written of love like
this."[10] About the departure from his original story and
appropriating source material from other Hemingway texts
the author's own outburst seems to be the best comment
on the arbitrariness of screen adaptations:

> I sold Fox a single story, not my complete works. This
> movie has something from nearly every story that I
> ever wrote in it.[11]

Apart from the *Gun Runners* released in 1958 directed by
Don Seigel that same year saw the release of the celebrated
The Old Man and the Sea. It was this very profound and
powerful novel that won Hemingway the Nobel Prize but
the film version personally supervised by Hemingway from
script to technicalities was a box office failure. It was
directed by John Sturges with Spencer Tracy in the lead
role. Tracy seemed appallingly miscast, even physically
overweight and a disgusted Hemingway who had expended
a lot of time and energy in the making of the movie wrote
in a letter to Wallace Meyer in 1956:

> I bitterly regret ever having participated in the film
> in any way but it seemed best for all of us that an
> attempt be made to make a decent picture of the
> book.[12]

Hemingway committed suicide in 1961. In 1962

Hemingway's Adventures of a Young Man was released directed by Martin Ritt with Richard Beymer as Nick Adams. The film was based on ten Nick Adams stories cleverly and sensitively adapted into a single composite whole by Aaron E. Hotchner, who wrote the screenplay. But the film failed to be a success as Beymer was too inexperienced to do justice to the complexities in Nick's character. In 1977 the film version of Hemingway's posthumously published novel *Islands in the Stream* was released. It was directed by Franklin J.Schaffner and George C. Scott and Claire Bloom were cast in the lead roles. The novel written in three sections is brilliantly pared in the screen adaptation thereby giving it a remarkable cohesiveness. Scott was remarkable as Thomas Hudson and his make-up made him resemble Hemingway complete with salt and pepper beard.

I am tempted however to look back at two very different films based on the same contextual data. I am referring to the documentary film *The Spanish Earth* (1937) that was scripted by Hemingway along with his voice-over commentary and the film fiction *For Whom the Bell Tolls* (1943) which was an overwhelming success. It received Academy award nominations for best picture, cinematography, art direction, editing, musical score as well as acting nominations for Gary Cooper, Ingrid Bergman, Paxinou and Akim Tamiroff. Katina Paxinou who acted as Pilar won an Oscar and the movie was one of the top grossers of 1943. The film was directed and produced by Sam Wood. While *The Spanish Earth* was filmed as part of the fund raising campaign for the Loyalists with which Hemingway was actively engaged and focused on a Spain threatened by the sinister shadows of Franco and Fascism the Hollywood film, *For Whom the Bell Tolls* deliberately elided the political groundings and prioritized the love story in troubled times. Phillips comments,

..that since the Fascists under Franco had won the civil war and were now in power in Spain producer-director Wood and the studio bosses wanted to soft-pedal the political implications of the story in order to avoid running the risk of having the film boycotted by the Spanish government or by Spanish groups in the United States—just as the same studio's officials had worried about offending Italians with the 1932 version of *A Farewell To Arms*.[13]

Conforming to the norms of the establishment sustains democracy. Critical reception of Hemingway's novel however was a mixed one and he seemed to have dissatisfied both the Left and Right, while the former accused him of ideological uncertainty the latter found his narrative prolix and biased.

This reminds me of another American film released around the same time which won considerable accolades whereas the original text was subjected to adverse responses. I am thinking of John Steinbeck's *The Grapes of Wrath* published in 1939. The novel was virulently attacked and also banned for a while but the film released in 1940 was praised. The film was produced by Darryl Zanuck and directed by John Ford. Jane Darnell who was cast as Ma Joad won an Academy Award and Nunnally Johnson won a prize for his script. In the course of the transference from fiction to visual fiction the ideological impact of the text's historicity was elided and the film instead emphasized the re-birth of hope and the viability of the American Dream. Where Steinbeck's fictional discourse interrogated, exposed and threatened revolt, John Ford's filmic discourse was affirmative. Ford had stated without embarrassment " I never read the book"[14] and the film version vindicated his frankness! Another interesting instance of even re-inventing the historicity of a text is the third re-make of *To Have and Have Not* titled *The Gun Runners* (1958). The film makes use of the Cuban revolution without mentioning Castro for Cuba was very much in the news then. The agenda, whether hidden or obvious, for the re-make was a commercial one. So Harry Morgan renamed Sam Martin is coaxed into selling arms illegally to the Cuban revolutionaries. The film however was not successful.

It is an accepted fact that film adaptation can never replicate the fictional text. "In the cinema, aesthetic expressiveness is grafted onto natural expressiveness-that of the landscape or face the film shows. In the verbal arts, it is grafted, not onto any genuine prior expressiveness, but onto a conventional *signification-* that of language- which is generally inexpressive."[15] The original fiction is source material for the screenwriter, it influences and inspires, it guides and limits the screenwriter to work out the script within a certain framework. George Bluestone observes,

> Like two intersecting lines, novel and film meet at a point and then diverge. At the intersection, the book and shooting script are almost indistinguishable. But where the lines diverge, they...lose all resemblance to each other, for each works within the framework of its own conventions.[16]

Bluestone further states that a conscientious filmmaker constructs a cinematic paraphrase of the original work.

While the good news is that serious fiction by serious writers have been crafted into visual fiction the bad news is that the historicity and political power relations represented in the fiction are deliberately elided, ignored, subverted or parodied in a commercial film production. The fictional text transferred into the film medium through a process of mutation and sublimation becomes a commodity for the gratification of mass culture. Frederic Jameson points out this dehistoricizing in visual fiction while E.L. Doctorow in a recent article in the *New York Times* expresses his alarm about the dominance of films in mass culture that discourages discourse and relies on visual impressions:

> Literary language extends experience in discourse. It flowers to thought with nouns, verbs, objects. It thinks. That is why the term film language may be an oxymoron. Film de-literates thought; it relies primarily on an association of visual impressions or understandings. Movie-going is an act of inference. You receive what you see as a broad band of sensual effects that evoke your intuitive nonverbal intelligence. You understand what you see without having to think it through with words.[17]

Often the diegetic and extra-deigetic reality in filmic representations maintain their exclusiveness from the fictional text despite efforts to privilege the impressions and perception of reality that a fictional text represents. As a result, it would not be inappropriate to distinguish between Hemingway's fiction and visual fiction in Barthesian categories as the difference between the fictional text of *jouissance* (bliss) and the filmic text of *plaisir* (pleasure) respectively. Film versions of Hemingway's fiction have invariably left an unsatisfactory impression in varying degrees if the keenness has been for identifying textual fidelity and mirroring of sequences in the fictional text. But it should be remembered that most of the Hollywood productions have been immensely successful as films in their own right (irony unintended). Similarly, Hemingway's inimitable kinetic prose when used as film dialogue did not have the same impact. Literary language and the filmic language have very different demands and Hemingway's fiction and visual fiction repeatedly vindicate the distinction. As there can be no simple equation between information and knowledge so too arguments that a picture is worth a thousand words does not always seem to be the right answer. I conclude with this extract from chapter 27 of *For Whom the Bell Tolls* where El Sordo the guerilla leader realizes that he is trapped and that death is inevitable. I feel it is not possible to translate into filmic language the resonance of this deeply emotive passage where prose is excited into poetry and this despite the visual images that the words create:

> Dying was nothing and he had no picture of it nor fear of it in his mind. but living was a field of grain blowing in the wind on the side of a hill. Living was a hawk in the sky. Living was an earthen jar of water in the dust of the threshing with the grain flailed out and the chaff blowing. Living was a horse between your legs and a carbine under one leg and a hill and a valley and a stream with trees along it and the far side of the valley and the hills beyond.[18]

NOTES & REFERENCES

1. Baudrillard, Jean. *Simulacra and Simulation*. U of Michigan P,1994.

2. *Ibid*. 2

3. *Ibid*.47

4. Hemingway, Ernest. *A Farewell to Arms*. Harmondsworth: Penguin, 1976.8.

5. *Ibid*.256

6. *Ibid*.143-4

7. *Ibid*.144

8. Phillips, Gene D. *Hemingway and Film*. New York: Ungar, 1980. 30-1.

9. Mandal, Somdatta." Ernest Hemingway and Hollywood". *Studies in American Literature*. Calcutta: American Center, 1999.136

10. *Ibid*.136

11. Phillips op. cit.109

12. Hemingway, Ernest. *Selected Letters*. Panther. 1985.857.

13. Phillips op.cit.43

14. Collado, Francisco R. *Flashbacks* University of Zaragoza.1992.202.

15. Bluestone, George. *Novels Into Film*. Berkeley: U of California P,1957. 62-3.

16. Metz, Christian. *Film Language*. Chicago:U of Chicago P,1991.77.

17. Doctorow, E.L. " The Novel Follows Film into World of Fewer Words" *The New York Times* March 15, 1999.

18. Hemingway, Ernest. *For Whom the Bell Tolls*. Harmondsworth: Penguin,1965. 296.

The Indian Critical Reception of Ernest Hemingway : A Bibliographical Overview

Somdatta Mandal

Over the years, American studies in India have evoked a stimulating debate between both the American and Indian scholars. The growing interest in American subjects among the younger generation of Indian researchers perhaps warrants a close examination of the whole question of American studies in India in retrospect as well as prospect. Studying literature in English in India meant basically syllabi relating primarily to British writers – a phenomenon that can be attributed to the indirect imposition of more than two centuries of colonial rule. Since the last three or four decades, the scenario has rapidly changed. Stalwarts at the helm of setting up University curriculum have introduced American literature in both the graduate and under-graduate syllabi and Ernest Hemingway is one of the most representative authors featuring in them.

The Indian critical response to Ernest Hemingway is unique. On the one hand, the writer is appreciated for his depiction of rugged outdoor life, full of action and violence.

The settings of his stories again provide the armchair traveller a window of the world. The exotic locations of Pamplona, Italian warfront, Africa, Constantinople, Michigan, Cuba, Paris or elsewhere, all add to this appeal. As a true supporter of democratic causes, his involvement in the Spanish Civil War against the Fascist forces, is a praiseworthy characteristic too. But what is more significant is the affinity that Indian readers find with Hemingway's world-view and that endorsed by our oriental philosophy. Santiago's stoical endurance is what exactly the *Bhagawat Gita* preaches. Even Robert Jordan's suicide mission is interpreted according to the law of '*karma*' endorsed by the scriptures. The 'code-hero'/'apprentice hero' relationship is in tune with the '*guru/sishya*' tradition. Further, in a traditional patriarchal society like ours, the male chauvinist hero and his masquerades are fully justified in all his actions, where issues like androgyny (like that depicted in *The Garden of Eden*) are dismissed as temporary aberrations. How we have Indianized 'Papa' is clearly evident from the kind of articles written upon him by Indian scholars.

Before concluding it must be mentioned that the following bibliographical list is not foolproof. Hemingway's influence is so all-pervasive that I am sure there are several articles on him in other Indian regional languages which I could not access. I have concentrated only on Bangla, my mother-tongue. Also, the list should not mislead any serious researcher that all the articles and books published upon the author are of superior standard. Many of them are rehashed material, warmed-up fare, so to say. On the other hand, there are also really committed Indian scholars whose works of criticism are in no way inferior to those produced by the first-rate American scholars at the major American universities. Several books are revised and published versions of doctoral dissertations. What is really significant is the writers' popularity. How far Hemingway is popular in this part of the world also becomes clear from another interesting phenomenon. Among the several 'special' Hemingway issues of magazines and journals published to commemorate his birth centennial, at least three are state-sponsored journals and as West Bengal has been under Marxist rule for the last twenty-three years, with a lot of anti-capitalistic issues on its agenda, it is no mean achievement. Ernest Hemingway has enabled scholars like us to explore avenues for a true cultural synthesis.

ERNEST HEMINGWAY: AN INDIAN BIBLIOGRAPHICAL OVERVIEW

A: BOOKS

Arumugam, A.E. *Ernest Hemingway : A Critical Bibliography.* Madurai: Twayne Publishers, 1980.

Chandel, Surendra Singh. *Violence in Hemingway.* Jaipur: Printwell Publishers, 1991.

Dahiya, Bhim S. *Hero in Hemingway: Study in Development.* New Delhi: Bahri Publications, 1978.

————. *Hemingway's 'The Sun Also Rises': Critical Introduction.* New Delhi: Lakeside Publishers, 1986.

————. *Hemingway's 'A Farewell to Arms': A Critical Study.* Delhi: Academic Foundation, 1992.

Das, Satyabrata. *Ernest Hemingway: The Turning Point.* New Delhi: Atlantic Publishers & Distributors, 1996.

Dasgupta, Sanjukta. *The Novels of Huxley and Hemingway: A Study of Two Planes Of Reality.* New Delhi: Prestige Books, 1996.

Dimri, Jaiwanti. *Ernest Hemingway: A Critical Study of His Short Stories and Non-Fiction.* New Delhi: Anmol Publications, 1994.

Ghosh, Tapan Kumar. *The Old Man and the Sea: An Indian Response.* Calcutta: G.J. Book Society, 2000.

Hamid, Syed Ali. *Short Fiction of Ernest Hemingway: Study in Major Themes.* New Delhi: Asia Publishing House, 1985.

Jain, Satya Prakash. *Hemingway: A Study of His Short Stories.* New Delhi: Arnold Heinemann, 1985.

Mathur. U.S. *Ernest Hemingway: The Old Man and the Sea.* New Delhi: Aarti Book Centre, 1994.

Mundra, S.C. *Ernest Hemingway: Novelist.* Bareilly: Prakash Book Depot, 1972.

————. *Hemingway's A Farewell to Arms.* Bareilly: Prakash Book Depot, 1977.

————. *Hemingway's The Old Man and the Sea.* Bareilly: Prakash Book Depot, 1977.

——————. *Hemingway's For Whom the Bell Tolls*. Bareilly: Prakash Book Depot, 1986.

——————. *Ernest Hemingway: The Impact Of War on His Life and Works*. Bareilly: Prakash Book Depot, 1988.

Nahal, Chaman. *The Narrative Pattern in Ernest Hemingway's Fiction*. Delhi: Vikas Publication, 1971.

Nair, N. Ramachandran. *The Hemingway Arc*. Delhi: Pencraft International, 1994.

Paul, Sukrita. *Man, Woman and Androgyny: Study of the Novels of Theodore Dreiser, Scott Fitzgerald, and Ernest Hemingway*. New Delhi: Indus Publishing Company, 1989.

Rao Nageswara, E. *Ernest Hemingway: A Study of His Rhetoric*. New Delhi/Atlantic Heights, N.J.: Arnold Heinemann Academic Press, 1983.

——————. Ed. *Ernest Hemingway: Centennial Essays*. Delhi: Pencraft International, 2000.

Rao, P.G. Rama. *Ernest Hemingway: Study in Narrative Technique*. New Delhi: S. Chand, 1980.

Singh, Jaspal. *Semiotic Analysis of Hemingway's The Old Man and the Sea*. New Delhi: Bahri Publications, 1990.

Srivastava, Ramesh Kumar. *Determinism in Hemingway*. Amritsar: Guru Nanak Dev University, 1975.

——————. *Hemingway and His 'For Whom the Bell Tolls'*. Amritsar: Guru Nanak Dev University, 1980.

Tripathi, J.P. *Ernest Hemingway: A Study in His Evolution*. Bareilly: Prakash Book Depot, 1990.

B: ARTICLES:

Abraham, T.V. "The Role of Action in Hemingway's Concept of Victory". *Modern American Literature* eds. A.A. Mutalik-Desai & T.S. Anand. N.Delhi: Creative Books, 2002.

Agnihotri, Pratima. "Mirrored Image: Self-reflexivity in Hemingway's *Across the River and Into the Trees*." *Ernest Hemingway:Centennial Essays*. Ed. E.

Nageswara Rao. Delhi: Pencraft International, 2000:107-111.

Arora, Viswa Nath. "The Hemingway Industry." (Review) *Indian Journal of American Studies* 5 (1&2): Jan & July'75: 82-87.

Bandopadhyay. Deb Narayan. "TheUndefeated": Conceptualising 'Pundonor'. *West Bengal* XLI.23 (Dec 16,1999): 103-106.

Banerjee, Soma. "Fisher Kings of a Fecund Land." *Ernest Hemingway:Centennial Essays*. Ed. E. Nageswara Rao. Delhi: Pencraft International, 2000: 31-39.

——————. "The Ancient Mariner, The Tainted Mariner and Hiawatha: Studies in Pride." *Journal of the Department of English, Rabindra Bharati University* V (1998-99): 158-166.

——————."Living out the Nada: Destroyed but not Defeated." *West Bengal* XLI.23 (Dec 16,1999): 99-102.

Barua, Dilip Kumar. "*The Old Man and the Sea*: A Humanist Parable." *Journal of the Department of English, Rabindra Bharati University* V (1998-99): 142-148.

Bharathi, T. "Hemingway's Robert Jordan: A *Karma-Yogi.*" *Ernest Hemingway:Centennial Essays*. Ed. E. Nageswara Rao. Delhi: Pencraft International, 2000: 64-70.

Bhattacharya, Chidananda. "World War I and its Aftermath in the Early Novels of Hemingway." *Journal of the Department of English, Rabindra Bharati University* V (1998-99): 29-52.

——————. "Hemingway's incremental vision." *West Bengal* XLI.23 (Dec 16,1999):33-42.

Bhattacharya, Ramkrishna. "*The Fifth Column:* 'but today the struggle.' *West Bengal* XLI.23 (Dec 16,1999): 125-128.

Chakraborty, Basudeb. "Hemingway's short story "The Undefeated": A Study of Its theme and language." *West Bengal* XLI.23 (Dec 16,1999): 107-112.

Chakraborty, Santosh. "*The Old Man and the Sea:* A Story of Conviction." *Journal of the Department of English, Rabindra Bharati University* V (1998-99): 194-198.

——————. "Hemingway as a War Correspondent."*West Bengal* XLI.23 (Dec 16,1999): 81-88.

Chakraborty, Ujjal. "Masculinity/Femininity –Feminine Presence/ Absence in a Male World: Hemingway's *Men Without Women." Journal of the Department of English, Rabindra Bharati University* V (1998-99): 64-73.

Chakravarti, Sudeshna. "Two Writers of the Spanish Civil War: Hemingway and Malraux." *West Bengal* XLI.23 (Dec 16,1999): 53-66.

Chakravertty, Tania. "Engendering Gender: Hemingway and Women." *West Bengal* XLI.23 (Dec 16,1999): 169-80.

Chandra, Lakshmi."Existentialism in *The Old Man and the Sea.*" *Literary Voice* 1 (Dec'94): 21-24.

Das, Satyabrata. "From the Bullring into Politics: A Study of Hemingway's Changing Response." *Literature and Politics in Twentieth-Century America.* Eds. Plakkoottam, J.L. & Prashant Sinha. Hyderabad: American Studies Research Centre, 1993: 99-105.

Dasgupta, Hemendralal. "Ernest Hemingway and the Spanish Builfight.' *Indian Journal of American Studies* 6:1&2 (Jan-July'76): 55-64

Dasgupta, Sanjukta. "Rape of Spain: Ernest Hemingway's Ideology." *Journal of the Department of English, University of Calcutta* XXVI.1(1998-99):15-24.

——————."The Crack-Up: Scott Fitzgerald, Ernest Hemingway and the Lost Generation." *F. Scott Fitzgerald: A Centennial Tribute (Vol 1).* Ed. Somdatta Mandal. New Delhi, Prestige Books, 1997; London : Sangam Books, 1998: 30-38.

——————. "Huck and Nick: Mark Twain and Ernest Hemingway's Bohemians." *Journal of the Department of English, Rabindra Bharati University* V (1998-99): 53-63.

——————. "'A Writer is like a Gypsy': Hemingway and Politics." *West Bengal* XLI.23 (Dec 16,1999): 13-22.

Dey, Pradip Kumar. "The Hemingway Hero and the Poetics of Combat and Love." *West Bengal* XLI.23 (Dec 16,1999): 89-94.

Dhar, Subir. "Infantry of the Mind: The Poems of Ernest Hemingway." *West Bengal* XLI.23 (Dec 16,1999): 95-98.

Ghosal, Goutam. "Hemingway's 'Maria' and Stephen Crane's 'Maggie': Two Attitudes to Women – A Consciousness Approach." *Journal of the Department of English, Rabindra Bharati University* V (1998-99): 115-119.

Ghosh, Tapan Kumar. "The Play's the Thing: Hemingway's *The Fifth Column.*" *West Bengal* XLI.23 (Dec 16,1999):43-46.

Girdhari, V.T. "Love-Religion-Death, Triumvirates of Human Life: Hemingway's *A Farewell to Arms.*" *Modern American Literature* Eds. A.A. Mutalik-Desai & T.S. Anand. N.Delhi: Creative Books, 2002.

Guha, Sourin. "The World of Ernest Hemingway." *The Calcutta Review* (Aug'65):

————. "The Old Man and the Sea." *The Bulletin of the Department of English, Calcutta University* 1.2 ('65-'66):

————."The Old Man and the Sea." *Ripples.*(1963):

————. "Men Without Women: Four Long Short Stories of Ernest Hemingway." *Journal of the Alumni Association of Presidency College 1991-1992.*

————. "Three Short Stories of Ernest Hemingway." *Journal of the Alumni Association of Presidency College 1994-1995.*

————. "*To Have and Have Not:* A Proletarian Fiction?" *Journal of the Alumni Association of Presidency College 1995-1996.*

————."On Hemingway's Play: *The Fifth Column.*" *Theatre International* (1996):

————. "Reflections on the Hemingway World." *West Bengal* XLI.23 (Dec 16'99):129-32.

————. "Comments on Two Prose-Works of Ernest Hemingway." *Comsomath* 2000

————. "Hemingway and Myself." *India Yesterday.*

Haldar, Indrani. "Hemingway's In Our Time: The Writer's Continuing Relevance." *Journal of the Department of English, Rabindra Bharati University* V (1998-99): 11-19.

——————"Picasso, Hemingway and the Bull." *Indian Journal of American Studies* 16.1 (Win'86):27-32..

——————. "Between Cezanne and Picasso: Hemingway's Artistic Inheritance." *West Bengal* XLI.23 (Dec 16,1999):23-32.

Jaidev. "A Note on the Narrational Perspective in *A Farewell to Arms.*" *Indian Journal of American Studies* 15.1(Win'85):85-88.

Jain, Satya Prakash. "Hills Like White Elephants: A Study." *Indian Journal of American Studies* 1.3(July'70):33-38.

Josh, S. "Foregrounding the Sea: A Reading of Hemingway's *The Old Man and the Sea* and Thakazhi's *Chemmeen.*" *Ernest Hemingway:Centennial Essays.* Ed. E. Nageswara Rao. Delhi: Pencraft International, 2000: 71-77.

Kaur, Kiranjeet. "Hemingway's Perpetual Message Through Obsessive Visions." *Modern American Literature.* Eds. A.A. Mutalik-Desai & T.S. Anand. N.Delhi: Creative Books, 2002.

Kumar, Sanjay. "The Question of Gender, Power and Possession in Hemingway." *Moderm American Literature* Eds. A.A. Mutalik-Desai & T.S. Anand. N.Delhi: Creative Books, 2002.

Kumar, Sukrita Paul. "Towards the New Woman: The Shifting of Sex Roles in Dreiser, Fitzgerald and Hemingway." *Indian Journal of American Studies* 17:1&2 (Win'& Sum'87): 65-73.

Kundu, Rama. "*The Torrents of Spring*: Anxiety of Influence: A Case Study." *West Bengal* XLI.23 (Dec 16,1999): 151-156.

Lahiri Chowdhury, Sheila. "Re-inventing the Whale: Hemingway's *The Old Man and the Sea.*" *Journal of the Department of English, Rabindra Bharati University* V (1998-99): 174-183.

Lal, Malashri. "The Spanish Civil War and Ernest Hemingway: From Reportage to Novel." *Indian Journal of American Studies* 10.1(Jan'80):65-77.

Maini, Darshan Singh. "American Literature: Miscellany." New Delhi: United States Information Service, 1967.

Malhotra, O.P."Ernest Hemingway's *The Old Man and the Sea* : An Appraisal." *Modern American Literature* Eds. A.A. Mutalik-Desai & T.S. Anand. N.Delhi: Creative Books, 2002.

Mandal, Somdatta. Book Review: *Less Than a Treason: Hemingway in Paris* by Peter Griffin. *Indian Journal of American Studies*.20.2 Sum 90: 102-3.

————. "Hollywood and the Motion-Picture Industry: Multifarious Responses of Some Twentieth Century American Writers". *American Literature and Culture: New Insights*. Ed. L.Parasuram. New Delhi: Prestige Books, 1995.

————."Hemingway's *The Spanish Earth*: A Case for a Documentary Film". *Journal of the Department of English, Calcutta University* XXVI.2, 1998-99:59-68.

————."Ernest Hemingway's *The Old Man and the Sea*: An attempt at teaching the novella through the audio-visual method of the film". *Literary Voice* 3: Win 1997.

————. " 'Fascism is a lie told by bullies': The Spanish Civil War and Ernest Hemingway". *Journal of the Department of English, Rabindra Bharati University 1998.* "Ernest Hemingway and Hollywood" *Studies in American Literature* (Anniversary Edition) Calcutta: American Literature Study Circle, USIS, 1999: 134-144.

————. "The Itinerant American Traveller: Settings and Locales in Ernest Hemingway's Fiction" *Journal of the Department of English, Rabindra Bharati University* V (1998-99): 83-97.

————. "Mount Kilimanjaro Revisited: Africa, the Lion's Roar and Ernest Hemingway". *West Bengal* XLI.23 (Dec 16, 1999) (Special Hemingway Number):113-124.

————. "From Page to Screen: Hemingway, *To Have and Have Not* and Hollywood." *Ernest Hemingway: Centennial Essays*. Ed. E. Nageswara Rao. Delhi: Pencraft International, 2000: 136-147.

Mishra, Kalidas. "Writing Under Fire: The Legacy of Hemingway." *Ernest Hemingway:Centennial Essays*. Ed. E. Nageswara Rao. Delhi: Pencraft International, 2000: 40-45.

Mukherjee, Tutun. "Hemingway and Hollywood: An Uneasy Relationship."*Ernest Hemingway:Centennial Essays*. Ed. E. Nageswara Rao. Delhi: Pencraft International, 2000: 125-135.

Nair, N. Ramachandran. "Re-Emergence of the Artist in 'The Snows of Kilimanjaro'." *Ernest Hemingway:Centennial Essays*. Ed. E. Nageswara Rao. Delhi: Pencraft International, 2000: 90-98.

Nanda, Aparajita. "Gender Crisis, Androgyny and the Length of Hair: A Look at *For Whom the Bell Tolls, A Moveable Feast* and *The Garden Of Eden.*" *Journal of the Department of English, Rabindra Bharati University* V (1998-99): 107-114.

—————. "Hemingway's search for identity – from *The Sun Also Rises, A Farewell to Arms, For Whom the Bell Tolls to The Garden Of Eden.*" *West Bengal* XLI.23 (Dec 16,1999): 157-162.

Paul, Ajanta."Hemingway's Short Fiction and the Problematics of Peregrination." *Journal of the Department of English, Rabindra Bharati University* V (1998-99): 120-125.

Prasad, Murari. "The Sea as Symbol in *The Old Man and the Sea.*" *Journal of the Department of English, Rabindra Bharati University* V (1998-99): 184-193.

—————."The Sea as Symbol in *Moby Dick, Lord Jim* and *The Old Man and the Sea.*" *Indian Journal of American Studies* 22.2 (Sum'92):89-95.

Rahul. " 'No Man is an Island': The Relevance of Ernest Hemingway In Our Time."*Ernest Hemingway: Centennial Essays*. Ed. E. Nageswara Rao. Delhi: Pencraft International, 2000: 17-25.

Rao, B. Gopal. "Cinematic Adaptations of Hemingway's *A Farewell to Arms:* The Problem of Ending." *Indian Journal of American Studies* 25.3(Sum'95):142-46.

Rao, Nageswara, E. "Syntax as Rhetoric." *Indian Linguistics* 38 (1975): 296-303.

_____. "Note on Catharsis in Hemingway." *Indian Journal of English Studies*16 (1975-76):189-91.

_____. "Hemingway and the American Tradition.' *Essays and Studies: Festschrift in Honour of Professor K. Viswanathan.* Ed. G.V.L.N. Sarma. Machilipatnam: Triveni, 1977. 61-4.

_____. "Forms of Irony in Hemingway." *Littcrit* 4.1(1978): 44-6.

_____. "The Motif of Luck in Hemingway." *Journal of American Studies* (England) 13.1 (1979): 29-35.

_____. "Style as a Mirror of a Writer's Vision." *Issues in Stylistics.* Ed. Ramesh Mohan. Hyderabad: CIEFL, 1980. 139-48.

_____. "The Quest for Happiness in Hemingway." *Indian Journal of American Studies* 13.1(1983): 119-25.

_____. "Hemingway Criticism, American and International: An Evaluation." *Indian Journal of English Studies* 24 (1984): 141-50.

_____. "Ethnic Attitudes in Hemingway." *English Association Journal* 8 (Sum'94): 109-115.

_____. "The Impact of the Spanish Civil War o Ernest Hemingway." *Literary Spectrum.* Ed. D.J.P.N. Reddy. New Delhi: Arnold Associates, 1994: 179-186.

_____. "Frederic Henry's "Embarrassment": Rhetorical Devices in *A Farewell to Arms." Ernest Hemingway:Centennial Essays.* Ed. E. Nageswara Rao. Delhi: Pencraft International, 2000: 84-89.

_____. "The Hemingway Cattery: The Feline in Hemingway's Life and Letters." *Ernest Hemingway:Centennial Essays.* Ed. E. Nageswara Rao. Delhi: Pencraft International, 2000: 99-106.

_____. "Noah's Ark: The Hemingway Menagerie." *Journal of the Department of English, Rabindra Bharati University* V (1998-99):74-82.

Rao, P.G. Rama. "Hemingway's Second Thoughts: Some Inserts in the First Draft of *For Whom the Bell Tolls." Ernest Hemingway:Centennial Essays.* Ed. E. Nageswara Rao. Delhi: Pencraft International, 2000: 54-63.

————. Book Review. S.C. Mundra, *Ernest Hemingway: The Impact Of War on His Life and Works*. *Indian Journal of American Studies* 22.1(Win'92):100-01.

————. Book Review. J.P. Tripathi. *Ernest Hemingway: A Study in His Evolution. Indian Journal of American Studies* 22.1 (Win'92):104-5.

————. "A Note on the Structure of 'The Snows of Kilimanjaro'." *Indian Journal of American Studies* 1.2 (Jan'70) :13-20.

Rao, P. Subba. "Hemingway's *A Farewell to Arms* and *For Whom the Bell Tolls:* Two Classic American Novels as War Movies. *Indian Journal of American Studies* 25.2(Sum'95):147-54.

Ray, Mohit Kumar. "*The Old Man and the Sea*: An archetypal perspective." *West Bengal* XLI.23 (Dec 16,1999): 71-74.

Roy, Amitava. "Controversial Hemingway: Ways of Reading." *Journal of the Department of English, Rabindra Bharati University* V (1998-99): 20-28.

————."What is American in American literature: Ernest Hemingway: A Case Study." *West Bengal* XLI.23 (Dec 16,1999): 47-52.

Rudra, Arup. "The Ways of Images and Languages in Hemingway's *The Old Man and the Sea*." *Journal of the Department of English, Rabindra Bharati University* V (1998-99): 149-157.

Sangwan, S.S. "Money and Morals in Hemingway's Short Stories." *Punjab University Research Bulletin (Arts)* 21.2 (Oct'90): 69-73.

————. "Hemingway's Humanist Outlook: A Study of *A Farewell to Arms*." *Punjab University Research Bulletin (Arts)* 21.1 (Apr '90): 55-62.

Sanyal, Jharna. " 'No man should be alone in his old age' A gerontological Reading of *The Old Man and the Sea*." *West Bengal* XLI.23 (Dec 16,1999): 75-80.

Sarkar, Subhas. "A Modernist quest for martyrdom: Hemingway's *The Old Man and the Sea* and T.S. Eliot's *Murder in the Cathedral*." *West Bengal* XLI.23 (Dec 16,1999): 67-70.

Saxena, Alka. "The Theme of Love in Hemingway's Short Stories: An Analysis." *Journal of the Department of English, Rabindra Bharati University* V (1998-99): 98-106.

Sen, Krishna. "(Re)Constructing the Iceberg: Narrative and Praxis in "Hills Like White Elephants"." *West Bengal* XLI.23 (Dec 16,1999): 5-12.

Sengupta, Pallab. "The Isomorphs of Santiago-Myth." *Journal of the Department of English, Rabindra Bharati University* V (1998-99): 167-173.

Shende, Dharamdas M. "Does Santigo Reflect Siddharth?" *Modern American Literature* Eds. A.A. Mutalik-Desai & T.S. Anand. N.Delhi: Creative Books, 2002.

Singh, Aviram. "Threshold Angel and War: Three Case Studies of Heroines From American Fiction." *Ernest Hemingway:Centennial Essays*. Ed. E. Nageswara Rao. Delhi: Pencraft International, 2000: 46-53.

Sinha, Amitava. "The Interactive Conflicts in *For Whom the Bell Tolls*." *Journal of the Department of English, Rabindra Bharati University* V (1998-99): 136-141.

—————."On Hemingway's *A Farewell to Arms*." *West Bengal* XLI.23 (Dec 16,1999): 181-83.

Sridhar, M."Why Should We Read Kesava Reddy's Hemingway in English?" *Ernest Hemingway:Centennial Essays*. Ed. E. Nageswara Rao. Delhi: Pencraft International, 2000:78-83.

Tuli, Uma. "Interview with Mrs. Mary Hemingway." *Ernest Hemingway:Centennial Essays*. Ed. E. Nageswara Rao. Delhi: Pencraft International, 2000: 148-151.

Uma, Alladi. "Hemingway: The Quintessential American?" *Ernest Hemingway:Centennial Essays*. Ed. E. Nageswara Rao. Delhi: Pencraft International, 2000: 26-30.

C : M.PHIL & PH.D. DISERTATIONS:

Abraham, T.V. "Ernest Hemingway: A Study of the Concept of Victory in His Fiction and Short Stories.' Nagpur: Nagpur University, 1994.

Arora, Viswa Nath. "Search for Identity in the Novels and Short Stories of Ernest Hemingway." Chandigarh: Punjab University, 1971.

Banerjee, Anupa. "Portrait of the Artist in Hemingway's Fiction.' Kurukshetra: Kurukshetra University, 1992.

Chellappa, T. "Hemingway's *A Farewell to Arms* and *For Whom the Bell Tolls:* Comparative Study." (M. Phil thesis)ᵗ Palayamkottai: Madurai Kamraj University, 1988.

Das, Satyabrata. "Literary Responses to the Spanish Civil War: George Orwell And Ernest Hemingway." Bhubaneswar: Utkal University, n.d.

Dasgupta, Hemendralal. "Hemingway: Expatriate in Search of Life in Europe." Kharagpur: Indian Institute of Technology, 1974.

Dimri, Jaiwanti. "The War and the Wound: Ernest Hemingway's Short Stories And Non-Fiction." Meerut: Meerut University, 1980.

Garg, Vandana. "Hemingway and Human Suffering: Study of *For Whom the Bell Tolls, The Old Man and the Sea,* and *Islands in the Stream.*" (M.Phil thesis) Kurukhsetra: Kurukshetra University, 1981.

Hamid, Syed Ali. "Short Fiction of Ernest Hemingway: Study in Major Themes." Lucknow: Lucknow University, 1980.

Jain, Satya Prakash. "Short Stories of Ernest Hemingway: Study in Meanings." New Delhi: University of Delhi, 1976.

Kumari, Little K. "Ernest Hemingway's *The Old Man and the Sea:* Study of Santiago as an Existentialist Hero." (M.Phil thesis) Palayamkottai: Madurai Kamraj University, 1988.

Mandal, Somdatta. "Interrelations: Film and Fiction: Cinematic Themes and Techniques in the Fiction of F. Scott Fitzgerald, Ernest Hemingway and William Faulkner." Calcutta : Jadavpur University.

Mangathayaru, G.A. "The Theme of War in the Novels of Ernest Hemingway with Special reference to *The Sun Also Rises, A Farewell to Arms* and *For Whom the Bell Tolls.*"(M.Phil thesis) Guntur: Nagarjuna University, 1989.

Mishra, Ajit Kumar. "Theme of Loneliness in Modern American Fiction, with special reference to Sherwood Anderson, Ernest Hemingway, and Thomas Wolfe." Bhagalpur: Bhagalpur University, 1977.

Mishra, Kalidas. "The War Novel in America: A Study of Changing Response." (Chapter 3: Hemingway, cummings, Dos Passos) Bhubaneswar: Utkal University, 1988.

Mundra, S.C. "The Impact of War on Hemingway's Life and Works." Agra: Agra University, 1976.

Nair, N.Ramachandran. "Critical Study of the Thematic and Formalistic Anticipations of the later Hemingway as seen in his early writings." Calicut: University of Calicut, 1979.

Pagey, Sulabha. "Ernest Hemingway: Interpretation of the Themes of His Novels." Ujjain: Vikram University,1974.

Paul, Ajanta. "Intercontinental Affinities in the Modern Short Story with special reference to James·Joyce, Katherine Mansfield, William Faulkner and Ernest Hemingway." Calcutta: Jadavpur University, 1996.

Paul, Sukrita. "Man-Woman Relationship in the Fiction of F. Scott Fitzgerald, Ernest Hemingway and Theodore Dreiser." Aurangabad, 1975.

Raju, G. Chandra Sekhara. "The Apocalyptic Vision of the 'Lost Generation' with special reference to Fitzgerald and Hemingway." Tiruchirapalli, 1993.

Rajyalakshmi, A. "War Novel of Hemingway: A Study." (M.Phil thesis) Visakhapatnam: Andhra University, 1991.

Rao, E. Nageswara. "Rhetoric of Hemingway." Hyderabad: Osmania University, 1980.

Rao, P.G. Rama. "Narrative Technique of Ernest Hemingway." Bhubaneswar: Utkal University, 1970.

Reddy, D. Jayaprakash Narain "Nature in Ernest Hemingway's Novels." Waltair: Andhra University, 1978.

Saxena, Alka. "Theme of Love and Violence in the Fiction of Ernest Hemingway." Kanpur: Kanpur University, 1989.

Sengupta, Sanjukta. "Two Planes of Reality: Study of the Major Novels of Aldous Huxley and Ernest Hemingway." Calcutta: University of Calcutta, 1984.

Sharma, Dilbagh Rai. "Empirical Ethics of Ernest Hemingway." Chandigarh: Punjab University, 1969.

Sharma, Prem Kumar. "Study of Some Journalistic Writings of Ernest Hemingway." Patiala: Punjabi University, 1988.

Sharma, Purnima. "Ernest Hemingway: Critical Assessment as a Novelist." Jabalpur: Rani Durgawati Viswavidyalaya, 1987.

Sharmah, Narayan. "Ernest Hemingway: Critical Study of His Novels with Special Reference to his Treatment of Love." Meerut: Meerut University, 1974.

Srivastava, Ramesh Kumar. "Hemingway's *For Whom the Bell Tolls*: Critical Introduction with Annotations." Salt Lake City: University of Utah, 1972.

Sunderrajan, R. "Impact of War on Hemingway With Special Reference to *A Farewell to Arms* and *For Whom the Bell Tolls*."(M.Phil). Madras: University of Madras, 1987.

Tuli, Uma. "Symbolistic Technique of Ernest Hemingway." Delhi: University of Delhi, 1978.

D : IN OTHER LANGUAGES (BANGLA):

a) Articles

Bandopadhyay, Deb Narayan. "Pampalonar Manolo O Hemingway.' (Hemingway and Pamplona's Manolo) *Paschim Banga* 33 (Vol.29-30) Jan-Feb'2000: 743-5.

Bhattacharya, Chidananda. "Hemingway: Bichitra Chinta." (Hemingway: Multifarious Thoughts."*Jubamanash* (Aug'99): 14-18.

Chakladar, Manoj."Ekhon Ar Keu Eka Noy" (Now No one is Alone) *Paschim Banga* 33 (Vol.29-30) Jan-Feb'2000: 750-7.

Chakraborty, Santosh. "Andhokar thekey aloye: Hemingwayer jibonbiksha." ("From darkness to light: Hemingway's Worldview." *Paschim Banga* 33 (Vol.29-30) Jan-Feb'2000: 737-42.

Charaborty, Tania. "Hemingwayer A Farewell to Armsey Nari-Purush Samparka." (Man-Woman Relationship in *A Farewell to Arms*." *Paschim Banga* 33 (Vol.29-30) Jan-Feb'2000: 746-9.

Chattopadhyay, Sadhan. "Tritiya Bishwa Ebong Hemingway." (Hemingway and the Third World).

Paschim Banga 33 (Vol.29-30) Jan-Feb'2000 :758-61.

Chowdhury, Paromita. "Juddho, Mrityu, Hemingway." (War, Death, Hemingway). Jubamanash (Aug'99): 11-13.

Guha, Sourin. "Hemingwayer Rachonar Prathamik Alochana." ("A Primary Discussion on Heminway's Works." Anrinya (1981):

—————."Hemingway: Shatobarsher Alokey." ("Hemingway: In the Light of His Centenary.") Kobitirtha (1999):

—————. "Heminwayer Chotogalpe Samajik Abokhoyer Chobi." ("Social Decadence in Hemingway's Short Stories."Antarjatik Chotogalpo (2000):

Mandal, Parthapratim. "Bashotti Bachar probolbhabe bechechilen Hemingway." (Hemingway lived passionately for 62 years) Jubamanash (Aug'99): 3-4.

Mandal, Somdatta. "Challachitra, Hemingway Ebong Hollywood." (Films, Hemingway, and Hollywood). Jubamanash (Aug'99):5-10.

Roy, Amitava. "Ernest Hemingway: Ek Bitarkito Sahityik." (Ernest Hemingway: A Controversial Novelist) Paschin Banga 33.29-30 (28 Jan-4 Feb2000) : 735-6.

b) Translation of Short Stories in Bangla.

Basu. Soma. "Indian Camp" Jubamanash (Aug'99): 21-22.Guha, Sourin. "The Killers." Kobitirtha (July'2000):

Mukhopadhyay, Kalyan. "The Capital of the World." Jubamanash (Aug'99): 32-36.

Naser, Kazi Kamal. "Why Will You Die?" Jubamanash (Aug'99): 39-40

Roy, Amitava, et al. Eds Hemingwayer Kobita: Bhumika, Alochana O Anubad.(Hemingway's Poems: Introduction, Discussion and Translation.) Calcutta: Writer's Co-Operative, 2000.

Roychowdhury, Amiya. "In Another Country." *Jubamanash* (Aug'99): 27-29.

Sarkar, Dipak. "The End of Something." *Jubamanash* (Aug'99): 37-38.

Sen, Debolina. "In Our Time." *Jubamanash* (Aug'99): 23-26.

Sengupta. Chandramalli. "Hills Like White Elephants." *Jubamanash* (Aug'99): 30-31.

Ernest Miller Hemingway Chronology

1899   Born on the 21st of July at Oak Park, Illinois, second of six children of Dr. Clarence Edmunds Hemingway and Grace Hall Hemingway.

1917   Graduated from Oak Park High School; rejected by Army because of eye injury in boxing; works as a cub-reporter in Kansas City *Star*

1918   Goes to Italy as Red Cross ambulance driver. Legs severely injured by mortar fragments and heavy machine gun fire on July 8, two weeks before his nineteenth birthday, near Fossalta di Piave. Decorated for his services.

1919   Returns to America.

1920-23   Reporter and foreign correspondent for Toronto *Star* and *Star Weekly*.

1921   Marries Hadley Richardson; leaves for Europe. Settles in Paris where he renews earlier friendship with Ezra Pound and Gertrude Stein.

1923   Publishes first work : *Three Stories and Ten Poems.*

1924   *in our time*, thirty two pages of miniatures published in Paris.

1925   *In Our Time*, U.S. edition published by Boni & Liveright. Contains fourteen short stories plus miniatures of the Paris edition, which are used as inter chapters. Meets F. Scott Fitzgerald in Paris for the first time.

1926   The satirical novel on Sherwood Anderson *The Torrents of Spring*, published in May by Charles Scribner's Sons. New York. *The Sun Also Rises* published in October.

1927   Divorces Hadley Richardson; marries Pauline Pfeiffer. Publication of *Men Without Women*, fourteen short stories ten of which had appeared in magazines.

1928   Hemingways make first visit to Key West, Florida in April.

1929   *A Farewell to Arms*, the first commercially successful novel published in September. In November, account of the Hemingway-Callaghan bout appears in *New York Herald Tribune*.

1932   The non-fictional work on bull-fighting, *Death in the Afternoon* published.

1933   Publication of *Winner Take Nothing* in October containing fourteen stories. Published first of the thirty-one articles and stories to appear in *Esquire*. Leaves for a safari in Africa in 1899, December.

1934   Continues the safari till February.

1935   Publication of *Green Hills of Africa* in October. During 1935- 37 he writes, speaks and raises money for the Loyalists in the Spanish Civil War.

1937   Goes to Spain as a war correspondent for North American Newspaper Alliance in March. In October, *To Have and Have Not* published.

1938   *The Fifth Column and the First Forty-Nine Stories* published.

1940   *For Whom the Bell Tolls* published in October. Pauline Pfeiffer divorces him; marries Martha Gelhorn in November. In December he buys the Finca Vigia outside of Havana, Cuba.

1942   *Men at War*, a collection of war stories and accounts edited and with an introduction by Hemingway published from 1942-45 he covers the European wars as newspaper and magazine correspondent.

1944   Divorced from Martha Gelhorn.

1946   Marries Mary Welsh in March.

1950   *Across the River and Into the Trees* published in September.

1952   *The Old Man and The Sea* published in September.

1954   Awarded the Nobel prize in October. Cited for "forceful and style-making mastery of the art of modern narration."

1961   Dies of self-inflicted gunshot wound on July 2 in his home at Ketchum, Idaho.

1964   Publication of A *Moveable Feast.*

1969   Publication of *The Fifth Column and Four Stories of the Spanish Civil War.*

1970   Publication of *Islands in the Stream.* edited by Carlos Baker. *Ernest Hemingway, Cub Reporter: Kansas City Stories.* Ed. M. J. Bruccoli.

1971   Publication of *Ernest Hemingway's Apprenticeship: Oak Park, 1916-/917.* Ed. M.. J. Bruccoli.

1985   Publication of *The Dangerous Summer ; Ernest Hemingway, Dateline: Toronto* (The complete *Toronto Star* Dispatches, 1920-1924.) Ed. William White.

1986   Publication of *The Garden of Eden.*

1987   Publication of *The Complete Stories of Ernest Hemingway: The Finca Vigia Edition.*

1999   Publication of *True at First Light: A Fictional Memoir* edited by Patrick Hemingway on 22nd July, as a centennial tribute.

List of Contributors

Chidananda Bhattacharya
Professor of English, Rabindra Bharati University, Calcutta.

Dipendu Chakrabarti
Sir Goorudass Professor of English, University of Calcutta.

Sobha Chattopadhyay
Professor of English, Jadavpur University, Calcutta

Sanjukta Dasgupta
Reader, Department of English, University of Calcutta.

Scott Donaldson
College of William and Mary, Williamsburg, Virginia.

Indrani Haldar
Reader in English, (Retd.) Jadavpur University, Calcutta

Peter L. Hays
Professor, University of California, Davis.

Judy Henn
Department of English, University of Haifa, Israel

Alexander Kelley Dupuis
Journalist, San Diego, California. A regular contributor to www.ernest.hemingway.com website devoted to Hemingway studies.

Pralhad A. Kulkarni
Teaches English at Sangli, Maharashtra.

Somdatta Mandal
Reader, Department of English, Vivekananda College, Madhyamgram. University of Calcutta

Miriam Mandel
Professor of English, Tel Aviv University, Israel

Priyadarshi Patnaik
Department of Humanities & Social Sciences, Indian Institute of Technology, Kharagpur, W.B.

Ajanta Paul
Reader in English, St. Paul's Cathedral Mission College, Calcutta.

E. Nageswara Rao
Professor, (Retd.), Osmania University, Hyderabad.

P. G. Rama Rao
Professor (Retd.), Utkal University, Bhubaneswar.
Former Academic Associate, American Studies Research Centre, Hyderabad.

Amitabha Sinha
Reader in English, (Retd.) University of Calcutta.

Bickford Sylvester
Professor, (Retd.) University of British Columbia.